GETTING IT FOR LOVE
IN OLD SAN JUAN

A Journey

Peter Gabor Ernster

Published by London Grove Publishing

Cover photograph by J.K. Byass

ISBN: 0615881564
ISBN-13: 9780615881560

For my mother, Klara Ernster. Years before I was born,
a Gypsy fortune teller told her that she would have
a son who would become a writer. So many
years later the jury is still out.

Preface

This book is a dramatized memoir based on my experience in the U. S. Merchant Marine. Although directionally accurate, I have taken some liberties in filling in the gaps of my memory in creating dialogue, created some composite characters, and occasionally enhanced the story for dramatic effect. In that sense it is not strictly a memoir. I have also changed the name of the ship and the names of the real people with whom I interacted to protect the guilty and innocent alike.

The Appendix is an essay about the state of the U.S. Merchant Marine in 1962, the year I shipped out, and how and why it evolved as it did to that point. It provides useful context for the attitudes of the men on the ship and in the union. Without intending a literary comparison, its purpose (but not its position in the book) is akin to that of the whaling chapters in Melville's *Moby Dick.* Like those chapters, although not critical to the story line itself, the Appendix is useful in understanding it.

Some perspective on dollar figures in the book: For historical accuracy, amounts are expressed in 1962 dollars. Because of inflation since then, $10 in the book is equal to $76.50 today.

CHAPTER 1
Setting Out

As I walked up the hill from Riverside Drive in the cool spring morning, the rising sun on my face felt good. The 60-pound duffle bag on my right shoulder did not. Halfway up the block the bag was getting heavy and I had a long way to go. But that was the whole point. I was going a long way, and the bag being heavy and uncomfortable was very much a part of it. Each step of this voyage needed to be felt. It was late May, 1962: I had just turned twenty, and I had a ship in the Unites States Merchant Marine.

The newly laminated card issued by the U. S. Coast Guard qualified me to serve as Ordinary Seaman and Wiper, the lowest functional levels on deck and in the engine room of a merchant vessel. Diagonally stamped in large red letters across the front of the card were the imposing words, "VALIDATED FOR EMERGENCY SERVICE." What this meant in fact was that if the United States went to war, instead of being drafted, merchant seamen, who otherwise were employees no different than bus mechanics or short order cooks, would serve their military duty in virtually unarmed cargo ships and tankers, becoming perpetual targets for the bombs and torpedoes of enemy warplanes, ships and submarines. What it meant to me, with no war in sight, was that my card (my "Seaman's Document") was real, and I was really in the merchant marine.

And "really in" also meant that although my parents and friends thought it was a summer job, in fact, I was leaving college for at least a couple of years to ship out and see the world.

To be real I had to look the part—at least as I imagined it: tan pants and shirt, white web belt, and black work shoes. And to carry all the rest, a white canvas duffle with an opening at one end, with four grommeted holes held together by a long-necked padlock. The salesman at the army/navy surplus store assured me that it was a real seaman's bag: it had no handles. A seaman didn't use handles; he walked with a white duffle bag slung over his shoulder, as I was doing—I had seen it all in World War II movies.

The bag, shoes, shirt and some of what was stuffed into the bag were *bon voyage* gifts from Lorna, a pretty brunette nine years older than I whom I had met in the park a month before. They represented the first delivery on the promise I imagined to be on the horizon, though my focus was on erotic rather than material gifts. The previous evening had blown a large cloud on that horizon, but I still held out hope.

The 5:30 A.M..bus from the Port Authority Terminal to Port Elizabeth was largely empty. "Main Wharf," I told the driver feigning tired experience, found two seats, and leaned on my sea bag. I wondered if any of the other men on the bus—and they were all men—were seamen. Maybe one of them would be on my ship. They sure didn't look like me. They were in their thirties and forties and looked more like the salesman at the surplus store than my image of seamen. They didn't appear anxious to make new friends. Paying no attention to me–or each other—they slept.

I was too excited, nervous, to sleep. Yet the forty-minute ride wasn't long enough to conjure up even a few of the fantasies that had consumed me in the time leading up to this day. I tried to think about the "adventure," people I would meet, storms, women in ports— seamen meet women in ports. But these thoughts were fleeting and couldn't hold my focus. So I looked out the window. Even in the bright, blooming spring, the view along the New Jersey Turnpike was bleak. The swampy terrain with its intermittent land-fills made of garbage still visible near the surface jarred against my image of the sea not far away.

As the bus sped along, I focused on small things: the cracks in the beige vinyl of the seat in front of me, a smudge on the window. I clung to these details the way a condemned man might before he was to be executed. I thought of falling off the ship and drowning and being killed in a fight. A less fanciful fear, concentrated now that actually getting on the ship loomed close, was the reality that I didn't know how to do anything on a ship. That I had no idea what my job entailed—what I was actually supposed to do—didn't help.

I would later learn more about container ships in general and a lot more about the *Rufus Saxton*. Then I only knew that containers were the cargo-carrying boxes attached to truck cabs and made up what I knew as trailer truck bodies. The idea—new at the time—was that instead of loading cargo piecemeal into the holds of ships, a driver would drive a truck up to the ship's berth, detach the loaded container, and a very large crane would place the container in the ship's hold. Once the holds were filled, more containers were stacked two, three or four high on the deck. The process was repeated in reverse at the other end of the voyage.

In the months that led to getting this ship I had been told by the old hands at the Seafarers International Union hall that the job of "coastwise wiper" was the worst in the merchant marine. They meant that in relative terms. The best job for someone with no experience—what would now be called "entry level" —was that of ordinary seaman on an around the world run. A trip like that was said to take four months and ten days. That's the job I had hoped for, fantasized about, and told my friends I would have. I had no reason to think that I would get it, but I had used the elemental glamour of steaming around the world and the long time away as a line to impress Lorna, and I soon started to believe it.

The next best job was ordinary seaman (any job really) on a northern or southern European run in the summer. Steaming into a fiord in Norway or past the Little Mermaid in Copenhagen or into any harbor in the Mediterranean had to be any seaman's dream. It was certainly mine. You didn't have to be a seaman to imagine and appreciate the scene, but it would certainly legitimize your presence. There would be bars near the port and in the bars there would be women. There wouldn't be much time, but there would be enough.

Coastwise wiper may have been the worst job relatively, but on an old container ship—and all container ships at the time were old even though the container use was new—I would learn that it was also a bad job in an absolute sense, a really bad job. And I was lucky to get it. As in, "Look kid, turn down this job, you can get the fuck outa here." What the hell, I had thought, it was my first ship; it wouldn't last forever. Next ship… around the world! Besides, I would be back in New York for a night every week or so, and Lorna offered a lot of promise, though it was going a lot more slowly than I had expected.

Sitting on the bus that morning, all I thought about was that I was going to be a wiper on a ship, and that I had no idea what a wiper did, though the name was certainly suggestive. Of course, I could have found out. It wouldn't have taken much. I could have asked any number of people at the union hall. Someone would have given me straight information even if it was surrounded with "stuff to scare the kid." But the fantasy of the adventure was clearly more appealing to me than the details of the reality, and an emphasis on fantasy over day-to-day reality was very much a part of my "fuel mixture."

The bus stopped for the third time. When I didn't move, the driver turned to me and said, "Last stop, kid. From here it's by boat." And following the four remaining sleepy men I staggered down onto a long wharf, lined with berthed ships—and into reality.

None of the men had heard of the *Rufus Saxton*, but they all agreed it was probably the last ship in the line. The sea bag was going to get heavy again, I thought.

And it did—no fantasy there. As I walked, I tried not to think about whether I looked like I belonged on that wharf. Did I look like a college kid, a phony? This was no summer job for me. Maybe for some others, but not for me. This was going to be my life for at least a couple of years.

I needn't have worried then. Whatever I looked like, there wasn't a soul around to see me. The four men all went aboard the first ship and after about a thousand feet I finally noticed that the wharf was empty—no one walking on the road, no trucks, carts or any moving vehicles, and no one visible on the decks of the ships I passed. It was 6:30 in the morning. Where was everyone? Maybe I had the wrong wharf. Damn, was I going to have to haul the bloody sea bag around all of Port Elizabeth? Then I saw a stack of containers and what looked like a ship with cranes large enough to move them. Right! At the very end of the wharf.

Shifting the sea bag from shoulder to shoulder, I thought that the dark olive army duffle with handles that the surplus salesman had recommended might have been a better idea. Why did seamen use bags with no handles while soldiers used bags with handles? Maybe it was because soldiers walked a lot and seamen didn't. Well, this seaman was doing a lot of walking and carrying a very heavy bag with no handles. As I wondered about bags, soldiers and seamen, the gangway of the *Rufus Saxton* suddenly appeared ahead.

Up close, the ship looked enormous, over 400 feet long. In fact it wasn't large at all by then current cargo ship standards. I was surprised at how close to the water the deck was, no more than 15 feet in the middle of the ship. Wouldn't the waves just wash right over the deck? I had seen passenger liners and their decks were much higher off the water. There were already containers on the deck, so the ship was being loaded—or was it being unloaded? It would be a lot higher, I thought, if it were empty. But the whole idea of cargo ships was to be full in both directions of a run. So the waves were going to be a problem. But it was an old ship, so it couldn't have been too much of a problem since it was still afloat.

With that measure of reassurance, I started up the gangway. I had expected someone with a whistle—something like what greeted sailors onto Navy ships in every war movie I had ever seen. Two notes, high to low, or was it low to high? Or someone at the top, demanding, "Who goes there?" Or at least someone barking, "What do you want, kid?" No one. No one at all.

Very hesitantly I stepped onto the deck through the opening in the railing. Maybe I was supposed to wait until an officer or someone told me to come aboard. I put the bag down and called out "Hello" a few times, softly at first, then louder until it seemed way too loud in the unexpected silence of the ship and the wharf.

I really didn't want to get this wrong. I could be breaking some rule or some ancient seafaring tradition. Nobody had invited me onto this ship. Maybe I shouldn't be on it. So I got off. Shouldering the bag, I trudged back down the gangway, put the bag down, sat on it and stared up at the ship.

After 10 minutes it was clear that willing someone to appear on deck wasn't working. What the hell was I doing? I had a job on this ship. I was—or soon would be—part of the crew. Of course I could be on the ship.

I was supposed to be on the ship. Maybe I was already late. Back up the gangway I went. Once on deck I shouted several times, "Anyone home?" and "New crew member." I walked here and there looking at doors, not daring to open any, when suddenly a man emerged from one of them. He was about six feet tall, dark blond hair and a craggy face. He looked more used than rugged, and appeared to be in his fifties. He was dressed just like me. So I had gotten it right after all, I thought.

He glanced at me briefly and his short chuckle didn't give me much confidence. "You the new wiper?"

"Right," I replied. "Peter Ernster," I added.

"Peter what?" I spelled it. "OK, so what do you go by?"

I wasn't prepared for this. Clearly, Peter wasn't a seaman's name, but I was no more a Pete than I was a Mike, Bill or Joe. It just wasn't my name. No one had ever called me Pete. When I was ten I moved to a new neighborhood. A group of kids asked me my nickname, I told them "Rusty." It was the only nickname I could think of. The problem was I had dark brown, almost black hair. Quick thinking!

In the intervening years I hadn't thought about it again, but Rusty wasn't going to fly any better this time. So Pete it was. Of course, it didn't matter what I told him, as he replied, "OK kid," and rolling his eyes, said as if reciting from a script, "Welcome aboard." Then, "Your first ship, kid?" So I didn't look like an old hand, huh. "Yeah," I muttered, trying to convey a toughness that although not born of years in the merchant marine, had been earned through many scrapes with life.

He missed that effort as he turned and told me to wait there while he got the ship's articles for me to sign. The ship's articles! Horatio Hornblower had signed ship's articles. Whatever anyone thought of me, I was about to become a full-fledged member of the crew of the *S.S. Rufus Saxton.*

He returned with what looked like a ledger, opened it to a page half filled with signatures and dates, and pointed to the next empty line. I wasn't sure whether to be careful and clear or to make an illegible scrawl. I wondered if on some of the pages in the "articles" there were Xs. I didn't imagine that literacy was a requirement for being a wiper or for any other non-officer position on the ship. I signed carefully. I wanted it damn certain that I was a crewman on this ship.

"I'm the Second Mate. Call me Second."

He told me that breakfast was at 7:30 and that I was to "turn to" at 8:00. By that I gathered that I had to find the engine room by then. He then pointed to the stern of the ship and said that I should stow my gear in my fo'c'sle. It was the last one on the starboard side. "Stow," "gear" and "starboard" were snaps. "Fo'c'sle" threw me. My ignorance was clearly expected. But I didn't ask. I wasn't giving anyone that kind of satisfaction. Instead, I turned and headed to the stern of the ship as he shook his head slowly and walked the other way. Screw him, I thought. It didn't take a brain surgeon to work on a goddamn ship.

A little research might have helped. A little preparation of any kind—instead of my incessant daydreaming—would have given me at least an even start. I might have learned a bit earlier that "fo'c'sle" was derived from "forecastle." But then again, whatever that had meant on an 18th century British frigate, it now meant my cabin, and it wasn't in the "fore" of anything, castle or otherwise; it was in the back. So back I went, lugging the sea bag and wondering how I would balance myself with the bag on my shoulder as the ship rocked heavily in a storm. Why I would be walking around the deck of the ship in a storm carrying my sea bag was not obvious, but that's the kind of thing I worried about.

The ship had two buildings—superstructures. By far the larger was in the middle of the ship and was several stories high. That was where I had come on board. The second was near the stern of the ship, much smaller and lower, and looked like an after thought. In between, on what would have been the open deck of a regular cargo ship, were rows of containers stacked three high. Passing these I opened the door (it would be another two hours before I was instructed, not for the last time, that the ship had no doors, only hatches) to the back of the stern "house" (was it the stern of the stern house?) and walked very quietly down the short hall. The doors to the four fo'c'sles were closed. There wasn't a sound. I guessed everyone was already out, or they were all still sleeping.

Opening the first door on the right, I peered inside. On the left was a double-deck bunk built into a space in the wall of the fo'c'sle. On the right, under the only porthole and about five feet from the double bunk, was a single bunk. The upper and lower bunks were occupied. That is, there were clearly bodies in them, though no sign of a head in either. I was surprised, ecstatic really, that the single bunk was empty. This had to be prime real estate on a ship: no one above and right under the porthole. I imagined lying in that bunk after a long day, enjoying the breeze and the fading light coming through the porthole. More important, though, was that these guys, my new fo'c'slemates had left me the best bunk. Maybe they didn't want to be that close to the porthole, but no matter, they seemed to have gone out of their way to be welcoming to the new wiper. This wasn't going to be so bad. A good start, I thought.

With that I walked over to my bunk. A standard, though rather thin, mattress with blue and white ticking was rolled up at what seemed to be the head of the bunk with a pillow of the same material on top of it. I unrolled the mattress. It was stained and had a pronounced though undefined smell. It was definitely going to need some airing. I placed the sea bag on the mattress at the head of the bunk and put the pillow on top. As I sat down, I swiveled my body, swinging my legs to the right and my upper body to the left. I crossed my arms behind my head and slowly lowered my head and shoulders onto the pillow, a grin on my face. At the moment just before I made contact with the pillow, the body in the lower bunk turned over, revealing part of a face. The face mumbled in a sleepy Irish brogue, "Guy died in that bunk yesterday."

CHAPTER 2

Maybe Not

The words "guy died in that bunk yesterday" hit me like a two-by-four, and I jumped forward and to the left to get away from the death bed. The awkward movement in changing direction so suddenly, together with the force behind it, landed me on my left knee on the metal floor. "Goddamn it," I yelled as the pain traveled up from my kneecap like lightning, "thanks for telling me. Damn!" The pain and the news competed for my attention.

"Yeah," the face said, "maybe you can get new stuff. I wouldn't sleep on that shit."

"How come they didn't just throw it away?"

"They don't throw nothin' away on this ship. Figure it's your problem."

"So where do I get the new stuff?"

"I dunno, maybe ask Second; he's the guy probably signed you in."

"Yeah. What'd he die of?" I asked, still reeling.

"Man, I dunno. He sure died messy. That I do know. We stayed the hell outa here until it was over. But me and Raul," pointing up to the top bunk, "we had to clean it up."

"But was he hurt— an accident— or was he sick?"

"Oh he was sick all right. He was always sick, coughing all the time. Man, he made me sick. He was on this fucking ship forever. I've been here for 14 months, and he was sick all that time for sure."

"Maybe he had lung cancer," I offered. "You know, with all that coughing."

"Yeah, probably. I think he bled to death somehow, inside."

The face had sat up, swung his legs over the side of the bunk and seemed to ponder for the first time how this guy, this guy who had lived in the same small room with him for 14 months had died.

"What was his name?"

"Stanley. Just wanted to be a wiper on this ship. Nuts. He was old, man, had an A book, could have worked any ship he wanted. And he was an AB!"

He saw my surprise. An AB was an able body seaman, the most common rank in the merchant marine, though it took years to attain; and it meant you could do pretty much everything on the decks of a ship, including steering it. And an A book was the top level of seniority in the union. Why in hell would he want to work as a wiper on an old coastwise ship?

Reading the question in my eyes, he answered, "Said he wanted to be in port often. He didn't want to stand watches, wanted to work during the day and sleep at night. Well, he didn't sleep that much. Read all the time, read and coughed. Said he had a daughter lived in Brooklyn. I dunno if he lived with her or just saw her a lot, but he was in a damn big hurry to get off the ship when we got back to port and finished work"

Sounded like I had missed an interesting guy. I wondered what he read. I hadn't expected reading to be a favorite pastime on the ship. Anyway, he was dead, and though it seemed strange that his death hadn't generated more emotion from his fo'c'slemate, I wasn't going to lose any sleep over a guy I hadn't even met. That is, if Second would give me another mattress and pillow. I was going to lose a lot of sleep if I had to keep what was on the bunk.

Not the greatest introduction to my fo'c'sle. I was going to be thinking about the guy dying in my bunk for a while even with another mattress and pillow. And I had a really sore kneecap. But I had learned something important. I was a day worker. It seemed that whatever wipers did didn't have to be done at night. That was just fine with me.

Later I learned that other than wipers and the guys in the galley (and the Captain and Chief Engineer) basically everyone on the ship—and there were 33 in all—worked watches. Four hours on, eight hours off, four hours on. 8:00 to 12:00, 12:00 to 4:00, and 4:00 to 8:00. First and third watches had their supposed advantages. 8:00 to 12:00 you got to sleep at night, get up at a normal time and have time to do whatever you wanted during a lot of the day. 4:00 to 8:00 you got up early, but you saw the sunrise, had time during the day and went to sleep at a normal time. They kept the dinner hot in the galley for those guys. 12:00 to 4:00 seemed to have no advantages. You went to work when you should be going to sleep and slept during much of the day. You had to be out of kilter with that schedule. It was the lower seniority guys who worked the second watch. While I certainly wasn't happy about being a wiper, it was a sure bet that if I had the ordinary seaman job I had been hoping for, it would have been 12:00 to 4:00, and that, I thought, might have been worse. It turned out I was wrong, way wrong, at least on this ship.

Face slowly emerged from his bunk. He was about 5' 9" with curly, sandy hair and a broad face with smiling eyes and a wry wary look. He shook Raul, who hadn't moved a muscle since I had arrived.

"Michael Flaherty," he said, sticking out his right hand while picking up the dirtiest pair of pants I had ever seen with his left.

"Stanley," "Michael," not "Stan" or "Mike." Perhaps I could be Peter after all. But what came out as we shook hands was "Pete, Pete Ernster."

"What kind of a name is that?" he asked absently.

"German, but I'm Hungarian." His lack of attention made it clear that I had just offered way more information than he wanted. I reminded myself that this wasn't some fraternity. No one was going to give a damn about me, and that was just fine. Just shut up, Peter.

Poking Raul hard in the back, Michael said, "This shithead is Raul Fuentes," followed by "Get the fuck up you lazy spic. I'm not covering for your ass."

Instead of turning and kicking Michael in the head for the insults, Raul turned over grinning and in a heavy Puerto Rican accent said, "Come on, Michael, you son of bitch, get me some toast." And then, with no expectation that his request would be granted, "I didn't think they could get a new wiper for this stinkin' ship so fast."

"They told me I didn't have a choice. If I didn't take this job, they'd rip up my C card. But I guess they got lucky too, because no one else bid on the job."

"Bullshit man," Raul replied. "Maybe they get lucky but we don't. You don't show up, no wiper; no wiper, we sit here. We sit here forever, man. Engine off, not so hot down there. Chip some paint—bullshit work, then go into city at night, every fucking night. They gotta pay us the same. Everybody gonna be pissed at you, man." He said all this with an expression on his face that was a cross between a grin and a wince. I was to see that expression many times and not know what it meant any more than I did then. I didn't know if he thought the situation was funny or if he wanted to kill me.

What I'd learned was that I was not a welcome addition. What Raul said would be echoed by everyone on board. The crew had been counting on, or at least hoping for, a long layover in port while SeaLand Service and the union tried to find a sucker for this wiper job in one of the other East coast ports. I knew I'd get quite a reception in the mess hall at breakfast.

During the introductions, Michael and Raul grabbed more clothes from the floor and finished getting dressed. It wasn't just that they wore the same stuff they had thrown on the floor the night before; their clothes looked like they had been worn for a month. What had once been gray pants and white t-shirts were so covered with paint, oil and tar, in most places overlapping, that the material was hardly visible. I thought their pants could stand by themselves. Looking down at my spotless tans, I realized that though I might be dressed like Second, a senior officer, I sure wasn't dressed like these guys. I was going to look like a jerk, and the crew would have quite a target.

I don't know what I had been thinking. I wasn't an officer. I was a goddamn wiper. I wanted desperately to change into a t-shirt. I couldn't make it all dirty, but at least I could get rid of the tan shirt with the now ridiculous-looking epaulets. But I had trouble with the lock on the bag, and Michael said it was past 7:30 and we had to get some food. I wasn't going to go to that mess hall alone. So off I went with my new "buddies," dressed like some kind of merchant marine cadet.

CHAPTER 3

North to Alaska

Although at the age of twenty my life was certainly at sea in the figurative sense, I had not long harbored any ambition to go to sea. I was doing adequately in my second year at NYU's Washington Square College. My major was European History with a minor in International Economics, though at that point I had really only completed most of the required courses in a variety of subjects needed for a Bachelor of Arts degree. My plan was to go on to law school and then further study to pursue a career in international law.

I lived occasionally at my mother's apartment on Riverside Drive in New York City—it was from there that I had embarked with my sea bag that morning. But mostly I lived with an assortment of roommates in dilapidated, walk-up apartments in and around Greenwich Village. I studied, went to classes at the urban campus surrounding Washington Square, played tennis in Central Park, and worked at various part-time jobs—mostly delivering groceries—and worked harder at picking up women.

Since the real work in my academic major and minor would only begin in earnest during my junior year, I majored in women in general and the pursuit of sex in particular. I should note that I use the word "women" not in some politically correct manner to describe the girls at NYU, but specifically to distinguish my targets from that group, since given my main objective, it was with women, not girls, that I had the best chance of success.

Another focus was Air Force ROTC. I joined as a way of avoiding a gym class requirement when it became clear that despite some athletic ability and accomplishments in a variety of sports, membership on a university-wide varsity team was unlikely. Once in AFROTC I pursued the flying program and did so with a passion. On weekends I flew with reserve pilots on C-47s, the military version of the DC-3, and planned on becoming a jet fighter pilot. At this point I had pretty much decided to defer going to law school until I had completed a four-year tour of duty in the Air Force.

If it appears that my plans were rather fluid, they were. And my decisions were generally precipitous. Because I recognized this, I usually didn't include my mother or father in the process. My father lived in Europe. He was an opera singer, and I saw him only when he came to New York to sing. Although always a looming figure in the background, he wasn't a part of my day-today life and had no real role in guiding it.

My mother was a very different matter. We had a close relationship and I was her main preoccupation. I tried to avoid worrying her. So, for example, when I decided to attend NYU I hadn't discussed my acceptances at various eastern colleges that my boarding school advisor had made clear to me were far more prestigious. To me they were replicas, albeit on a grander scale, of the small bucolic boarding school I had attended for four years, and I wanted the anonymous adventure of life in New York City.

Nor had I discussed various summer jobs—dishwasher at a camp, bellboy at a resort—before I left for them. She might well not have been concerned, but I didn't want to take the risk. Likewise, when I twice left the European tour I had been given as a high school graduation present—the second time resulting in a nine-day hospital stay in Rome, the result of a motor scooter accident—I didn't mention it to my parents until well after the fact. So I certainly wasn't going to discuss my flying activities—or plans.

My mother knew I was in AFROTC–the uniform I wore once a week was hard to miss when I was living at home–but she seemed to understand little of the activities and commitment involved. I figured she thought it was a kind of extension of the Boy Scouts. I meant to keep it that way for as long as I could.

All of that would have to change as I got closer to the point, at the end of my sophomore year, when I would have to apply for the Advanced Corps and, if accepted, get paid for the next two years. In return, I would need to commit to the four years of active duty—and, of course, the jet fighters. As I was the top student in the Air Science program, I knew I would be accepted, and I assumed I would pass the various tests required to fly jet fighters. So the only issue would be my mother's reaction—and ultimately my father's. I spent a lot of time worrying about the various scenarios.

I also spent a lot of time being consumed by a general feeling of unease, not with the present but with the future. It was too set. High school, college, law school, a job, a career, a wife, a family—it was all too predictable. Even if it were all wonderful, where was the adventure? The four years flying jet fighters would certainly provide that—the old C-47s were already providing that. Then I would contentedly and with enthusiasm pursue the rest of my life in the ordered progression everyone expected. But what if I didn't pass the flying tests? And more likely, what if my mother really objected?

On the other hand, the potential dangers involved were not a concern, largely because I was nineteen and because in 1961/1962 the United States was not involved in a war.

As I said, my plans were fluid. And in the winter before I had to make my decision, a new possibility, a way of delaying decisions, entered the picture. During Christmas vacation in 1961, John, a friend from boarding school, visited for a few days. We spent most of our time together walking around the city and talking. He shared my restlessness. We were walking along 42nd Street when it began to snow lightly. It was very cold, and the wind blew from the Hudson River down the broad street turning the snow into needles in our faces. We passed countless movie marquees. Then we saw posters for *North to Alaska,* with John Wayne. The suggestive power of the snow and the cold made the decision for us; we had to see this movie.

After the Elmer Fudd cartoons, *Movietone News,* and Audie Murphy single-handedly defeating the Nazi war machine, *North to Alaska.* It was a mild gold mining adventure, nothing special. But the image of John Wayne stripped to the waist, swinging a pick, mining for gold in the Alaskan springtime, was inspirational. As we were leaving the theater, John and I mused about Alaska, the last frontier, although the blinding vista that greeted us when we emerged onto the street should have dampened our enthusiasm. In the more than four hours since we had entered the theater, 42nd Street had accumulated ten inches of snow. We were in the midst of the great blizzard of '61.

It took us over three hours to walk through the deserted city back to my mother's apartment where John was staying. The effort of wading through the drifts, the wind and the snow in our faces, should have been exhausting, but the excitement of our emerging plan made it exhilarating. If for any reason my flying plans were derailed, John and I would leave school at the end of the spring term and go to Alaska to work on the Alaskan pipeline, one of the greatest construction projects of all time. We would swing picks, become really strong and get into bar fights. With all the money we made—and it was well-known that workers made a fortune on the Alaskan pipeline—we would meet beautiful women in (or above) saloons. Just like in the movie. It might be the middle of the twentieth century, but some things don't change. And in the winter? We would find work moving the snow, exchanging picks for shovels. In other words, we would have the adventure of a lifetime. And when we were done we would go back to school.

Despite our enthusiasm, the life of this plan was not much longer than the snowy aftereffects of the blizzard. I wrote to the Alaska Chamber of Commerce and a few other organizations. I told them that we were "experienced, highly motivated and fit workers seeking manual work on the pipeline and would be ready to begin at the end of May when our current contracts expired."

Remarkably—and for our purposes, regrettably—two of the agencies responded immediately. The responses were almost identical form letters enclosing the same brochure, entitled "Employment Opportunities in Alaska:" Given the surplus of manual workers already in Alaska, it read, we should consult the brochure for the types of opportunities that did exist—and there were many. Some that I recall were for accountants, dental assistants and taxidermists. Not jobs for John Wayne. On the phone John and I agreed to stay in touch about ideas, but the disappointment dissolved our commitment.

As the winter started to recede, my meeting with the AFROTC authorities approached. As did my inevitable confrontation with my mother. Did I really want to do this? Was I sure? Flying jet fighters would be great; I was sure of that. But four years? I thought about the impending decision most of the time. I had already told some of the officers that I would apply, and they in turn talked about the possibility of a regular commission—as opposed to a reserve commission—if I were to graduate at the top of the AFROTC class and therefore receive the Distinguished Military Student award. Heady stuff.

I imagined that I would manage the meeting with my mother on my terms. Like so many things I imagined, reality was different. During one of my stints at home–my roommate and his girlfriend had decided to move in together in his apartment–I was scheduled for a weekend at Mitchell Air Force Base, where I had been flying, to undergo a battery of tests—medical, physical and mental—that would determine my aptitude for flying in general and for the quick response-based requirements of flying jet fighters.

I told my mother I was going to an Air Force base as part of the AFROTC training. She looked at me intensely and said nothing. Her stare held my eyes.

"Look Mom, I've got to go...uh...now."

This was definitely not on my terms.

"Sit down, Peter.

She could always read me like a book, and my getting older and more devious hadn't changed that. That I could avoid and dissemble but not lie to her made it easier. She was more than prescient; she had a sixth sense.

"What are you going to do at the Air Force base?"

"Tests...you know, mental tests, take a physical, stuff like that."

"Why there and not at school?"

"They've got special machines"

The rest of the cross examination went in an inexorably downward spiral.

"Do the machines have something to do with flying planes?"

"Well, some of them do."

And then the killer: "Do you think you are going to fly war planes?"

"Mom, that's what they do in the Air Force. I'm in AFROTC."

"But you want to be an international lawyer."

"Yes, Mom, after the Air Force."

"You can't do this."

"I *am* doing it. I've been doing it"

With that she went back to staring at me. So I explained everything, that I didn't want to go straight into my future with each step laid out after the other, that I needed adventure, that I needed to prove myself. I told her I had been flying for a year and a half and that I enjoyed it. I even added that America had been good to us since we had emigrated from Hungary, and I owed it to the country.

She wasn't having any of it. She got up and stood with her back to the front door of the apartment. She was very small, and I towered over her.

She cried. This small, strong, wonderful woman who had been through so much in her life cried. I had seen many emotions from my mother but I had never seen her cry—and she had had many reasons to cry.

"I won't let you go. I won't let you do this, she sobbed."

"I have to go or I'll be in big trouble"—of that I was quite sure.

Then she explained that she had spoken to people about AFROTC and had known about the flying for weeks. So much for her sixth sense. But then she used the ultimate weapon in her arsenal. She said she had a premonition in which she saw me crashing a plane into the side of a mountain. And then, with her voice cracking from the crying,

"I didn't go through the horrors of World War II in Hungary to keep you alive so that you could go and kill yourself fulfilling a stupid fantasy. If there is a war, you go and fight because you have to. If there isn't, you don't."

She wasn't exaggerating about the war; she risked her life for me many times. And we each had suffered, although I didn't remember all of it. And the stuff about the premonition might sound hokey, but it wasn't to me. I was in no position to dismiss any of it out of hand. I had experienced–and benefited from—her premonitions in the past. The details aren't important here, but they were very important to me then. The reality was that I could no more disobey or even disregard her than I could hurt her, and this was hurting her.

Still, I told her not to be so dramatic. No decision was being made that weekend. This was just a bunch of tests. We would talk about it again. And with that, I hugged her and left.

I passed the tests, whether with flying colors, I never found out. All I knew was that I had cleared one obstacle. But I was in deep turmoil. I had avoided talking with my mother about the flying precisely because I knew exactly what her reaction would be. I was all she had, all she really cared about, and she always feared for me. But how could I live like that?

Come what may, I would be completely forthcoming about AFROTC with my mother. I had no doubt she would ultimately engage my father on the subject, but his views would be far less predictable. At the ripe age of sixteen he had run away to join the Hungarian army in the First World War, was captured by the Russians after six weeks, and taken deep into Russia. Two years later he made a daring escape, holding on to the frozen undercarriage of a train. He understood adventure and what it meant to prove oneself.

In any event, even if I decided to do something they were both fervently opposed to, I would keep her in the process. So we talked about it over and over during the next weeks, without resolution but with a lot less emotion.

***

One night in late March while I was playing chess in the basement of Café Figaro in Greenwich Village, a friend mentioned that his cousin, who was in college in Boston, was shipping out in the merchant marine.

"Where's he going and what's he going to do 'on the high seas?'" I asked sarcastically.

"I don't know. I don't think he knows, he's just going to be some kind of seaman on a merchant ship until he figures out what he wants to do with his life."

I lost that game and the next, my thoughts wandering around vague images of merchant ships and adventure on the high seas and in far off ports. A new plan B began to form.

CHAPTER 4

Breakfast and the Inferno's Gate

The scene in the mess hall was not inviting. Some eighteen men were spread around six tables for four. The tables and chairs were attached to metal posts bolted to the floor. The gaze of the men as they stared at their plates was no less fixed. No one spoke. Michael and Raul, who a moment before had been joking and talking to me about how good the food was, now looked down at the floor as if observing some somber ritual, quickly found seats together at a table with two men and ignored me completely.

I stood for what seemed an eternity and focused again on my absurd costume. My pressed khaki pants and shirt—with epaulets no less—stood in sharp contrast to the casual, disheveled, dirty clothes of the other men. The uniform of the day was clearly old tee shirts, stained work shirts and very faded and dirty blue jeans. Well, I had no shortage of these, just as it happened, not on me. Here I was the most junior member of the crew by every measure–position, union status and age–dressed up like the second mate.

But I didn't stand there for an eternity, and these thoughts were fleeting. Uninvited, I sat down at a table with three men, thinking I would meet several at once. Without looking up, the man opposite me, a man with unusually narrow shoulders, very pale skin and wispy blond hair, spoke.

"Guy's coming in from watch; his seat."

Well, too bad for me. The hostess must have forgotten to put out the place cards.

"So, any empty seats?" I asked, imagining Alice and the scene with the Mad Hatter and the March Hare at the enormous empty dining table shouting, "No room, no room."

Still without looking up, he said, "Dunno. Ask."

So I went to a table in the back where only two men sat and asked. They shrugged their shoulders, got up and left. I sat down. I looked out the porthole directly in front of me and wondered gloomily what circle of Dante's *Inferno* I was in or whether this was just Hades and Hell awaited me down below. Then I realized that I was the only one in the room not eating.

Just sitting there wasn't going to help. And there was no one to ask at my table. I thought of turning and asking someone behind me but abandoned the idea. After a couple of minutes I got up and walked back out into the hallway. The kitchen was across from the mess hall and I went in. As I did, a solidly built fellow of medium height and around my age carrying a tray backed into me.

He yelled, "Shit," as I tried to get out of his way.

"What the fuck you want in here, man?" he asked with a Puerto Rican accent matching Raul's.

"I was just looking for some food, some breakfast," I replied.

"Well you just sit and wait. I ask you what you want and I bring it. You sit. Got it, man?"

"Got it" I said, but he wasn't done. "You don't work in the galley you don't go in the galley."

"Got it," I said again.

So I went back to the empty table, this time in a seat facing into the room, and waited. Eventually, true to his word, he came to the table. "You want eggs, bacon, toast," he said more than asked. I wondered, out of curiosity rather than desire, whether there were alternatives like pancakes or waffles, but as I looked around, those still eating were all hurriedly consuming bacon and scrambled eggs.

"Yeah, sounds good. Scrambled, OK?"

But the waiter had already turned to go. I looked at the large clock on the wall and saw that it was 7:49. I had eleven minutes to get my food, eat it and show up in the engine room at 8:00. I had a choice: forget the food and go back to the fo'c'sle and get out of my long-sleeved, tan officer's shirt with the epaulets and into a tee shirt or stay and eat. For better and worse, I chose the food.

As I waited for the bacon and eggs, I looked around the room at the men silently eating. Maybe I shouldn't take it personally, I thought. It's not just me; they're not talking to each other either. Still, a new crew member doesn't appear every day. You'd think someone would introduce himself or just ask, "What's your name?" But no one did. So Raul was right; they were all pissed at me because I had personally taken away their boondoggle by signing up for the lousiest job in the merchant marine. Well, damn them, I thought; what the hell can they do to me? On second thought, I really didn't want to find out.

The waiter must have looked at the clock too because the largest serving of bacon and eggs I'd ever seen appeared as I was finishing that second thought. He even brought coffee. I ate ravenously and fast. Fear seemed to have created a great appetite. And no mistake, I was afraid. With all my superficial preoccupations about my clothes and my fantasies about going to sea, I had no idea what awaited me in the engine room. I didn't even have any idea what it looked like.

It's hard to imagine a situation where you are about to enter a place, a place where you are going to work and spend a great deal of time, and have no idea at all what it looks like. I had seen pictures of extraordinary places—the more extraordinary the place, the more pictures there seemed to be, but I'd never seen a picture of the engine room of a ship. My life would be defined by this place that I couldn't even imagine. Yes, I was afraid.

At some point while I was eating, head down like the rest, Michael and Raul left. That certainly didn't help. Apart from my inchoate fear of this particular unknown, I had no idea where to find the engine room. I imagined there would be a door, a large imposing door, probably marked "ENGINE ROOM—KEEP OUT." But if there was such a door, I couldn't find it when I left the mess hall. I knew it was below me, so I headed down the steps of the main building from the mess hall to... as low as I could go. As I was wandering around, the second mate—"You call me Second" —came out of a cabin—OK, fo'c'sle.

"Looking for the engine room kid?"

"I figure the engine room is somewhere at the bottom of the ship; it's the door to it that I can't find."

My importune, whistling-in-the-graveyard response was not appreciated.

"One deck down. And kid, nobody needs a wise guy."

"Sorry," I said, as I headed down the next set of steps two at a time.

And then there it was, the only door in the hallway, large and heavy-looking. Painted the same medium gray as the rest of the hall, it was flanged at the edges …to keep it water tight, I supposed, or to keep a fire in the engine room contained—an inviting thought as I grabbed the large handle, turned it and pulled.

I opened the massive door and stepped inside…and a blast of the hottest air I had ever experienced in my life hit me like a truck. It was so hot that it hurt. I had been in midtown New York City in 104 degrees and that was certainly uncomfortable. But nothing like this. This was unimaginable heat. And I was going to work all day in this? It couldn't be. This was, in fact, Hell!

CHAPTER 5

Earlier Joys of the Sea and Jousting Against the Windmills of Bureaucracy

Plan B crystallized quickly. If nature abhors a vacuum, I didn't feel comfortable in one either. But a plan of any kind involving the sea or a ship was not an obvious choice for me. My only experience at sea had been a round trip voyage to Rotterdam on a Dutch student ship as part of a European tour when I was eighteen. My memories of those voyages were still as vivid as they were negative.

My cabin was on the "E" deck, which though it had a porthole, could just as well have been below the water line. The porthole was covered, latched and sealed.

With four double-deck bunks—each occupied—the cabin was so cramped that two people could not pass between bunks. There was only one small sink in the cabin, and only one person at a time could be anywhere near it.

If the crowding was bad, the food was worse. To this day I still don't know if the Dutch have a particular fondness for ox or if it was just on sale the week we left port–in both directions! But ox in one form or another, always with a taupe or gray hue, was the staple fare for every lunch and dinner. We ate ox steaks, ox roasts, ox soup, ox gravy, ox burgers, along with less ascertainable ox parts made no more palatable by having royal suffixes, like Elizabeth, Maria Theresa and Beatrix.

Perhaps not as a direct consequence of the food— but certainly not prevented by it—there was a great deal of seasickness. This made the bathrooms and hallways, to say nothing of the cabins and even the dining room, reek. And as the heavy seas (unusual for summer crossings) were frequently accompanied by driving rain, there was not much opportunity for respite on deck. Given the crowding, the result was inevitable: an ever-expanding, downward spiral of nausea eventually overwhelming most of the passengers.

Despite these hardships the voyages offered two very real delights, at least in concept: the easy availability of girls and inexpensive alcohol, a heady mixture for sure. The ratio of females to males on board was three to one, and   Once in international waters—within a half hour of departure—mixed drinks cost a quarter and a bottle of Heineken twelve cents. Even in 1960 that was virtually free.

At the first night's social mixer pairings were almost immediate, fueled by the abundant alcohol and the girls' readiness to cut some corners in the mating ritual to assure a partner for the nine-and-a-half day voyage. The problem was where to go. The cabins were crowded and offered no privacy. Initially, ingenuity rewarded a few as they found nooks and crannies in odd corners of the ship. But for most, there was a great deal of frustration. This led to more and more drinking. Then the heavy seas came, along with the Ox Beatrix, and the rest inexorably followed.

How did I fare in all this? What I have described is based, for the outward voyage, on reliable, albeit second-hand reports, as I spent all but one night in the ship's infirmary. After finding an attractive girl from the University of Iowa and consuming my share of beer that first evening, I eventually found my way down to my cabin and went to sleep. Waking a few hours later in a cold sweat, I got down from my top bunk to get a drink of water from the sink. What greeted me in the mirror above it—even in the dimness of the night light—was frightening. My face and chest were covered with spots. The conclusion was obvious.

Covering my head with a wet towel, I wended my way through semi–lit passageways and around drunken passengers, some ambulatory, others passed out on the floor, and eventually found the infirmary. My case of measles was accompanied by an initial fever of 106 degrees. I spent the remainder of the voyage quarantined from the rest of the passengers. Although uncomfortable and weak, I avoided the general chaos and unpleasantness. I couldn't avoid the ox.

The return voyage was better in that I didn't have the measles and could therefore participate in the onboard activities of pairing up and drinking. But this time I couldn't avoid the inevitable seasickness all around me. I found to my surprise that I wasn't inclined to being seasick, that is, not from the motion of the ship even in rough seas. That didn't immunize me from the effects of vomit everywhere I turned. It also made the female to male ratio a lot less attractive as the denominator was no longer the total population of girls on the ship but only the girls who weren't seasick, a much smaller number due to an inverse correlation between hardiness and attractiveness. So, as I said, it was not at all obvious that my one roundtrip experience on a ship would inspire me to adopt a Plan B at sea.

My interactions with the crew certainly didn't motivate me either. The only times I saw them they were either cleaning up vomit or serving their endless cavalcade of ox parts. Eventually those functions blurred.

I didn't even like fish. I had never even gone fishing, or been on a sailboat. In fact my only other nautical experiences had been on the Staten Island Ferry, on a tour boat cruising around Manhattan Island, and in a row boat.

But reality wasn't going to interfere with fantasy. I wasn't going to be influenced by my experience or by my lack of it. I was looking to join the merchant marine that worked on freighters, not that group of unfortunates that had to deal with seasick passengers and gray ox meat. Mariners on freighters wouldn't get seasick. They were tough and seasoned. I was sure I could pass that test.

So with my head filled with colorful images of Marseilles and Istanbul dredged out of vaguely remembered movies, I decided to go to sea. That is, I would commit to the advanced corps of AFROTC, stay with the flying program, assuming they would have me, get a job on an American merchant ship when my spring term exams ended, letting everyone at the university, my mother and father and my friends believe it was a summer job, and then stay at sea, postponing my education—and the eventual confrontation about the flying program—until I was ready. Really the same plan as the Alaska pipeline, but with an opportunity to see the world. And to see it the way it should be seen, not as a tourist but with a purpose.

***

So much for the plan. Joining the merchant marine and getting a ship turned out to be a good deal more problematic. But I had time; it was only February. Of course, I had no idea how to go about any of it, or even where to begin. All I knew was that I needed seaman's papers, whatever they were. I knew that because my highly eccentric fourth year Latin teacher in boarding school had been a purser on passenger ships for 27 years, and had spent part of a class otherwise devoted to the fifth book of Virgil's *Aeneid* explaining how difficult it was to get seaman's papers. Out of the four people in the class, he must have been talking to me.

Seaman's papers were issued by the United States government. Was it the Navy, the Department of Commerce, the State Department? In a time of computers and Google, such an inquiry would be a snap. In 1962, not so easy. I had no one to ask. I figured the Navy would be my best bet. But the Department of the Navy was in Washington D.C., and I wasn't going to make a long distance call. So I went to the Navy recruitment booth at Times Square.

When I explained what I was looking for, the petty officer in charge (I was familiar with all service ranks from the AFROTC training) laughed.

"You don't want to join the merchant marine kid; you want to join the Navy."

Explaining that I was already sort of in the Air Force didn't seem a useful response. I insisted that it was the merchant marine I wanted, and he replied that the Navy had nothing to do with it. Further, he had no idea where one got seamen's papers, and he couldn't imagine why anyone would want to.

"The merchant marine is a bunch of skags that can't get into the Navy, and their ships are crap."

Thus chastened, I went to the library and looked up "merchant marine," and after a few false starts found the National Maritime Administration. That was the federal agency responsible for the merchant marine. Assuming that it would be the one issuing seamen's papers, I found the number in the phone book and called. No answer. I called several times over two days. This was the government; they had to be home. No answer.

But they did have an address, somewhere in lower Manhattan. A few days later I had no afternoon classes, and still very much buoyed by my fantasies, I headed by subway down to the southern tip of Manhattan to visit the National Maritime Administration.

The offices were nondescript beige. There was nothing about them to suggest the sea or the merchant marine. There was also no one there. That would explain the phone problem. But the doors were open, and there was a small reception area, so I sat down. A quarter of an hour later a woman emerged from another door, and as she walked by me toward her desk, she asked whether I had an appointment. I told her I didn't. Looking around the empty room, I added that I hoped they could squeeze me in. She ignored my sarcasm.

"I'm here to get seaman's papers," I said.

"Well, you're in the wrong place."

"Isn't the National Maritime Administration in charge of the merchant marine?"

"Yes."

"Well then, why not?"

"Because we don't."

"Then who does?"

"I don't know."

"Is there someone here who does?"

"You say you don't have an appointment?"

"Yes, that's right, I don't. But since you're not the right government agency, you wouldn't have given me an appointment anyway once I told you what I wanted, right?"

We were nearing a stalemate.

"Could you just ask someone," I asked, indicating the door through which she had emerged. She thought about that for a few seconds, got up and went through the door. The absurdity of the situation didn't amuse me.

A few minutes later a middle-aged man burst through the door, closely followed by the woman. Annoyed and agitated he said, "She told you we don't issue seaman's papers."

Clearly, my persistence had upset the office routine. "Yes she did. Would you be kind enough to tell me who does?"

"The Coast Guard," he said with some effort, rolling his eyes.

Well, that was progress. Then, pressing my luck and with some trepidation,

"Their address?"

"Whitehall Street," he exhaled, as if I had choked it out of him, and pointed vaguely in the direction of the elevator. I didn't think I could get more, so I thanked them and started to leave. As I opened the front door the man said, "You're wasting your time you know. You'll never get a ship."

I turned to ask why, but he and the woman had gone back into the other room.

Why couldn't I get a ship? Why were these people so unhelpful? Well, some bureaucrat being a jerk because I interrupted an office meeting wasn't going to stop me from joining the merchant marine and shipping out. And now I finally knew who issued seaman's papers and sort of where they lived.

Thus undaunted, I set off in the direction the man had pointed. The fourth person I asked was able to direct me to Whitehall Street, six blocks away. On the way, I thought about the name. I remembered "Whitehall" often being referred to in British war movies as the home of the "Admiralty." It couldn't have been a coincidence that the American Coast Guard was located on another Whitehall Street. I felt as if I were going somewhere historic. Somehow this made my quest more important, more dramatic. And in my head I always created my own fantasized, dramatic context.

Whitehall Street didn't disappoint. It was indeed near the water, at the very bottom of Manhattan Island.

But there was nothing in sight that should have been the historic home of the United States Coast Guard. After trying the lobby of several high-rise office buildings, there it was in small white plastic letters set in a black board listing the many tenants of the building: "U.S. Coast Guard——3rd fl." Certainly not what I had expected.

The Coast Guard office, like those of the National Maritime Administration, was almost entirely two-tone beige, its walls, its metal desks and chairs. But it looked like it actually dealt with people. Just beyond a reception area was a large room with several thick square pillars and a long counter with clerks on one side and short lines of waiting men on the other, much like a post office or bank. I joined one of the lines.

Whatever these men were here for—perhaps getting seaman's papers—the process involved lots of discussion, and progress was slow. As I looked around I saw that taped to each pillar was a sheet of paper roughly fourteen inches by eighteen inches with columns of dense print. From where I stood I couldn't make out any of it. I asked the man in front of me to hold my place and walked over to look.

What I read would inspire a new set of fantasies about shipping out. Below a heading that read, "Members of the World's Merchant Marines Currently Missing at Sea," was a five column list of several hundred names in telephone directory-size type. They were listed alphabetically, irrespective of nationality or of the merchant marine to which they belonged. It was impossible to tell how many were from the American merchant marine.

The list was frightening, as much for its matter-of-factness as for what it displayed. There must have been almost a thousand names. These people didn't die in an accident or from sickness. They were missing! How could they all be missing at sea? How did you become missing at sea? Did they fall overboard? Were they pushed? How long did they stay missing before they were taken off the list? In other words, how old was the list? I had a lot of questions. But I had a new and real fear: a lot of seamen had become missing at sea and are never accounted for. How they got that way was now my new preoccupation.

As I was staring transfixed by the terrifying list, a clerk called, "Can I help you?"

I hadn't noticed that my line was now just me. I rushed over to the counter, and still thinking about the list, I said with a lot less enthusiasm than I had had a few minutes before, that I wanted to apply for seaman's papers.

"You got your committal letter?" he asked.

"I'm sorry; I don't know anything about a committal letter or really anything else involved in the application. I had enough trouble just finding where to apply."

"Well, at least you're in the right place. We issue seaman's papers, but only when you've got a committal letter from a steamship company saying that they're willing to employ you. That and all the other stuff: vaccination record, health certificate, and of course, the completed application."

"So how do I go about getting one of these committal letters?"

"Can't help you there. Don't really know, and if I did I wouldn't tell you."

"Why not?"

"Because the merchant marine isn't looking for more seamen. There aren't enough jobs as it is. Too few ships, that is, ships flying the American flag."

"Look, I'm not trying to be a pain, but I really want to ship out. I've wanted to do this all my life. I need this chance." The lie rolled off my tongue effortlessly. "I just need a direction, not names."

"Look, kid, I'm not trying to be a pain either. I'm just telling you how it is. You're not going to get a ship. You're wasting your time. Even if somehow you got a ship company to write you a letter, you still have to get into the union. You want to know pain. They're a pain."

"Union? What union? I thought it was part of the Coast Guard or the National Maritime Administration. I have to join a union?"

"For someone who wanted to ship out all his life you sure don't know anything. The merchant marine is private just like the ships they work on. And there are two unions that matter, one mainly for passenger ships, the NMU, and the other for cargo ships and tankers, the SIU. It's more complicated than that, but that's the general idea. What were you looking to do, as if it mattered?"

"Not passenger ships, for sure."

"Well that's good, 'cause the SIU may be a bit easier." Then he thought for a moment. "Maybe not. They're all a pain. But they run the show. They give you a ship, or not, and they lead those shipping companies around by the nose."

"But if the union gives me the ship, then what's the use of a letter from the ship company that they'll hire me; I mean if they end up not having any choice?"

"Figure it out. You look like a smart kid, too smart for this stuff."

"Thanks," I said, rolling my eyes this time. "I will figure it out and I will get a committal letter. I've got the vaccination certificate and I'm healthy. I'll be back." Then, as I turned to leave,

"I figure NMU stands for National Maritime Union, and the IU ought to be International Union. So what's the 'S,' seamen?"

"Seafarers."

"Looking at that list of missing seamen, it ought to be "sea fearers.""

"Yeah, well, who knows what and where most of those guys are. Dregs of the earth. A lot of those on that list were wanted by the law in whatever hellhole of a country they came from. They jump ship; I mean into the goddamn water. They get knifed in fights. Who knows? You're not dealing with the Sea Scouts, you know, and that goes for ours too." And then for good measure, "Why don't you go talk to the recruiter," he said pointing behind the counter, "and join the Coast Guard?"

"Thanks all the same. I appreciate your help and your time." At least regarding his time, I meant it.

I left the Coast Guard office defiant. This bureaucratic bullshit was not going to keep me from shipping out, from doing what suddenly had become the most important thing in the world.

My typical attitude: I was generally imbued with a totally unreasonable belief that I could accomplish whatever I wanted if I wanted it enough and therefore worked hard enough at it. Mostly I believed that I could talk my way into or out of just about anything.

My performance record, on the other hand, was rather erratic. But I rationalized any failures simply by declaring to myself—I was the only player in these games who mattered—that I hadn't wanted it enough. Within this superficial overconfidence, I had a particular disdain for authority, bureaucracy and other interference from rules, regulations and procedures of any kind. I seemed to make a point of doing things late, and then talking my way out of whatever problem I had created for myself. These "victories" over all manner of administrators at the university and elsewhere gave me surprising satisfaction.

It was with this attitude that I approached what I saw as a ridiculous bureaucratic impediment, the problem of the committal letter. The horrible fates of the missing seamen temporarily receded from my consciousness.

Both would have to wait. I had a history paper to write and a geology exam to study for. I was, after all, a student—at least for the moment. In fact I enjoyed my studies and intermittently concentrated hard on them, although I was easily distracted by thoughts of my future and by life in general.

One of those life distractions was Lynn. Although my focus was on women, not girls, women weren't so easy to come by, while girls—students at the university—were. So I made a lot of exceptions. Generally this involved the pursuit of redheads.

But I grew weary of this pursuit as I learned a demographic/geographic law to which I had not found an exception in eighteen months: the prettier the redhead, the further she lived from me. So for each incremental prettiness point on a scale of 6 to10, I had to count on an additional half hour of travel time.

Since I was able to connect with some 8s and 9s, my commutes to pick them up for a date, do something in Manhattan, take them home, and then get home myself—and that was the drill—could be six hours not counting the date itself. Inevitably these girls lived either in deepest darkest Brooklyn or the furthest reaches of the Bronx. Far enough to require a bus *after* several subways.

I clearly needed to be saved from redheads, and Lynn was auditioning for the savior's role. A brunette, of course she lived in Manhattan, albeit on the lower east side. We had had one date. She was an 8, but more important, very sexy. She acted much more like a woman than a girl. When I took her home, I kissed her good night in the vestibule of her building. What she did with her tongue over the next fifteen minutes was beyond anything I had experienced and brought kissing from the level of benign foreplay to what I thought embodied the very essence of sex.

The promise of more was intoxicating. It was the upcoming second date with Lynn that was on my mind, easily edging out the history paper and the geology exam, and certainly the committal letter.

The Saturday night date came, and it was most of what I had hoped for. We had dinner at a place I knew near Times Square that didn't cost too much. She made a point of telling me that she had cancelled a date with another guy to be with me. Though it was meant to make me feel good, I was uneasy. I thought of an expression that I had heard but never used myself: "There but for the grace of God go I."

My trepidation didn't last long. When we finished eating I asked if she would like to see a movie. She looked at me intently and said no. We looked at each other some more, and I quickly splurged for a cab. I was staying at the apartment of a friend and he was out. We were in.

Unlike many of the "girls," Lynn did not insist on the ritual of a step by step invasion of each successive layer of armor. She shed most of her clothes right in the living room as I got her a drink. We spent the next couple of hours playing with each other as we went through the levels of foreplay from 101 to 404, stopping just short of graduation. I wasn't sure why, but I wasn't pushing it. This was too good to screw up.

The history paper and geology exam were a reasonable success. I had other course work, and of course, AFROTC and flying the C-47s when the weather was favorable.

I was also in a military fraternity called the Pershing Rifles. Its principal activity was a trick drill team, and that also took a lot of my time. We drilled and performed complex maneuvers while twirling, throwing and otherwise manipulating eleven pound M-1s with fixed bayonets, to the amusement of audiences at Madison Square Garden during the intermission of basketball games, sometimes even televised. My relationship with Lynn was in stable mode, and eventually I returned to the problem of the committal papers.

Propelled by an attitude more of annoyance than desperation, I consulted a truly esoteric source to deal with my problem: the Yellow Pages. I called twelve ship companies, from very large ones with big ads to ones with no ads. I imagined that the large ones dealt with these requests all the time and would refer me to the appropriate person who would drop everything and write me the letter. The small ones would get few requests and therefore view mine as an opportunity to help an aspiring merchant seaman, one that might one day work on one of their ships.

As usual reality was different. The large companies most often said that as a matter of company policy they didn't write committal letters. One said that the person who handled such things was on vacation. When I asked when he or she would return, the response was "who knows?"

Another came up with what I had recently learned was called a "catch 22": asked if they could write a committal letter for me, the woman on the phone asked if I had my seaman's papers.

The small ones didn't even seem to know what I was talking about. They told me they didn't hire seamen, and that I should talk to the union. So much for the straightforward approach.

I asked my friends if their parents had friends who might know someone in a ship company. I came up empty. But I couldn't accept the notion that this stupid bureaucratic impediment, this catch 22, was going to keep me from shipping out.

The eventual solution to my problem came from a source so unexpected, so incongruous with every image of going to sea, of shipping out, of joining the merchant marine, that it embarrasses me to this day: my mother! I had told her of my plans to "work on a ship as a summer job." She didn't raise a fuss. Whether she wasn't concerned, knew she couldn't go to the wall—or the door in her case—on every issue, or thought that such an adventure would cure me of my suicidal idea of flying "war planes" I don't know.

I told her in passing about the committal letter problem, and she said she often played bridge with a man who owned a shipping company. And she would ask him. How about that!

Two weeks later I was on the phone with his secretary, and a week after that I received the committal letter. Just like that.

And just like that, my *mother* got me into the merchant marine. Armed with my committal letter, health and vaccination certificates and my completed application, I returned to the Coast Guard office on Whitehall Street. With a self-satisfied, smug expression, I waited on the line in front of the same clerk. He wasn't expecting me.

"You got everything?" he asked with a doubtful expression.

I handed him a stuffed envelope. As he took out the various documents, his shocked look was all I had hoped for.

"So how'd you get it?" Obviously not many people came back after his committal letter speech.

"No problem," I said with a dismissive wave, as if I overcame these administrative hassles all the time. I smiled as I imagined his reaction if I were to tell him my mother had arranged it.

He said the application and everything else were in order and that I would receive the *U.S. Merchant Mariner's Document*—that was its official name—in the mail.

"Can't I wait for it here?"

"No, you'll get it in the mail in about a week."

So, no instant gratification, but I was happy and it showed.

"OK, you got your papers," he said almost grudgingly, "but now you've got to go deal with the SIU to get a ship. You may not be smiling long. Good luck!"

I nodded in what I thought was a manly, knowing way, said thanks and left. Yes, the union, the SIU was next, but that would have to wait. If I got through that maze and they suddenly gave me a ship, I was in no position to take it. I still had six weeks of classes and exams before I was ready to go. So the rest of my life, my current life, would be my focus. And that would very much include Lynn.

CHAPTER 6

It Begins for Real

I stood on the steel grid landing just inside the main hatch to the engine room. The initial blast of heat, unbelievable heat, didn't dissipate at all. I stood frozen by it. I wondered how anyone could work in such heat, even for ten minutes, to say nothing of all day. Then an even more troubling realization hit me: we were still in port. The steam engine, the thing that must be generating all this heat, was either shut down or at least on a low power setting. How hot would it be when we were out at sea?

I needed to get down there, down to hell, and go to work. *Don Juan in Hell!*

I reached for the stainless steel railing.

Then hell erupted. I let out a yell. "What the...! Damn!"

Searing pain went through my hands. They felt burned though I couldn't see any immediate marks. I'd forgotten my work gloves. Heavy leather work gloves. They were in my sea bag along with my tee shirts and jeans—another gift from Lorna. But they weren't on my hands.

How the hell was I going to get down this ladder—
and what could I do once I got there—without the
gloves?

But down I went, leaning back against the ladder
and keeping my arms out, as if I were walking on a tight
rope.

Three levels below the main hatch I arrived at the
bottom, the main deck of the engine room. Above, steel
bridges, ladders and landings, most with machines of
some kind on them, hardly filling the vast vertical space.
The ladder had deposited me near what appeared to
be the boilers. There were two of them, immense steel
containers about ten feet high and eight feet wide and
deep. Their steel-covered portholes—that's what they
looked like to me—faced each other. In between was a
panel of dials and gauges.

A man, dressed as I should have been, studied the
panel. He didn't notice me. The noise from the boilers and other machinery was far too loud. I realized it
would get a lot louder when we were moving.

As I stood gazing around the engine room, trying
to take in as much of my new surroundings as possible,
I felt a hard tap on my shoulder. I had heard nothing.
Lesson number one: with noise at this level you can't
hear someone coming up behind you with rubber-soled
work shoes on a thick steel deck.

I turned around and saw what I thought was Second,
the mate I had met when I boarded the ship. It wasn't,
but it sure could have been his brother.

"I'm the Second Assistant Engineer, 8:00 to 12:00
watch. Call me Second." That would be convenient.

He probably had a name, I thought, but I clearly didn't warrant knowing it.

"I'm the new wiper."

"Well, I kinda guessed that," he said with a smile, "but I wasn't sure. You're dressed like...I don't know what." He didn't ask my name.

"Yeah, well, I didn't have time to change. Got on the ship, had something to eat and...."

He cut off the explanation. "You're going to get hot, and that rig you got on, well it's not going to look like that for long."

"Hey, I'm hot already and don't worry about my clothes. I'll deal with it."

In a far corner I could see Raul chipping paint with a chisel. Michael was nowhere in sight. The guy at the boilers must have heard us—though I don't know how—since he turned around. He was tall, almost my height, thin, stooped with a crew cut. In his mid-thirties.

"Glen, fireman" he offered, extending his hand.

"Peter." We shook hands. He pointed in the direction of another guy, who seemed to be just walking around, a bit older, shorter and wearing a pink baseball hat with blue flowers, and said "Oiler, Tony."

That was it for introductions, but at least someone had made an attempt. Certainly an improvement over the mess hall.

Second motioned to me to follow him. He led me around behind the boilers to a machine attached to the deck and surrounded by a sheet metal crib about eighteen inches high and eight feet square. The machine made intermittent noises like a pump. It was almost

completely submerged in oil. The steel crib was almost
overflowing with oil leaked from the machine.

"So here's what you do, kid. Empty the oil out of
the crib and pour it into the tank by the bulkhead, then
clean the pump and the deck so they're spotless."

He pointed in the general direction of the other
side of the engine room, waived at some empty ten gallon paint cans and a stack of rags, and turned to leave.

"Uh, do you have an extra pair of work gloves around
that I could use?"

"I guess you weren't planning on working today, kid.
You thought maybe today would be a guided tour of the
ship and a nap? Well, kid, you don't start with a day
off. So here, use these," He took a pair of brown cotton
work gloves from his back pocket and handed them to
me.

I wanted to respond, to say I wasn't expecting a day
off, that I was expecting to work, and to try to explain
again about my bag and running out of time. But this
wasn't my father or some teacher. He wasn't interested
in my explanation or in me for that matter. I was going
to have to get used to the fact that this wasn't some
kind of camp. While it seemed they were going to call
me "kid," they weren't going to cut me any slack. So
I just said "Thanks. I'll wash them and get them back
to you."

He nodded with a half smile, probably wondering
what I was wondering: how the hell would I get the oil
out of these gloves? Then he left and I looked at the
pool of oil. I thought he must have given me this job
just to make sure that my tans got ruined, and maybe he
did. Then again, the oil was no more than a half inch

below the top of the crib. Someone had to do it and soon. I didn't know how long it had taken to fill the crib, but I clearly had arrived just in the nick of time. I went to get the cans and rags. You're a wiper; you wipe.

The job looked easy enough. Just dip two cans into the oil until they were full, carry them around to the other side of the engine room and dump them into the tank. So that's what I did. Carrying two ten gallon cans full of oil turned out to be heavier than I had expected, but lack of strength wasn't my problem.

Oil had dripped on the sides of the cans as I filled them. Also, I had filled the cans almost to the top to save trips. When I started to walk, the oil from the sides of the cans dripped onto the deck. And as I continued, the oil sloshed back and forth and eventually over the top edge of the cans and again onto the deck. As I turned to go back after emptying the cans, I saw that I had left a trail of oil the whole way.

Second saw it before I did. As I looked up he was standing on a ladder staring at me. I nodded at him and then in the direction of the trail.

"I know. I'll take care of it."

I felt like the sorcerer's apprentice. With a rag in each hand, I crawled back along the deck cleaning the trail I had left. I was finding a way to screw up everything I did. I was going to have to think and be careful. I didn't know what I had expected—I really hadn't expected anything. But if I didn't get my act together, I'd be kicked off the goddamn ship before it left port.

I used a third can to dip into the oil and pour into the two others. And I filled the cans to the three-quarter level. I took more trips, but I didn't spill a drop. This

was stupid, mindless work, but it was my job, and I was
going to do it perfectly.

When there wasn't enough oil left to use the cans,
I used the rags and wiped. My shirt was completely
soaked with sweat and pretty much covered with oil, my
pants not far behind. I tried to use clean rags to wipe
my head, but the gloves were covered with oil, so my
face, neck and hair were covered with oil as well.

Periodically the machine came alive and shuddered
for twenty seconds. When the crib had been full the
shuddering created waves in the oil. Now that it was
empty and I was wiping the deck near the pump and the
machine itself, I stayed away from it when it shuddered,
as if it were some kind of quirky animal.

Finally I was finished. The old pump—and it looked
old—and the deck and crib were spotless if not exactly
gleaming. I found Second and he followed me back
to the scene of my great achievement. I was beaming
and must have looked as if I was expecting a medal for
wiping valor. He nodded. I asked him what I should do
with the three cans filled with oily rags. He pointed at
the tank I had gotten to know so well.

"You'll deal with those later."

After that he introduced me to some of the other
machines around the engine room, though not to what
they did. I attacked them with my rags. I wanted to ask
about the machines, but I thought he was about as interested in talking to me as I was in wiping, so I just wiped.

After the wiping, I swept.

Then Second came over and said it was time for
lunch. I realized that for nearly four hours I hadn't

looked at my watch. How one could be so absorbed in such mindless work I don't know, but I was.

***

Lunch was not at all like breakfast. The place seemed more alive. People talked. There was noise. Even after washing up—we used industrial solvent and then soap— I was in the mess hall a few minutes before noon. There were several guys already sitting, but most of the room was empty. Remembering the morning's experience, I sat at an empty table, with my back to the portholes. A few minutes later Michael came in, saw me and sat down in the seat opposite.

"So how did it go? Second had you doing the fucking pump. Did it to Raul when he came on. He wants you to get used to the mess, to get you dirty. Not a bad guy though. Doesn't give you a lot of shit. First is a pain in the ass. All the time looking at his watch, telling you you're taking too long whatever you're doing. Yells a lot. He's an unhappy sod. Miserable bastard really; got no friends. Second, he's a decent sort. You notice how much he looks like the Second Mate?"

A lot to take in. "Yeah, they look like brothers, if not twins. And Second does seem OK. He got me dirty alright. I can probably throw these clothes right out."

"You crazy man? Eventually you wash the sweat out so they don't stink—guys'll give you a hard time if you stink. Shit man, I'll give you a hard time if you stink. But oil stains, paint, they're fine. Look, all we do is get dirty. No point in wearing clean clothes."

"Yeah, yours look like they've seen some activity." It made sense, of course. You washed your clothes so they didn't stink, and when they became so stiff with paint and everything else—which, looking at Michael, they clearly eventually did—you got rid of them, or tore them into rags, and got new stuff.

"What about the other officers?" I asked.

"Oh, they're alright I suppose. Don't see Third too often and Junior is pretty quiet."

"Junior? What or who is Junior?" But before he could answer, the guy from the galley this morning came over with sandwiches. As he put them on the table he looked at me, glared really, and then down at my feet. Then he left.

"What's his problem?" I asked.

"Who knows? He's always pissed off about something. Anyway, "Junior" is Junior Assistant Third Engineer. Screwy title, you know. There's no sense to it. There's the Captain, the Chief Mate—he really runs the show, and the Second, Third and Fourth Mates. But with the engineers, there's a Chief Engineer—he's like the Captain of the engine room. Captain doesn't really tell him what to do. Then First, Second and Third Assistant Engineer, and instead of a Fourth Assistant, they call him Junior Assistant Third. Why? Who knows? Second, he always stands the 8 to 12 watch. The others sometimes trade watches. Even though they're mostly on in daytime, you never see the Chief Engineer or the Captain. And by the way, they're not called officers anymore; 'licensed personnel' they're called now."

"What about the other guys, the firemen and the oilers, do we work with them?"

"No, if we work with anybody—and mostly we don't because we do such shit work that nobody else does— we might work with an engineer. You know, if he's fixing something."

"So, do we clean the engine? And where is it anyway? I could sure hear it but I didn't see anything that looked like it should be making all that noise."

"The turbines, they're in a compartment behind the tool boards, along with the propeller shafts and the steering gears and the like. And no, we've got nothing to do with that stuff. They don't want us going in there. If something breaks, the engineers fix it, maybe with an oiler."

The off-limits warning, just made getting into that compartment my new imperative.

Just then Glen the Fireman came over and sat down. "So how do you like the SS fucking *Rufus Saxton?*"

"Not much to compare it to. My first ship. I'm telling you that just in case you had some doubts. How old is this ship? Is it as old as it looks?"

"Yeah it's old. Maybe twenty years old, maybe more. Built during the war, and it saw a lot of service in the Atlantic. But that's not the problem. It was built cheap, from an old design, and they made lots of them. It was a regular C-2 cargo ship. Then just a few years ago Sea-Land—your employer if you didn't notice—started this container business and they converted this ship and a few others into container ships. But they weren't built for this, not originally. Now these things are top heavy, use a lot of ballast. Anyway, ship's had a lot of wear. Engine's still good, but most everything leaks. And that, my friend, is where you come in."

We continued talking, and I learned a few more things about the ship. I asked when we were going to pull out, get going. I didn't know the right term for it. I knew it wasn't "set sail!" He didn't offer any help on the vocabulary but said we wouldn't be loaded up until around dinner time, and that we would leave about an hour after that. Then after a sandwich and a soda, I went back to the fo'c'sle, got rid of the thick shirt and put on a white tee shirt. It wasn't going to stay that way, but it sure was a lot cooler. I also got my gloves.

The afternoon passed more slowly, as I did lots of small wiping jobs around the engine room and then joined Raul chipping paint. Chipping and painting are the mainstays of all seagoing activity. On deck the salt air and the almost constant sea spray as the bow cuts through the water breaks down the paint and, if left unchecked, corrodes the metal. Rust is the main enemy of a metal ship, outside and in. In the engine room it was the humidity and extreme heat that ate away at the paint. I never did find out why the paint adhered so unevenly to the metal of the ship. Within the space of a few inches some of the paint was peeling spontaneously. A touch with the broad chisel was enough to dislodge good-sized pieces. Next to that the paint was intact and required the business end of the chisel helped by a hammer.

I asked Raul about this. But Raul turned out not to be a source of information on just about anything. He seemed to know very little and cared even less. His response to most of my questions—and I had a lot and he was the only one within earshot—was "I don't know."

He just shook his head and stared at the paint. After another question he had had enough.

"Who knows about that shit, man," the "man" pronounced "maaaan." "Don't ask me that shit man; I don't care. OK? I don't care about any of this. I hate this stinking ship. OK? This just a job, a shit job, but it pays; it pays for me. But you, you could get a real job, not a shit job like this, and make money. But no, you here. You ask stupid fucking questions. Nobody give a shit. OK?"

"Look Raul, I got this job because I wanted to ship out, and the union said I take this job or nothing. And I ask you questions because I want to know what I'm doing. That's it. No big deal."

He took my proffered hand and gave it a limp shake; and that was the end of that. We didn't talk the rest of the afternoon. Side by side we chipped until he disappeared for about ten minutes. At 4:30 Michael, who had been painting all day on another level of the engine room, showed up and we all washed up, again starting with the solvent. I wondered what effect using an industrial solvent on your hands and arms twice a day would have, but now I knew enough not to ask.

***

As hungry as I was, eating was not my priority. I had time, so I went back to the fo'c'sle, got out of my clothes and found the shower. It was wonderful. I had never enjoyed a shower so much. Whatever might be wrong with the ship, and there appeared to be plenty, the shower wasn't one of them. Clean clothes felt good too.

As I walked back to what I thought of as the main house, I realized how thirsty I was. Although I had several drinks from the water fountain in the engine room, it couldn't have replenished all the water I had lost sweating. I had never sweated so much in my life, not even close. I wished I had a scale because I would have bet that I had lost more than five pounds The heat would never abate, and I would never get used to it.

Dinner was a very pleasant surprise. There was a menu with many choices: three main courses, salads, different vegetables, potatoes. Not only was there a variety, but it all looked really good. This was a restaurant, not a cafeteria. But the best thing was that you could have as much as you wanted. In fact you could order the entire menu. It was called "a full house." It turned out that steak was always one of the main courses, and you could order two steaks or even three.

As Michael told me all this, he issued a warning: "But If you order extra, don't order more than you're going to eat. 'Cause if you don't finish the second steak or whatever, Cook's going to get mad, and you don't want to see Cook mad. He'll kill you, man. I mean it."

"The cook is going to kill me if I don't finish my dinner? Sort of like my mother, huh?"

One of the guys from breakfast, the one who had said the seat was taken, heard me from the next table, and said, "Yeah he might, kid. Hell, he might kill you anyway, just because he doesn't like you. Did seventeen years for manslaughter. Killed a guy right in his galley."

"For not eating his second steak?" I asked, feigning bemusement.

"I don't know why he killed the guy. Why don't you ask Cook, kid? I'm sure he'll want to discuss it with you and maybe other things too. Who knows, maybe you'll strike up a lasting friendship."

At this, Michael and Raul made dismissive gestures, and turning to me, Michael said, "Cook doesn't talk much, and I think he did kill a guy. Said it was self-defense. I don't know how big the dead guy was, but Cook is every bit of six foot eight and weighs, I don't know, maybe two eighty. Said he was standing in the galley—not this galley; on another ship—and the guy pulled a gun on him and supposedly told him to put his hands up. So cook did that and there happened to be a meat clever, you know, hanging on a hook through that hole at the end of the blade, just where his hand was. And Cook just grabbed the clever and brought it down on the guy at the point where your shoulder meets your neck, and just about split the guy in two. Problem was, they never found a gun, so Cook did seventeen years. Anyway, that's how I heard it; and heard it and heard it! Cook's a legend. And he's one legend you can stay away from."

With that happy advice, dinner was over. You could eat dessert right then or wait until "Pie Watch." Pie Watch involved going back to the mess hall around 8:00 or later and eating freshly baked pie left there by the cook. Of course, not just one pie, but three kinds of pie. Sounded good to me, so I left and walked back to the fo'c'sle. But before I did, I asked one of the guys where I could find another mattress and pillow. I didn't want to go looking for Second. Turned out there was an open store room right near the mess hall that had all sorts of stuff. Whether I was supposed to or not, I took what I needed. I would deal with Stanley's stuff later.

At the stern house I looked around. There wasn't much. Another fo'c'sle, pretty much like mine, some store rooms, the shower room and toilets, and next to that, the washing machine. There was no dryer. Instead the washing machine had a device attached to the top called a mangle: two rollers set close together through which you fed the wet clothes. It got most of the water out. With a pair of pants you could fold them into position and the mangle almost ironed them. There were clothes on hangers all around the area and in the fo'c'sles. I wondered who bought the detergent. It turned out that we each did. No sharing. Each guy had his favorite brand, and they argued about which was best like a bunch of housewives. I would have to get some Tide, the only brand I knew, but that and my wash would have to wait until Jacksonville, three or four days later.

I found my harmonica stuffed in the bottom of the sea bag and put it into my pocket. I had started playing a couple of years before and thought it would be an appropriate activity on a ship, even for a wiper. I went out looking for a place to sit and watch the ship pull out of its berth. I sat on a small hatch cover between the stern house and the stacks of containers. There were four rows of containers stacked three high. Below deck level they were stacked four deep. From what I had seen earlier, there were a lot more at the bow end of the ship. I thought about taking a look, but staying out of the way seemed a better idea. So I sat and watched the shore.

The loading must have finished, because stevedores were undoing the massive lines from the pilings, and seamen on the ship were pulling them back aboard and coiling them on deck. This at least looked like what I expected to see aboard a ship. I went to the other side of the deck and saw a tugboat getting ready to pull us away. So this was it. This was the real beginning. It was a little after 6:00 pm, and I was finally going to sea.

Once away from the pier, we went south down Arthur Kill, a channel that connects Newark Bay to the north and Raritan Bay to the South. We made a left turn at the bottom of Staten Island into the Kill van Kull—the one thing I had done was look at a map—and then under the Outerbridge Crossing, the bridge that connects New Jersey with Staten Island. I had driven over that bridge a few times. It was strange to see it overhead. Then we made a right turn, entering Upper Bay, as the sea breeze picked up noticeably. Ahead was the new Verrazano Narrows Bridge, connecting Staten Island with Brooklyn. Although it was far from finished, you could see the grand scope of the project. It was going to be the biggest bridge in the world. Seeing it this way, from the water, seemed very special, even historic. I wanted to shout, "Wow, look at that," and share it with someone. But there was no one around, and everyone on the ship had seen it many times before.

Passing under the Verrazano we were in New York Harbor. As it began to get darker, we continued straight ahead for a few more miles, now truly at sea. We made another right turn and headed south along the coast toward Jacksonville, Florida, my first port of call.

The night came quickly. Although we were on a coastwise run, we weren't close enough to the coast to see the shore. Occasionally I could see distant lights, but mostly it was dark. I could hear the water and feel the breeze, but looking out at the water it was as if my visual sense was disengaged. I couldn't see anything. A not unexpected feeling of loneliness came over me. I played the harmonica.

CHAPTER 7

How I Get My Ship

It was a glorious spring. The flowering trees and bushes in Riverside and Central Parks were starting to bloom. The air smelled fresh. There was an alive feeling everywhere. I could play tennis in Central Park and ride my bike comfortably to most places I needed to go. Even my course work took on a new glow. I was fascinated with everything I was studying: 16th century Europe, the Reformation and the great convocation with the irresistible name, the Diet of Worms; Joyce's *Ulysses* that had bedeviled me in prep school was grudgingly yielding a few of its secrets; and economics was making a lot of sense. Although I didn't find the work of translating French poetry very rewarding, Baudelaire I could relate to. Finally, geology had produced a field trip on a beautiful day to a striated rock cut-through next to a busy highway in the Bronx to study Manhattan Schist, on which much of Manhattan rests. Life was good.

The best part, though, was Lynn. There was clearly more than a sexual attraction. I enjoyed every moment I spent with her. We had fun. We gave each other small presents involving elephants. When I wasn't with her I thought about her. She seemed to feel the same way about me, saying she had never felt about anyone the way she felt about me. I had never been in love, and I wondered if this was it.

I never found out. Although she had once stood me up at one of the trick drill team's performances at Madison Square Garden, she had a complex but credible explanation, which I wanted to believe. And when she couldn't go to the Equity Library theater the upcoming Saturday night because she was going away for part of the weekend with two girlfriends, I thought, fine, we were probably together too much anyway.

But the Saturday night after that she needed to stay home and study. I told her I would call her so she wouldn't get lonely. When I called, her mother answered the phone. There was an awkward pause and she said Lynn was out. I was more surprised than angry.

She hesitated and then added, Lynn has been going out with someone else regularly."

"Why are you telling me this?"

"You're too nice a guy and you deserve better."

How about that. I always had a way with the mothers!

I was dumbfounded. Hurt, yes, but mostly I felt stupid. I remembered our first date and what I had thought when she said she had canceled another date. Well, here I was. With surprising resolve, despite my very strong feelings of just the day before, I thanked her mother and decided, OK, *that's* done.

At 2:00 a.m., when Lynn called with another elaborate explanation involving a fight with her mother, it was still done. I said good-bye. And when she asked, I said, no I wouldn't throw away the little elephants she had given me. The next day I rode my bike hard for about thirty miles. And that was pretty much that.

***

Between studying for my exams, playing tennis, and a few dates, the days passed quickly. During the exam weeks when I needed a break I rode my bike in the parks trying to pick up women.

It wasn't that difficult. If you had thick enough skin it was like baseball: you had a batting average. Even if it was low, with enough at bats you would get some hits. I was tall, pretty good looking—according to females beyond my mother—and could make reasonable conversation. I wasn't frightening. I had learned from an older friend that it didn't really matter what you said to start. Either the attraction was there or it wasn't. Either she was interested and had the inclination to talk or she wasn't or didn't.

Although I had had a couple of successes with moving targets, it was easier if she was sitting on a bench. Usually she would be armed with a book for defense. I would be similarly armed, but for offense. Alighting from my bike at the next bench, I would begin with a clever "Hello," and one thing would lead to another. Or not.

That's exactly how I met Lorna. A pretty brunette— clearly a woman not a girl—about 5' 5", with a perfect figure quite visible in a white sleeveless blouse and tan cotton slacks. She was reading, with her bike leaning against the bench. She looked up and smiled when I sat at the next bench. She was still there after my "hello," so I asked what she was reading.

"*A Doll's House.*"

"Oh, Ibsen," I said way too eagerly, as if it were a quiz. "Do you like it?"

"Yes and no."

She looked at the book in my hand, Beckett's *Waiting for Godot.* "Are you reading that or do you just carry it around to impress women you're trying to pick up?" Her eyes smiled.

OK! This had never happened before, and I liked it. A girl wouldn't have the aplomb or the wit to say something like that, but a woman....

"Both. If I fail to pick up the woman, I still have something interesting to do."

Now she smiled fully. And so it began. We talked about plays—I mostly listened—and movies. I expounded on the two Bergman movies I had seen, skillfully avoided *North to Alaska,* and moved next to her. After a while we rode around the park together, then sat and talked some more. We talked about New York and what we each liked to do. I mentioned my usual haunts and even added Café La Mama, a currently "in" experimental theater café that actually bored me to tears. She liked museums and chamber music. Well, so did I.

Then she asked my age. Not a good sign. I could get away with a couple of years, but not much more.

"Twenty-two. Graduating from NYU later this month."

"I'm twenty-nine," she said with a laugh. I'm an assistant fashion copy editor at the *New York Herald Tribune.*"

Wow again! My self-confidence was suffering a seismic crack. I had been with women older than her—briefly—but it wasn't just age. She was in all ways on a higher level than the others...and me. She was educated, sophisticated, confident. She was all that I pretended to be. I struggled to feel older, to imagine myself with life experience somehow comparable with hers, to will myself into her league.

Perhaps sensing my unease, she continued the conversation.

"What are you going to do after graduation?"

What indeed? For the first time it occurred to me how my jumbled plans of the merchant marine, jet fighters and international law would sound to a person who actually lived life rather than just imagined it. It sounded too much like a four-year-old's response: "I'm going to be a fireman and an astronaut...and a cowboy too." My story needed a quick edit if I was going to have a chance with this copy editor.

"Eventually I'm going to study international law."

"Really! That's exciting." She leaned toward me. "Do you speak other languages?"

"French, Hungarian and some German." As part of the edit I skipped my four years of Latin, the promised 'gateway to all romance languages.' "But before I do that I need to see the world. I joined the merchant marine and right after graduation I'm shipping out, probably around the world."

She might have missed my feigned nonchalance. It was her turn for a "wow!" She seemed genuinely impressed. I was too. What I described was certainly not an every-day combination. Of course, I hadn't actually done any of it yet. For the moment neither of us dwelled on that.

"Wouldn't you see the world as an international lawyer?"

Now what? This wasn't the occasion for my "straight path through life" speech.

"Sure, but in a very different way. First I need to prove something...to myself." I hoped for an air of manly mystery.

She asked about the merchant marine and I passed on my fantasies. After about an hour she put her hand on my arm, smiled and said she had to go. Then she wrote her telephone number on the inside cover of Godot, got on her bike and rode away. I sat on the bench in a daze.

***

Lorna lived in a studio apartment on the ground floor of a brownstone on the Upper West Side. We got together every few days, either at some of my haunts in the Village or in her apartment. We talked a lot and did a lot of advanced making out. But for a woman who seemed so comfortable with everything, she held back. Stop and go, push and pull. All enjoyable, but somehow surprising. So I asked.

"I really don't know what to do with you. I'm attracted to you and I enjoy being with you, but I'm so much older. I really don't know why I'm doing this. It really can't work out." All this with her legs wrapped around me and her skirt up at her waist.

"If you mean we aren't likely to get married, maybe not. But can't we just enjoy ourselves? I've got no problem with your age. Hell, you're twenty-nine not fifty-nine. And it would work out just fine if you'd just let herself go." This was all too much like the perpetual, annoying games with the redheads in Brooklyn.

One night Lorna joined me on a foray to an army-navy surplus store on 42nd Street to buy some clothes for what I imagined to be my merchant marine "uniform." I had khaki pants, but I needed a couple of khaki shirts, a web belt, work shoes, work gloves, and most importantly, a white canvas sea bag. After making my selections I left her for a few minutes to look at some interesting cavalry sabers—another fantasy. When I returned and went to pay for my supplies Lorna had a smug expression.

"Your girlfriend already paid," the salesman said with a knowing look.

"Wait a second, Lorna, you don't need to buy my clothes." It reminded me of my mother buying me a summer suit before I left for prep school.

"You don't understand. It's not the clothes. I want to give you a "bon voyage" present and I can't think of anything else you could take along. I want to do this, so please let me."

I felt awkward but in the end just thanked her. That night we got very close. But this wasn't horseshoes.

***

And so it went. My exams ended, and with Lorna very much on my mind, I turned to the problem of the union, the SIU, and getting a ship. It wasn't likely that my mother played bridge with any labor leaders. The father of a classmate from prep school was the head of the ILO, the International Labor Organization which was part of the UN. But he lived in Paris. I had no connections directly or indirectly with anyone in a union. But I was sure the SIU had a phone number and an address, though it didn't occur to me that it would be in Brooklyn. So it took a bit of a search to find it.

The call itself was much easier than I had expected. I told the man who answered the phone that I had my seaman's papers and my committal letter and that I wanted to join the union and ship out. He passed me to someone else who turned out to be the executive director of the New York local of the SIU. He was pleasant enough, but not at all reassuring.

"How old are you?"

"Twenty." No lies here.

"What do you do?"

"I just finished my second year of college."

"Do you know anybody?"

"Well, I know the head of the ILO, Mr. Grey." I had stayed at his apartment in Paris for a night with his son when he wasn't there. We'd never met.

"Oh yeah, well, you're ahead of me there," the sarcasm evident. I didn't think the UN had much to do with this bunch.

"So how did you get your committal letter?"

"I know the guy, family friend."

"Well, kid, things are a bit slow these days, so I don't know when or even if you'll get a ship, but you can come by. Ask for me, Joe Williams, at the front door. There'll be a guy there."

"I'll be there tomorrow morning."

I dismissed his caveat. I would get a ship.

The next day I took the subway to Brooklyn. I hadn't been in that benighted borough since the Dodgers had moved to Los Angeles in 1958, the greatest betrayal in my life. Lynn was nothing compared to that. I really didn't know my way around Brooklyn, so the address meant nothing to me. Williams had said it was a couple of blocks from the subway station. The first man I asked pointed in the direction of a building standing alone at the end of a large vacant lot. As I approached what appeared to be a three story building, I felt fear for the second time since the merchant marine plan had surfaced. The missing seamen had created an inchoate fear. This stark semi-modern building, with no windows on the side I was facing and isolated from the surrounding community as if it were under siege and prepared for attack, was tangible and forbidding. This was the place where real seamen were, not college kids. This was the end of the line for my quest. This was where fantasy turned into reality, and this was where I would have to "put up or shut up." This fear was palpable.

What greeted me when I opened the only door facing the street replaced all these thoughts with something even more real and immediate. Between the door and a steep flight of stairs sat the largest and scariest person I had ever seen. As he was seated, I couldn't tell exactly how tall he was, but I was six four and I was sure he was taller than me. He must have weighed well over four hundred pounds. He was also unbelievably ugly. He had very short black hair and a low forehead. His face had been smashed in and was deformed. Surely no man could have done this to him; it had to have been a truck. I must have stared at him. He glared at me, though it might have been his only facial expression.

"What the fuck you want?"

"I'm here to see Joe Williams."'

"Bullshit! Get the fuck out a here."

"Look, I'm sorry to bother you, but I spoke to Mr. Williams yesterday, and he gave me an appointment. You can check with him. My name is…" But I didn't get any further.

"You didn't hear me asshole. Get the fuck outa here."

Arguing with a real life ogre—or was he some kind of giant troll?—was not on my agenda, and the thought that he might stand up was enough to make me turn to go. But I still had to add, "I don't know what your fucking problem is, but you've obviously got one."

Not waiting for an answer, verbal or otherwise, I went out the door and slammed it. Smart. Now what? I walked back toward the subway station, not to go home but to find a pay phone. I had the union phone number in my pocket and called. The same person answered as the day before.

"Look, Mr. Williams said to come by today. I came to the building but there's a very large…person…who doesn't seem to agree with the invitation. "

"Oh, Sal. Yeah, if he doesn't know you, you don't get in. Must have forgotten to tell him."

"Well, I sure would appreciate it if you could call him off. That way I won't have to hurt him."

"Yeah, right."

I assured him I was joking, and that Sal was without question the most effective guard the SIU could possibly have. He told me to come back and come up the stairs, go through the bid hall and come to the door on the far left. With that I retraced my steps. Hoping that nothing had come up in the mean-time to prevent the guy on the phone from defanging Sal, I tried my luck with the SIU a second time.

When I opened the door, Sal, still seated, rolled his chair from in front of the stairs. We made no eye contact as I went by him and up to the bid hall. Over the next two weeks Sal would grudgingly admit me to the inner sanctum without comment. He was a modern day version of the many monsters of Greek mythology that guarded important gates and doors. Each morning I felt heroic just making it past him.

The bid hall was a very large room, around fifty feet square, with a high ceiling. Its off-white walls were adorned with a few big, color photographs of cargo ships. The hall seemed to take up most of the horizontal dimensions of the building. Arranged throughout were more than a dozen square, wooden tables, each with four wooden chairs. Most of the tables were occupied with men talking, reading, playing cards or sleeping. At the far end, opposite the door, was what looked like a pulpit, and on the wall behind it was a blackboard about twelve feet high and ten feet wide, painted with a white grid. At the top was a heading: "Open Positions."

In the spaces on each line were listed the job title/ function, name and type of ship, name of steamship company, and whether the destination was foreign or coastwise. Only a quarter of the board was filled.

As I stood at the back of the room, I felt as if I were watching the world from another dimension. I wasn't physically part of it. It wasn't just that no one noticed me; it was that they didn't notice me because I didn't belong there. I was an image that didn't fit into the picture, theirs or mine. The pounding in my ears as I surveyed the scene in front of me drowned out all sound. What the hell was I doing here?

I snapped out of my reverie. I was here to get a ship, and the door to Williams' office was ahead on the left. I knocked, and when there was no answer, I opened it. There was a series of small offices sharing a common reception area. In it two men were standing and talking. One turned to me and asked if I was the one on the phone a few minutes ago. For a moment, I hesitated. It seemed a lifetime ago. When I said yes, he pointed to a closed door. "He's got someone with him. Have a seat."

Twenty minutes later the door opened and I couldn't believe my eyes. Coming out of Williams' office was my prep school roommate. He was just about the last person I could imagine on a merchant ship. We had certainly never spoken about it. Then again we hadn't spoken since graduation two years before, and a lot can change in that time. I was certainly an example of that. Still, he fit even less than I did. Yet here he was.

"Herbie," I nearly shouted. "What the hell are you doing here?"

"Shipping out. You too?"

"Well, trying to. Just getting started; had to finish exams. You know what you're going to do and where you're going yet?"

"Yeah, ordinary on a Mediterranean run."

"So you hit the jackpot. Way to go, man."

"Yeah, I got lucky I guess."

At that point Williams came out of his office and said, "I see you guys know each other."

When Herbie didn't answer, I said, "We were roommates the last two years of high school," avoiding the words prep school or boarding school.

"Yeah? How was that?"

"OK, but it was a bit tough living with the worst player ever to play on a varsity basketball team."

Herbie seemed in a rush to leave and he certainly wasn't dwelling on our two years together in front of Williams. So we said good-bye and that was the last time I ever saw him. I never learned how he made out on his ship or in his life for that matter. And with that, Williams ushered me into his sparsely furnished office. He sat behind a small wooden desk and motioned me to a chair next to it.

"Look, kid, don't get any ideas from your buddy. I mean, OS on a Mediterranean run, there's not a lot of those going to be available. If you want to ship out, you're going to have to take whatever comes...if it comes."

"I understand. I'll take what comes, but I'm still hoping for a European run of some kind. So he just got lucky like he said?"

"Yeah, when he was born. His father, he knows a lot of people."

And then I remembered his father. He was District Attorney of a fairly large city in Pennsylvania. He was, I now recalled, a figure in the Democratic Party. Unions supported Democratic candidates. OK, I got it. If that's what it took to get a good job on a good run then I would be lucky to get a deck job on a ship to Alaska in the winter. My prescience about a bad job was spot on; I just had the wrong end of the thermometer.

"So what do I do now, wait in the bid hall?"

"No, kid, that's not what you do. What you're going to do is go downstairs and out the back way. Outside you'll see a small building. You go up the stairs to the print shop. That's where you'll be until you get a ship or until you give up. Your choice."

We shook hands and he said, "Good luck." I followed his directions, passing behind Sal, to the print shop. For the next eleven days, not counting Sundays, I worked in the union's print shop, setting type manually for the union newsletter. There was more than one irony involved. First, I wanted to go to sea on a merchant ship and I was working in a print shop instead. Second, I was working, eight or nine hours a day, for a union, an organization dedicated to assuring fair labor practices, and I wasn't being paid a dime.

I was not alone in the print shop. In addition to the boss, a pleasant man in his forties who seemed genuinely embarrassed at the way we were being used, there were two other would-be seamen. One was a fellow who kept to himself, spoke very little and after three days was gone. He acted as if he had been instructed not to talk. Turned out he got a wiper job on a bulk freighter to northern Europe. I thought he must have had a deal

similar to my roommate, just a rung below on the connection ladder. The other indentured servant, the one
who stuck around long enough for me to get to know—
meaning that he was as low on the ladder as I was—was
Bob Johnson. He was a student at the University of
Nebraska who also had just completed his sophomore
year. He was a physical education major who was com-
mitted to becoming a basketball coach. As I had played
in high school and some on the Washington Square
College team, we had plenty to talk about.

Bob intrigued me. Other than the girl I had spent
a brief time with on the return voyage from my trip to
Europe, I had never met anyone from the Midwest,
that is, anyone I knew was from the Midwest. So I had
something of an anthropological interest. Beyond that,
of course, were the two overarching questions filling
the print shop: Since Bob had never played basketball
even at the high school level, why would he want to
devote his life to coaching the sport? And why would
someone from one of the most landlocked places on
earth want to go to sea? Whether Bob was stupid, just
couldn't find the words, or as he put it, really just didn't
want to talk about it, I don't know. I never did get the
answers. After a week he was gone: Ordinary Seaman
on a bulk freighter to Brazil. Not bad. My hopes rose
like a rocket, since between the two of us, no one in his
right mind would pick Bob over me to work on a ship.

Following my usual pattern, whether I liked the
work or not, even whether I was getting paid or not, I
dove into the work at the print shop with a passion. I
asked questions constantly, wanted to do it the "right"
way, and worked as fast as I could, even though there

was no benefit in doing so. If I finished before the boss expected, I didn't get to leave; I just got another project.

And so it went until the afternoon of the day Bob got his ship. A man I had not seen before came into the shop and had an intense conversation with the boss. After several minutes, he came over to me and introduced himself. He was an assistant vice president of the local. He asked if I knew that the SIU and the NMU had several what he called "jurisdictional disputes." I lied and said, "Of course."

"Now look, what I'm going to ask you is on a volunteer basis. Volunteer only." He paused to make sure I understood that. "We have a problem right now about certain ships and certain runs. We need to keep as many runs as possible. You know, the more we have the more jobs there are—and that includes you. So here's the deal. There might be a bit of a to-do tonight near a pier on the Hudson and 47th Street in Manhattan. We need to make sure we have some men there, you know, if there's a problem."

Jesus Christ! Was he talking about some goddamn gang war between unions? It sure sounded like it. I had managed to get through my entire formative years avoiding gangs and their inevitable fights, and now this? The print shop was one thing, a gang fight was quite another. But if I said, "Sorry, gang fights just aren't my thing, volunteer or no," I figured my chances of getting a ship would go from whatever they were to zero. So I asked how many men we would have, and he told me not to worry, there would be plenty.

"Now kid, it may be that nothing's going to happen at all. But just in case, if you've got a baseball bat or a bicycle chain, you'll probably want to bring it."

Oh shit! He couldn't be serious. A gang fight under the West Side Highway with bats and chains? Why no knives and guns? Was there some kind of code of chivalry that restricted the level of armament merchant seamen could use against one another? Was there going to be a referee? What if all the participants didn't understand the rules? I was going to get killed for this crazy job that I might never get anyway, for this stupid fantasy?

I was more mad than scared.

"You've got a union with thousands of members and you need me, someone working in your print ship who's not even a member of the union, to get into a gang fight for you?"

"Like I said, kid, it's up to you."

So I thought about it for about four seconds, carefully weighing the risks and all the consequences, and said, "OK, what time?"

With that I got special dispensation to leave, presumably to go to my personal armory and select the weapon of choice that would define my place in merchant marine lore. In fact I had few choices. I used a chain to lock my bike, though I would have to cut away the protective plastic covering. With the lock attached, it certainly made for an effective weapon—at least in the hands of someone with the will to use it. I had no confidence that I was such a person.

I decided that a bat would also be handy. Since I didn't know that I could use one weapon, how I would use two was even less clear. Nevertheless, at least I knew how to swing a bat and had done it tens of thousands of times. And though my anger—or more accurately, my frustration—had been directed at a ball not a person, I had done it.

Since going to get one of my bats would have meant going to my mother's apartment, I called a friend.

"Hi, I need to borrow that black bat of yours….No, the game's not this evening but I can only pick it up now. OK?"

An hour later I was fully armed. With no place to go. The rendezvous time was 9:30. It was not yet 7:00. So I went back to the apartment I had been sharing on Prince Street in the Village and waited. I had way too much time to think about the absurdity of what I was going to do. I was not a fighter. Yes, I had been in fights and all in all hadn't done that badly, but those had been unavoidable, one-on-one events that had escalated out of grudges or were the result of spontaneous combustion, usually in connection with a sport. This was nothing like those fights. I wasn't angry at anyone. Hell, I didn't even know any of them. And I was supposed to hit them with a baseball bat?

The first thing I decided was that I couldn't use the baseball bat. I couldn't really hurt someone like that. That the same someone might be more than ready to hurt me somehow wasn't my biggest concern. Besides, walking around the streets—or piers—of New York with a baseball bat, no glove, ball or sneakers wasn't exactly inconspicuous behavior. I would probably get stopped by a cop before I got to the subway.

I wanted to forget about the whole thing. The problem was I felt I had no choice. I became convinced that if I didn't show up, I wouldn't get a ship. So I decided the most important thing was showing up. If this was a test of some kind, just showing up should get me a passing grade. I didn't need an "A." I wasn't looking for a job as a union goon. What happened after showing up I would worry about later. And I would show up with the bicycle chain around my waist through the belt loops of my jeans. So, fortified by two hot dogs from a street cart, I headed for the Seventh Avenue subway.

I arrived at 47th Street and 12th Avenue, the North-South Avenue closest to the Hudson River, at 9:15. I wanted to reconnoiter and find a place to stand that offered a vantage point to observe how the situation developed—and to determine when I should make what I hoped would be a cameo appearance in this drama. I stood with my back to one of the metal pillars supporting the elevated West Side Highway, well into the shadows, and waited. I imagined the cavalrymen of the ill-fated light brigade must have felt this way before their obviously suicidal charge. I was damn scared. The bicycle chain around my waist offered no comfort. Fingering its metal links only served to remind me that I was supposed to fight with the damn thing. And I waited.

It was now well past dark and well past 9:30. Still I saw no one. Literally, no one at all. This area was where passenger ships berthed. The Dutch student ship with its load of students and ox parts had been berthed near here. But the berth was empty, and 12th Avenue, underneath the West Side Highway, was not a place for strollers. There were cars parked along the east side of the avenue, but there were none with lights or any indication of occupancy. I kept waiting. Maybe I got the place wrong or the union man had gotten it wrong. Maybe it was all happening somewhere else and no one would know that I showed up. I waited some more. I decided I would leave at 10:30. But when the time came, I stayed.

By 11:00 I had had enough. Whatever the reason, whether I was in the wrong place, the "to-do" had been called off, or the whole thing had been a goddamn joke on me, nothing was happening here and I left. And now that I was safe, along with a great sense of relief, I got mad. What a lot of bullshit! These guys were a bunch of jerks.

The next day, instead of going straight to the print shop, I went up to the bid hall to look for the union officer. I knocked on the office door and without waiting walked in.

"So where was everybody last night? I was there for an hour and a half and I didn't see anybody. You told me to be there, and I was there. What the hell, man?"

"Take it easy kid. I told you maybe nothing would happen and nothing did. It's not like I could get in touch with you. We appreciate you showing up. You're a good union man."

I was no union man. I wasn't even a member of the union. I didn't give a damn about his union. What I was, was a damn flunky. These guys must have laughed themselves silly while I waited under the West Side Highway for an hour and a half. Well the hell with them.

Back at the print shop I told the boss what had happened—or hadn't happened. He just shook his head and shrugged his shoulders. As I worked on the newsletter—it didn't mention any jurisdictional disputes—I thought mostly about leaving, just walking out. I'd wish the boss good luck with the newsletter, say fuck you to Sal, and head back to Manhattan and something resembling sanity. And so it went through lunch. As I was deciding just when to leave—at the end of the day would have no effect—the phone rang. It almost never did. The boss said, "Peter, you got a ship. Get over to the hall."

"What is it, OS, Europe, what kind of ship?"

"Didn't tell me. Just said to get you over there. And a word of advice. You're not a bad guy. I've had a lot worse back here. But whatever it is, you take it, and you don't say shit. You say you want to ship out. Well, whatever ship they give you, you say thank you. It won't be your last ship."

So warned, I was expecting the worst. And for once my expectations were met. It was Williams who met me in the hall. He pointed to the board, at the fifth and last entry. And there it was: wiper, SS *Rufus Saxton*, coastwise, SeaLand Service, C-2, Port Newark. I had gotten my ship and with it the worst job in the merchant marine.

In the print shop we spent a lot of time prioritizing the range of opportunities. My former roommate's job, ordinary seaman on a C-3 to southern Europe, was at the very top of the list. Coastwise wiper on a C-2, the smallest and oldest of the cargo ships still in ocean-going service, was at the very bottom. And there were quite a few in between.

Reading the disappointment on my face, Williams said, "I told you things were slow. You're lucky to get this ship, any ship. And kid, if you don't take it, you can just get the fuck out of here. And, you know, keep at it and with any luck you'll get another ship."

"Or if I get some political connections, huh? Anyway, I get the message. So, thanks; I'll take the job. What do I do, where do I go and when?"

"Port Elizabeth, though really it's part of Port Newark, main road wharf. Ask around for the ship when you get there. You take the bus from Port Authority. Be at the ship at 7:00 tomorrow morning."

I filled out some forms and joined the union. He gave me a union card imprinted with a big "C", my C card. It meant I had the lowest seniority in the Seafarers International Union. There were A, B and C books and a C card. I never learned how much time in service you needed to advance up the ladder of books or even to get your first one, but I assumed it would be a lot longer than I would be in the merchant marine. Williams wished me luck and I left. As I passed Sal I told him I had a ship. He was unimpressed. So was I.

But what the hell did I expect? Everyone had told me that I would never get a ship. Well, I got a ship. So why did I think I should get the ideal job, just because I wanted it? No, I told myself to cut the crap. I *was* lucky to get this ship. They didn't have to give me anything. Williams' initial greeting could just as easily have been the same as Sal's Williams'. Damn it, I was in the merchant marine. I did it—I tried not to think about my mother's role. And then I thought about the night before. They must have been testing me. My telling them that I had showed up at the 47th Street pier—assuming no one was there in one of the parked cars to see me—must be what got me the ship. As I rode the subway back to Manhattan, the thought comforted me. I would learn soon enough that I had it all wrong.

***

I called Lorna at her office to tell her that I had gotten a ship and would be leaving in the morning. Visions of a night in bed with her filled my head. After all, isn't that what seamen did the night before going off to sea in far-away places? That I was going only as far as Jacksonville, Florida did take some of the luster off that fantasy. Still, I was shipping out in the morning—albeit to return in eight days—we had known each other in all but the biblical sense for about a month, and she was twenty-nine. If not tonight, when?

I had romanced Lorna with tales of a four-month around-the-world run or at least a month to somewhere in Europe. This run wasn't going to cut it in the impressive department. As usual, though, my naiveté prevented me from seeing the real issue my actual seafaring status created. But I would learn that night—instead of getting laid.

Lorna agreed to meet me at a local Chinese restaurant for dinner. As I contemplated dessert only three blocks away, she started again on the theme of our age difference and that she was confused. She had hoped to use the time of my extended absence to figure it out.

In other words, she was very disappointed that I would be back in just over a week. Dessert was getting further away.

"What's the confusion all about? Either you're attracted to me or not. As you give every verbal and physical indication that you are, why the hell are we wasting time talking about it. Happiness awaits three blocks away."

"Well, it isn't that simple. I am in therapy, psycho-therapy to deal with some problems."

"I've seen a therapist a few times too about some trouble concentrating." I spend too much time think-ing about getting laid! "What does that have to do with us? Is your problem that you don't want sex?"

"No. It's that I want it too much."

"Well, you've found the right person. I do too. And since we both do, then it's not as if your desires are mis-directed. Obviously, I want you."

"But I haven't told my therapist about you. And that's a problem. It means I'm conflicted about you, and I really am."

"How often do you see the therapist?"

"Twice, sometimes three times a week."

"Jesus Christ! You've seen this therapist twelve or fifteen times since we met, since we've been fooling around on your couch, and you're there to talk about sex, and you never mentioned any of it to him?"

"Yes, that's right. And I know that's a problem. That's why I need time. I hope you can understand. For you it's just a conquest. It's simple. You want to get laid. For me it's a lot more complicated."

"No, I don't understand. But I understand this: you want to get laid too, and you won't let yourself. OK, it's unlikely we're going to get married. So did you think you were marrying every guy you went to bed with? Or haven't you ever gotten past this problem? Anyway, now I understand the presents at the surplus store. They weren't meant as *bon voyage*. They were meant as good-bye, period."

"No, I didn't mean it that way. I do want you, but I can't now. I have to think."

"And talk to the therapist. So now that I'm not going away for as long as either of us expected, what happens when I come back in a week or so? Do we get together, or do you want me to leave you alone?"

"Oh damn, Peter, I don't know."

"OK, we'll just leave it like that. You don't know. Right."

I walked her home. I was mad, confused, and damn frustrated, but I wasn't going to just leave her there alone at the restaurant. We said nothing the entire way. At her door I said good night and left. I was in no mood for more attempts at seduction. She wanted time. She would have it, plenty of it. These two nights had been a rollercoaster. First abject fear followed by nothing, then abject lust followed by nothing. Enough. I couldn't wait to get away from the City and on with being a merchant seaman, whatever the hell that meant.

CHAPTER 8

I Start to Meet the Crew

After playing my harmonica in the dark for a while—
which did nothing to ease my loneliness and my
entirely accurate feeling of being completely detached
from anything that was ever a part of my life—I went
to the mess hall to see what "pie watch" was all about.
As advertised, several men were sitting at tables eating
what looked and smelled like freshly baked pie—apple,
blueberry and coconut custard. They had taken huge
pieces, twice a normal-sized piece. They drank coffee
as they ate. And, to my amazement, they were watching
television, and baseball at that!

The TV was in the corner of the mess hall—somehow I hadn't noticed it earlier—and the men were
watching a Baltimore game against Detroit, sixth
inning. Baseball! These guys were watching baseball.
Well, I knew baseball; maybe not Baltimore and Detroit
so much, but I knew baseball. This was a big deal. I had
found one thing we had in common, something that
connected me to these men.

Apparently, if the ship stayed within a certain distance of the coast, the ship's antenna could pick up

local TV stations as we went by. We went slowly enough that if the weather was OK, you could see most of a game.

People don't watch baseball in silence. There is so much time between moments of action that the sport invites ongoing commentary to fill the void. And there are so many different points of entry for comment that I didn't need to wait long for an opportunity to join in.

Still I passed on several and waited. No one seemed to notice my arrival, so I ate my blueberry pie, drank my coffee and watched the game. It was a good one: Jim Bunning pitching for Detroit and everybody and his uncle pitching for Baltimore. The Orioles were weak that year and they didn't fare well against Bunning. As the Orioles were making yet another pitching change in the seventh inning, I seized my opportunity.

"You know, if it weren't for two of the oldest guys on their pitching staff, Baltimore wouldn't have a staff at all, and Roberts and Wilhelm can't pitch every game." Apart from the truth of the statement—Robin Roberts and Hoyt Wilhelm were still pitching well near the end of their careers—it sounded good, I thought.

A guy I hadn't seen before was the only one to acknowledge my comment. He was a good looking man with short, graying black hair, about 5' 10", medium build. He seemed intelligent and somehow different than the others. He would have looked more appropriate in a suit than in jeans and tee shirt.

"You're right," he said. "But they've got this kid Dave McNally coming up. He's only nineteen, but he could be good, real good."

I nodded. I hadn't heard of McNally.

He got up and moved to the table I was sitting at alone, extended his hand and said, "Jack Garrity, AB, four to eight."

I shook his hand and said, "Peter Ernster, wiper."

"Figured that much. Well, welcome aboard the *SS Rufus Saxton*! I don't suppose any of these bastards (gesturing around the room at the men watching the game) has bothered to talk to you. They're a real welcoming bunch."

At that, one of the men turned and said, "Jack's gonna tell the kid all about the ways of the sea, aren't you Jack? Or maybe you can get the college kid to read one of your books."

"Well, Max, if he can read, and I've heard it said that some people in college master that lost art, he'll double the literacy rate in this room."

So college it was. No mysterious history of working my way around the country doing odd jobs until I finally yielded to the call of the sea. My cover was blown.

We watched in silence as Detroit added a run in the eighth and ninth innings and Bunning pitched a complete game.

The game ended and we started walking out to the main deck.

"These guys don't seem too interested in talking to anyone," I said quietly. "Besides I gather they're all pissed off at me for taking this job and ruining their boondoggle in New York."

"Yeah, I heard that crap, and it's pure bullshit. Believe me; the union wasn't going to let this ship sit loaded in Port Elizabeth. They would have gotten somebody from somewhere, and quick, to take the job if you didn't. Listen, some of these guys are real stupid, and they'll believe anything, and I mean anything. Just last month a guy hears from some idiot that the union's worked out some kind of big raise for non-licensed crew. Now, we're losing ships to foreign flags every month and jobs are disappearing all the time, but this moron believes that we're going to get a raise. So he draws an advance and spends all his money because he's going to get much more next month. So now he's broke and has to borrow money from everybody. Yeah, some of these guys think—no they don't think, they believe—that they would have stayed in port having a ball for who knows how long. But don't worry about them. They're really not bad guys, just stupid."

I didn't know whether I should be relieved or more worried. Reasonably intelligent people can usually be reasoned with. Stupid people were always hard for me to deal with. Jack was clearly in the first group. I wondered what the other guy was referring to when he mentioned Jack's books. So I asked.

"What books was he talking about? Do you have a library on the ship?"

"No, no library. I write books, mysteries, detective stories."

"No kidding. You're an author? What the hell are you doing on this ship or in the merchant marine for that matter?"

"That's a long story. Maybe some other time. What about you? Shipping out for the summer? You thought you were going to see the world, right? Bet you didn't expect to be going to Jacksonville or Mobile. But you could get lucky and get to Puerto Rico!"

"Well, I'd like to hear that long story some time. But me, no, I intend to keep doing this for a few years and then finish school." I rehearsed my problem with living a well laid out life and my need for uncertainty and adventure. I told him about my flying plans. I had no intention of telling him about the issue of my mother, so he really couldn't understand why I didn't just go about graduating and flying. We left it at that.

Then he added, "You're not likely to find much adventure as a wiper on a coastwise container ship; I can tell you that. And your seniority is going to stay low enough that you'll be lucky to get any other kind of job, though it does happen. Round the world runs sometimes open up because guys don't want to be away for over four months at a time. But my advice is not to mention your plans around here. These guys don't want to see more long-term members of the union, even with C cards. Too much competition as it is."

I thanked him for the advice and for the general information. I really did appreciate it, although nothing anyone had yet told me amounted to good news. I went back to the fo'c'sle where the guys were in their bunks reading comic books. My first day and evening were over. I set my alarm for 7:00 and was asleep in seconds.

***

Waking up to the sounds and smells of the sea was a new experience. On the student ship, I was so far removed from either that it had felt more like waking up in an underground garage. I awoke before the alarm and before Michael or Raul. I dressed quickly and went out onto the deck. It was a clear day, overcast but somehow still bright, with a nice breeze. Without my sweatshirt I would have been cold. I breathed in the fresh air. There was a smell of paint and metal in the fo'c'sle that I hadn't noticed until I was away from it. There was certainly enough metal around. The whole ship was made of steel. But what about the metal created such a distinct but hard to describe smell? I never would find out.

I stood at the portside rail, looking further out to sea, puzzling over this and other mysteries. Suddenly, from no more than two feet behind me, "Nice day!" I nearly dove into the ocean. I had neither heard nor sensed anyone there. This was the second time I experienced the uncomfortable realization that the combination of background noise—this time of the sea and the wind–and rubber soles on a firm steel deck meant you couldn't hear someone approaching from behind.

I turned to the source of the voice. "Man, you scared the shit out of me. I was almost in the water!"

"Yeah, I can see that. Gotta stay awake to stay alive."

Scaring the new guy was obviously part of the daily drill.

"Max Lanier. I work the four to eight."

He put out his hand and I shook it. It was the guy that had kidded Jack about his books the night before. He seemed in his late forties, maybe older, about six feet tall, wiry with prominent veins in his arms, very straight medium brown hair, and a narrow face with a beak-like nose. But most noticeably he had what I had heard described—albeit only about old women—as a dowager's hump. I hadn't seen him before pie watch and then, but for his comment to Jack, he just watched the game. He seemed friendly enough now.

"Peter Ernster, wiper," still catching my breath.

"So, Jack tell you all you need to know about the sea?"

"That I doubt. But it was a good start. Nice guy."

"He is that. One of the best. He should get the hell out'a here and take advantage of his real life. But what the hell, it's his business."

I thought of asking him why a guy who had written a bunch of books that were actually published—nine he had said—would spend his time in the merchant marine going back and forth between Jacksonville and New York, but I decided that at some point I would ask Jack.

Instead I asked him the question I had been wondering about just before he had startled me and that I had started chewing on as soon as we were really at sea the evening before.

"What happens if someone falls overboard?"

"Depends if anyone's around to see it, and if that person gives a shit."

"Yeah, well, I get that. If no one knows then you're done. But..."

"Look, kid, nobody just falls overboard. What do you think we do here, pole vaulting? Unless it's some kind of major storm—and then you're just gone, simple as that. No, somebody goes over, he was helped, and who helped him ain't raising any alarms."

"OK, but just for argument's sake, suppose a guy slips and goes over and as he goes over he screams and someone who gives a shit hears him. Just suppose. Can the crew save him?"

"We got some time before breakfast. Wait here and I'll be right back."

Lanier turned and went in the direction of the main house. I wondered if he was going to get someone to help with a demonstration, something like throwing me overboard and then throwing a life preserver on a line after me. Thoughts of the missing seamen crossed my mind. But in three minutes he was back, alone but with a bright yellow cardboard box that unmistakably once held twelve bottles of Cutty Sark scotch. He held up the box for my examination.

"Now this is yellow, a real bright color. Not like you, say, dark brown maybe even black hair. So I'm going to throw this box over the side and you're going to watch the box without taking your eyes off it even for a split second. I'll time it on my watch. You keep watching it until the exact second when you can't see it any more. Then you say, 'now.' OK, you got that?"

I told him I got it, and he threw the box over the side. With no point of comparison it's hard to tell how fast a ship is going, so even though we were only about seventy feet from the stern of the ship, I was surprised how fast the box moved past the wash from the propellers. I stared at the yellow box as it bobbed on the slight chop of the rolling sea. It got very small very quickly, and then suddenly it was gone. "Now," I yelled, much louder than necessary, my excitement startling both of us.

"Eleven seconds, kid. Eleven seconds. And that's in three foot seas on a clear day. A bit higher seas, more chop, white caps, less light. Forget it. But suppose someone saw you as you went over like you said. He's got to tell someone else. They've got to get the ship turned, a hard turn, still maybe a mile circle. Get a boat down. Start looking. Good luck. Remember, eleven seconds for a yellow box a lot bigger and brighter than your brown head."

"So I guess you just don't fall in," I offered.

"That's pretty much it. You don't fall in. But you don't have to worry about it. You're down there where it's warm and cozy. Think about it this way: for all you have to do with the sea, you could be working in the boiler room of a factory."

Lanier's offhanded demonstration and accompanying narrative had two immediate impacts: I was now afraid of going between the fo'c'sle and the main house, to say nothing of anywhere else on the deck. At the same time he managed effortlessly to burst the romanticized bubble into which I had securely placed my entire merchant marine fantasy.

***

Just as I had expected, the engine room was hotter now that we were underway and the boilers were working at full tilt. How could anyone willingly spend his life in this inferno? But because it was familiar it wasn't quite as difficult to deal with as the first day.

I showed up, on time, with leather gloves, ready to take on whatever challenge Second threw at me. What he threw at me was a mop. He told me to mop the entire lower deck of the engine room and to make sure I got under the machines that were resting a few inches off the steel deck on short struts. "Aye aye sir," I said. I didn't know if I was supposed to observe naval formalities. But

I was going to make a go of this. Nothing they gave me to do was too low, too hard, too demeaning or too boring. No one was going to get any kind of reaction from me. Second just looked at me quizzically and pointed in the direction of the water tap and a stack of buckets.

Swabbing the deck. I realized that what I was doing was swabbing the deck, albeit of the engine room. I wondered if they knew that term. I had heard it in seagoing movies of all kinds since I was six—pirate movies, war movies. Then I remembered that in the movies they didn't use mops. They got on their hands and knees and used big brushes. That came next.

When I finished the mopping, Second came over and gave me a big brush and pointed to a few spots where my mopping had failed to dislodge some foreign substance. It looked to me like it had been painted over. I looked at Second and then at the first spot and then at Second. He nodded and left. I attacked the spots with a wire brush for almost an hour, hating the stupid, lazy son of a bitch that had painted over this crap in the first place.

Perhaps thinking I might need a bit of a break—but who knows?—Second came over when I had finished and pointed in the direction of the three cans filled with oily rags from the day before.

"Why don't you take those cans up to the main deck and put the rags on the big shelf."

It was a rhetorical question. Yet I had a good reason for not doing what he asked. I didn't know where in hell to find the big shelf. The main deck had lots of places and spaces; I had already seen that. Where was the big shelf? But there was no way I was going to ask him. No way. I would find it.

I nodded and grabbed the handles of the three cans, two in one hand—with great difficulty—and one in the other, and started for the ladder. Second stopped me.

"Remember this, kid: one hand for you; one hand for the ship. Remember that and you might have a chance of surviving. Don't remember it and you fall down that long ladder forty feet and break your neck. And I bet some people would be real upset." Of course, he was right—on both counts. I would have enough trouble getting up the ladder holding on with one hand with the roll of the ship. Yeah, I would need to remember that. But it meant three trips.

So, with one can in hand, I climbed the several ladders—they weren't called stairs—to the main deck. The relief of being out in the air again was powerful. The temperature difference must have been fifty degrees. Why the hell couldn't I have been an ordinary seaman? That's what I had imagined, breathing the salt air, out on deck, doing whatever ordinary seamen did. As I thought about the injustice of it all, I wandered about looking for something that looked like a big shelf. I found a big space above a group of four foot high lockers, but I couldn't imagine that anyone would want me to dump fifty pounds or so of oily rags there. So I wandered around some more.

As I rounded a corner, I nearly crashed into two men. Since I clearly didn't seem to belong there, one asked me what I was doing.

"I'm looking for the big shelf for these rags."

They looked at each other and nodded knowingly. One called over two guys chipping paint further along the deck.

"Hey, our new wiper is looking for the big shelf," said one.

"Maybe we should help him out and put him on it," said the other. Just then another guy rounded the same corner, and seeing the five of us, asked what was going on.

The first guy, stocky, rough black hair, around forty with a twisted, half smirk when he spoke, repeated what I was looking for, with more pronounced sarcasm but at the same time with a degree of deference to the inquirer. The new arrival looked at them, shaking his head.

"Why don't you leave the kid alone? You're so fucking smart, DeLeo. I guess you were born knowing every stupid term we use on this ship, and that's pretty much all you know after twenty years. I should just let the kid beat the shit out of you." Then, turning to me, he walked over to the rail. I followed. He pointed out at the ocean, looked at me with mock intensity and said with gravity, "*That* is the big shelf."

The other guys laughed and left. Feeling like a total idiot, I said, "Got it. Thanks," and dumped the bucket of rags over the side.

"Don't mention it; and don't let these shitheads get to you."

Though I had been set up, was embarrassed and felt like a fool, this guy had made an important point. I was bigger than most of the crew I had seen so far, and I was fairly strong. I probably could beat the shit out of a lot of these guys. The only advantage they had was they were older. As I thought about that some more, I added another, much more telling advantage: they sure looked a hell of a lot meaner.

My rescuer—I wondered how many I would need—turned out to be the Bosun. The Bosun is the equivalent of a chief petty officer in the navy, and is the senior non-licensed person on deck. He was in charge of all the ABs and OSs, on this ship a total of nine men. An important guy. Like Second, I was to call him Bosun. I wondered if that meant that people would call me wiper, but so far it had usually just been "kid."

He asked if I had seen the ship, and when I said no he turned and motioned for me to follow. I told him I had to get two more buckets of rags, but he dismissed that with a wave and said to tell Second I was helping the Bosun. So, on my second day I saw the ship, or at least some of it. We walked past the two huge forward holds with their stacked containers like small apartment houses, all the way to the bow. Some men were chipping paint along the bulkhead. The same work I would be doing in the engine room. Somehow I found that reassuring.

As we walked, he talked about the ship. "She" was 447 feet long and 76 feet wide, weighed 6000 tons empty and could weigh as much as 9000 tons fully loaded, and with its twin screws (propellers) could do seventeen knots. Anticipating my question Bosun said the ship was built in 1942, one of many built at the same time as the very similar Liberty ships. I said that I was born in 1942, and that maybe the ship and I shared a birthday. He just looked at me and continued. In 1958, SeaLand had the ship converted to its current configuration as a container ship. It could hold as many as 226 standard containers. The biggest change, he said, aside from the holds themselves, was a nine-foot increase in the ship's "beam" (width) to accommodate the dimensions of the containers. To me, the *Rufus Saxton* looked ancient, but its current form was only four years old.

He took me through the corridors of the main house, to the officers' deck. Though they all seemed to use the term "licensed" rather than "officer," this was still the "officers' deck." They had their own mess hall. I saw where the ABs and OSs bunked and the Bosun's fo'c'sle. He had his own quarters and it looked as if he had lived there for a while.

"Nice digs," I said, though apart from the fact that he didn't have to share it with anybody, it didn't look much different from the others. As I looked around I noticed a large silver-framed photograph on top of a partially built-in chest of drawers. It was of a pretty woman with short blond hair and four small children, none older than seven or eight. He saw the look of surprise on my face.

"My family."

"Nice picture, nice family, but…"

"But what, I can't have a family?"

"Yeah, well, sure, but…you're gone all the time."

"Not all the time. And kid," he added with a big grin, "each time I come home it's a honeymoon! Believe me, a honeymoon!"

"Congratulations! Sounds good to me. I may just have found a new philosophy of life." But in fact it wasn't new at all. It rather reminded me of my father with his dramatic arrivals and departures for singing engagements in New York and everywhere else in the world. Only his honeymoons sure as hell weren't with my mother.

***

Second wasn't around when I got back with the first bucket, so I took my time with the second and the third, leisurely enjoying the fresh air. Then I went back down to wash up and go up for lunch.

Since I had met a few of the guys, recognized a few more, and had eaten four meals there, I felt a bit more comfortable entering the mess hall. I saw Jack and sat at the table where he was sitting with Tony the oiler. We nodded. Old buddies. I stretched my feet just as the steward came over to take our lunch orders. Again he glared at me.

"What the hell is that guy's problem," I asked as he left. "He looks at me like I killed his mother."

"Oh, the kid, the kid's always mad about something or someone."

"Christ, I've been here all of what thirty hours. What the hell could I have done to him?"

"I wouldn't worry about it."

"'Yeah, well, fine, but this is my second lunch and it's the second time he looks at me like…like I don't know what. Next time I'm going to find out." Jack and the oiler just smiled to themselves as if they'd seen this movie before.

"By the way," I said, changing the subject to something I had noticed the night before. "How come there's no booze? I figured on a merchant ship every man would get, you know, his daily ration of rum, or at least a beer."

"Not on a coast-wise run you don't," Tony said with a wistful look. They figure we can be deprived for a few days."

Jack explained. "When you sign foreign articles, that's when a ship will not only be in international waters, but actually going to another country, then the ship carries liquor and beer. The powers that be figure we'd mutiny if we had no alcohol for that long."

"But that makes no sense. With a longer time at sea, wouldn't the booze make for more fights?" I asked.

Jack said, "You're right about that." Tony nodded in emphatic agreement. "On the longer runs there are fights all the time."

***

Back in the engine room, I moved to mopping and scrubbing the smaller second and third decks of the engine room. With each level the temperature was noticeably higher. I remembered: heat rises. Despite knowing that at least since ninth grade general science, I had never experienced it before.

Another inescapable truth was dawning on me. I was the only one in the engine room doing what I considered work. Though Michael and Raul might have been doing some, I rarely saw them. The others—the engineers, oilers and firemen seemed to just walk around (or just sit) checking things.

I finished after 4:00, and when I got back down I saw the First Assistant Engineer, "First" (you get the idea)— I had met him the day before—talking with Raul.

"Raul here is gonna show you how to blow tubes. Every third day—so tomorrow—it's your turn. You do it first thing in the morning and again before you leave, so around 4:30. He'll show you what to do now. Morning's really important. But don't miss either one. There's six around each boiler. You'll see. Raul's a good man.

He'll show you." As Raul looked at me with his inscrutable mix of a grin and a wince, I had my doubts.

I have to admit that I didn't like Puerto Ricans. That this was based on a stereotype is accurate, but that it was entirely a prejudice is not. That is, if a prejudice is a prejudgment, a judgment not based on any actual experience, I was not entirely prejudiced. I had had plenty of experience with Puerto Ricans, all of it negative: fights in grade school, gangs in junior high school, and roving bands of Puerto Rican teenagers on the Upper West Side and in the Village intimidating kids and anyone else that looked vulnerable. And my experience did not include the opposite side of that coin. At my prep school there were no Puerto Ricans and therefore no opportunity to develop any individual relationships or any balance in my perspective. So I tried to stay away from them, on the street, in the subway, everywhere. Living In New York City, I wasn't successful.

My problem had always been with Puerto Ricans in groups. I had never had any problem with an individual Puerto Rican. In fact, Raul was the first Puerto Rican with whom I had ever had any extended contact, if almost two days qualifies as extended contact. Anyway, this relationship was new ground for me, and Raul hadn't been the least bit friendly.

Despite sharing a cramped fo'c'sle, we had virtually no communication. He ate quickly and left the mess hall or grabbed a sandwich and ate somewhere on the deck. Michael said he was a buddy of the steward, the only other Puerto Rican on the ship. If they wanted the chance to speak Spanish, I could relate to that. I certainly remembered being a six-year-old in school, speaking only Hungarian. I sure had wished I had someone to speak to then. Anyway, the only conversations Raul and I had were on the morning I arrived and that afternoon chipping paint. Neither exactly encouraging. But since my attitude matched his, I didn't care. And I thought, it didn't matter. I was wrong.

The 10' by 8' fronts of the twin boilers faced each other on a large platform, which at the front—but not the back or sides—extended two feet to a single step down to the deck of the engine room. The back and sides dropped straight down to the bottom of the ship. If no one needed to be in back or at the sides of the boilers there would be no reason to spend the money on unneeded steel decking. But it turned out that someone did need to be there: me.

When a large ship steaming along on the ocean expels puffs of dark smoke out of its smokestack or stacks, someone is blowing tubes. In a ship of the *Rufus Saxton's* vintage, the combination of the heaviness of the fuel oil burned and the difficulty of getting the ideal fuel-air mixture sprayed into the fire box of the boiler results in some of the fuel not being entirely burned, leaving a soot residue in the tubes in which the boiling water was converted into steam. To eliminate the soot in the boiler tubes, some pressurized steam would be allowed to escape from the top valves and out the smoke stack— "blowing tubes" —as often as necessary. On this ship it needed to be done twice a day.

On more modern ships, which includes just about every ship built the day after the *Rufus Saxton*, this process is accomplished by pressing a button located comfortably near the fireman's station. On the *Rufus Saxton* the process was accomplished manually, that is, the button pressed was a wiper. The six valves were located at the top of each boiler, naturally along their inaccessible back and far sides. To each valve was attached a lever, and to that a long loop of steel chain.

The genius who had designed this system at some point recognized that there was no way to reach the chains, so attached to the back and sides of each boiler is a steel grid catwalk. Since there is nothing close behind the back and sides of the boilers but empty space, the catwalk could have been of any width, three feet, four feet. But no, it was fourteen inches wide. Apart from the fact that it was no wider than my shoes were long, the problem was the boilers. What was being burned inside their fire boxes was generating heat well over 1000 degrees. And though the boilers had some kind of insulating coating, if you touched them you still got burned.

The wiper's job was to walk along the cat walk, reach up and pull one length of the chain loop, releasing the jet of steam, pull the other length to close the valve, and repeat the process for the other five valves. To keep the gallant wiper from falling from the catwalk into the abyss below, the ship builders had thoughtfully installed a single, very thin steel rail situated at what would be the optimum protective height for the average wiper who, in their estimation, must have stood a strapping 4' 6". Risky for Michael and Raul who were in the 5' 8" or 9" range. At 6' 4" the railing assured that if I fell against it I would do a perfect half gainer. Beyond the height difference my problem was exacerbated by the fact that my shoulders must have been six inches wider than theirs.

Rather than show me by demonstration, Raul chose to show me by direction. Not only did this put me at the mercy of the extent and accuracy of his direction, it also meant that I took his afternoon turn. "You do it and I'll watch," would have been appropriate. Instead I stood on the catwalk, trying to stand in a way that would avoid my shoulders making contact with the boiler while not leaning so far away from it that I would lose my balance. I managed until he told me to grab the chain. As I reached upward, I bumped into the boiler. I let out a loud "shit" and "damn" as the metal burned the bare skin of my partially extended arm.

"You gotta be careful man, or you get hurt man," Raul offered laughingly.

I just glared at him. Because of the burn, I hadn't succeeded in grabbing the chain. I wondered how Raul reached it. Then I wondered why the chain wasn't four feet longer so even a midget could have grabbed it without reaching. But again the answer was clear. Why use extra steel when....? So with Raul grinning and wincing, I went at it again. This time I focused exactly on where to place my hands and arms to avoid the boiler. I reached up, grabbed it and started pulling. So far so good.

There is a natural tendency for people who are pulling on a vertically hanging chain or rope to keep looking up at whatever it is they are trying to accomplish by their pulling, unless, of course there is a reason not to do so. For example, a person hoisting a flag tends to look up at the flag he is hoisting even though he knows where it is going. In any event, I kept looking up at the lever I was eagerly pulling on with the chain. At first I didn't see anything—I wasn't expecting to. Then, too late to avert it, I did. A shower of scalding hot soot escaped from the valve and sprayed down onto my upturned face.

"Jesus Christ! Goddamn it to hell," I yelled as I fought to wipe the burning soot from my face with my tee shirt.

"Raul you shit head, why didn't you tell me the valves leak?"

"Man, you gotta be careful," he said with a giddy laugh. "I told you man. You don't know shit, man."

"I'll tell you this, Raul, you're a real asshole. You got that? If I knew, First wouldn't have told you to show me. You mess with me again, I'm gonna break your head, and now that you 'showed me,' *you* can finish blowing tubes. My turn's tomorrow."

As I walked away to wash up, he shouted after me. "Man, you don't tell me nothing. Think you some smart guy; come on this ship like you something. Man, you nothing here. And you don't fuck with me. Nobody fuck with me. You see, man. You see."

OK, my attempt at international diplomacy had not been well thought out. And true, I didn't like the guy. And yes, I may have overreacted a bit. But as I looked back at Raul to say something, who knows what—something to escalate the situation further, I suppose—Raul was taking a long-sleeved flannel shirt and a baseball cap off a hook near the boiler. I just looked at him and shook my head in wonderment. What the hell, couldn't I even expect a guy I worked and lived with to try just a little bit to help me avoid getting hurt? The answer: probably not.

CHAPTER 9

I Search for Meaning and Find Jacksonville

World War III didn't erupt that evening. I found a rickety, old plastic lawn chair in the locker where I had found the mattress and pillow, set it unsteadily on what was now *my* hatch cover and read *Waiting for Godot*. Lorna's immediate receptiveness had eliminated both the need and the opportunity to read it in the park, and I hadn't been in a reading mode since. I had seen a film of the play my senior year in prep school, and it had a powerful emotional impact on me at the time. I identified with the characters' constant search for meaning in life. I wasn't interested in existential philosophy, at least not what I had encountered of it in my superficial and limited readings of Kierkegaard and Camus and the pretentious discussions in the basement of the Café Figaro. I wasn't even interested in debating whether there was meaning to life in general, or if there was, discovering it. I was only interested in finding meaning in my own life. And to the existentialists who say you have to create your own meaning to your life, I was damn well trying to do that. But being a wiper on this ship wasn't getting me very far. So I read *Waiting for Godot* and waited, until the wind picked up, and it got dark, and I went back to the fo'c'sle and went to sleep.

***

The next day was the slowest in my life. All three of us, united for the first time in a common effort—the Three Musketeers of the engine room—were attacking the starboard bulkhead of the second level of the engine room with hammer and chisel. All day. Paint chips flew accompanied by the cacophonous sound of steel on steel. All day. It was impossible to have a conversation, though neither Michael nor Raul seemed the least bit bothered by that. Both were content to bang away and stare mindlessly at the steel wall.

We each worked on separate sections about ten feet apart, Raul on the far left, Michael in the middle, and I on the right. From time to time as I went by to get a drink of water, I could see the difference in our respective approaches to the work. It reminded me of the Three Little Pigs. Raul was the pig who built his house out of straw; he scraped off the paint that had flaked and could be knocked off easily. Michael was the pig who built his house out of sticks; he got the loose stuff but also went after some of the more resistant spots, though leaving as many as he removed. And I was the good pig who built his house out of bricks; I bore down feverishly on every spot of paint in my section, regardless of difficulty. What the hell was I doing? Was I looking for a gold star, somebody to come over and say what a good boy I was? Or did I think I was making a smooth canvas for a goddamn mural? I was working a lot harder than Michael and twice as hard as Raul.

When we finished chipping, whenever that might be—it was a very long bulkhead—we would paint it, the same beige color as before, and no one would ever look at it. It was the bulkhead of a cargo ship, on the inside of the engine room, on a level where no one spent any time. We were just protecting it from rust. I knew all this. Yet I continued to attack each detail. Why? Was I going to create meaning in my life by creating perfection out of meaningless work? A kind of existential alchemy. What the hell!

The day passed, as I said, slowly, and without incident. I watched Michael work, without emotion, neither careless nor careful, the distant, inconspicuous, self-sufficient Irishman. What the hell was he doing on this ship? Though always pleasant, he offered nothing. At some point I would try to find out if he was really just the second little pig.

But that afternoon I had a different goal. Just before washing up I asked First if I could see the turbines. To my surprise given Michael's warning, he said, "Yeah, OK, just don't get close to anything."

So through the taboo hatch I went. The noise behind the wall was overwhelming. The compartment, at the extreme stern of the ship was taken up mostly by the gleaming, spinning propeller shafts. I backed away as I imagined their spinning somehow pulling me toward them. The turbines were enormous and inscrutable. Looking at them, I couldn't imagine how they worked. I felt more cramped that on the catwalk, but with more dire consequences for a wrong move. I didn't get close to anything…or to having any idea how the ship worked.

I had lunch and dinner without encountering the usual glare of the steward, and in the evening I watched two poker games in the mess hall. No television. We would arrive in Jacksonville sometime during the night or early the next morning. The next day was a Sunday in port, and I would have the day off.

***

Work on the ship was governed by two opposing objectives: the need to do all the things that need to be done on a ship, every minute of every day, and the need to keep overtime at an absolute minimum. Finding the right balance between these irreconcilable objectives was the responsibility of the captain, and through him the licensed personnel aboard ship, the officers. Even though the captain, the mates and the engineers were themselves members of unions—two different ones, and neither being the SIU, they represented the interests of the steamship company. Technically we all did, as we were taking care of the company's ship, but obviously to a very different extent. Different enough that none of the non-licensed crew felt that way.

The point is when the ship was at sea, we worked, whatever day it might be. There were no days off. That was a good thing in principle: there was nothing else to do, and we got paid time-and-a-half on Saturdays and double time on Sundays.

But when the ship was in port over a weekend day not everyone worked. This was a directional policy. Who actually worked was determined by the officers, presumably under a budget. There seemed to be a lot of discretion. Most people wanted to work as much as possible. And in this, as in every other regard, seniority mattered. Apparently the budget allowed for one wiper, and Michael would work this Sunday. Raul and I would have the day off. What he would do with it I didn't know or care. I would see Jacksonville.

At the union hall I had been told that my salary was $335 a month plus overtime. Since I worked more or less seven and a half hours a day, not counting lunch and breaks, and there would be twenty-two or twenty-three regular work days a month, I figured I made about $2 an hour. So a Sunday chipping paint or painting could bring me $30. Not bad, I thought, for one day's work, especially compared to what I made at the supermarket. When I added the three very good meals a day, I was doing way better than I had expected. But this Sunday I was going to spend money rather than make any.

***

I woke up Sunday morning feeling on top of the world. I was a seaman going into port. No it wasn't Marseilles. But I was on my own in a place I'd never been, and everything was possible. I found Jacksonville on the glass-encased map of the lower half of the East Coast hung in the mess hall. It was at the intersection of the Atlantic Ocean and the St. Johns River. The port where

117

we docked was bright and looked nothing like dreary Port Elizabeth. This was the south; the air was fresher; the sun was brighter. I had a leisurely breakfast of sausages, eggs, pancakes, the works.

Jack came in as I was finishing and I stayed to have coffee and talk.

"So what's to do or see in Jacksonville?"

"Not much. There's a very big, very old tree somewhere in the middle of the city."

"Yeah, that would be a hell of a day off. 'Come to beautiful, sunny, historic Florida and see a big tree.' Aren't there some old buildings from when Florida belonged to Spain?

"There probably are, but I've never really spent much time in the town. I try to work the watches in ports like these, take off in others. I'll probably have lunch with an old friend who lives here."

"Why get a ship like this that just goes up and down the coast? With your seniority, why not a ship to Europe or around the world? Seems to me it's all about interesting port cities, you know, seeing the world."

"Yeah, well, I've seen them. Don't get me wrong, it's worth it the first couple of times, but then…it isn't. In the end it's just a job, not a very good job. It's good for getting away…and coming home.

I thought of the boson's honeymoons.

"But for me, now," he continued, not looking at me, I'm thinking about the future, and I don't want to commit to anything longer than these runs."

"Like I told you the other night, I'm here to think about the future too."

"Right. We're at opposite ends of that."

As I started to go on, he said, "Let's leave it at that." And then he added, "Why not go out to Jacksonville Beach, a bit north of Jacksonville itself? Nice beach, you'll have a good time."

Beaches meant women. That sounded preferable to looking at a tree.

I thanked him for the suggestion and went back to the fo'c'sle to get what I would need for a day at the beach: bathing suit, a towel, another book, *The Agony & The Ecstasy*, a thick, densely printed paperback about the life of Michelangelo, just in case, and a small canvas shoulder bag to carry it all in.

Dressed in clean jeans, white tee shirt, canvas tennis shoes and wearing aviator sunglasses—what would become my "uniform of the day" in port—I strode confidently down the gangway in search of a bus. A lot had changed in just four days.

The bus just went into Jacksonville. I would need another from there to Jacksonville Beach, or Jax Beach as the driver called it. So I would see Jacksonville after all. The bus deposited me in the center of town.

Walking around in no particular direction, I came to a park surrounded by large buildings. There, in the middle of the park was an enormous oak tree. A small brass plaque said it was the Freedom Oak, more than two hundred years old. Being a Sunday, there were very few people. But a few strolled by and some sat on the benches set in a large circle under the canopy of the tree. It was only 9:30, too early to go to the beach, so I sat on a bench, stretched out my legs, enjoyed the sunny, balmy day, and looked at the tree. And at the people.

Watching people, as I walked in the street and particularly in the park, produced a strange feeling. I felt like a spy in a far away place, an outsider, someone who wasn't supposed to be there, someone looking in from the outside. It wasn't unusual for me to watch people and to feel disconnected from them. Still, it was strange to be completely alone in a place where I knew no one at all. Even though I wasn't hiding, and given my size, hard to miss, I felt invisible. I watched the people and imagined their lives. Since I was invisible, in my mind I intruded on their privacy. I tended to focus on the women.

***

Though there is a small town called Jacksonville Beach, very few people lived there in 1962. What drew people to the area were the actual beaches. These were quite spectacular. I had only been to two beaches, both in New York, the one at Coney Island and the much larger Jones Beach. Neither was anything like this. The New York beaches were relatively narrow strips no more than three hundred feet wide, of soft, deep sand, crowded with people. This beach was enormous, perhaps a quarter of a mile wide. The sand was hard packed, hard enough to comfortably drive a car on. And rather than thousands of people on towels so close to each other that it was almost impossible to walk between them, a few hundred people were scattered over miles of beach.

The beach was so wide and its slope so gradual that there were no breakers, just gentle waves only a few inches high. I took off my tee shirt and walked along the edge of the water, the late morning sun beating down on me. I wished I had some sun lotion.

I walked about a half mile south and then back, reconnoitering. There were women, girls, alone and in groups among the people on the beach. But they were so isolated that there would be nothing casual about approaching them. I also felt as if they would somehow speak a different language.

As it got hotter I thought about going for a swim, but I couldn't figure out what to do with my clothes and, more important, my wallet. So I kept walking and from time to time sat down in the sand and stared out in the direction of what I thought was southern Portugal. And though, of course, I couldn't see anything, I thought it was probably the best view of it I would ever get. (Later, I looked at another map in the mess hall and saw that I was only looking toward the Azores. So I hadn't missed that much.)

Every 500 yards along the beach were wooden life-guard stands, about ten feet high, with built-in bench seats at the top. Over the almost two hours I had been there, none had been occupied, so I climbed up on one and sat down. The sun was shining directly in my face and I was probably getting burned, but it felt good, the contrast with the engine room glaring. I closed my eyes behind my sun glasses. Not long after, I was startled by a girl's voice.

"Excuse me."

I looked down and saw two pretty girls, probably a bit younger than me.

"Are you a lifeguard?"

"No, just sitting in the chair. Do you need something?"

"We're here with my little brother—he's four—and we left him digging in the sand over there," she said, pointing to a spot just a little way up the beach, "and took a walk. Now he's not there and we can't find him."

I climbed down from the chair. They were quite pretty, both with short light brown hair. They wore shorts and had nice tan legs and from what I could tell despite their loose shirts were otherwise well enough put together.

"Let's go find him. What's his name?"

"Sam. We've been calling his name."

"Well, I didn't hear you either." I took off my tennis shoes and rolled up my jeans. "I'll check in the water."

"Oh my God, do you think he drowned?"

"No, I don't think so at all. It's just that if he's sitting in the water it would be harder to see him. I'll go one way and you go the other; then we'll cross back. He couldn't have gotten far."

With that I walked into the water about a hundred feet. The water was still less than eighteen inches deep. Then I walked South, calling his name as loud as I could, which was a hell of a lot louder than the girls. I found him on his hands and knees in six inches of water. He was furiously digging in the sand with a small red shovel, watching the water fill and then level the hole he had just dug. A cute little kid, with the same light brown hair. He must have heard me shouting his name, but didn't seem to pay it any mind.

"Hi Sam. Having fun? Your sister is looking for you. Let's go find her." I reached down and he happily took my fingers. We walked back up the beach with me shouting, "I found Sam." Soon the girls came running back. His sister picked him up and hugged him.

"Thank you so much. Where did you find him?"

I told her as we walked back toward the lifeguard stand.

"Why don't you both come and sit up here? There's room for three. Sam can play right below and you can keep an eye on him."

Sharon and Jillie. Sharon was Sam's sister. They lived not far from the beach. They were each eighteen and had just graduated from high school.

"Fourteen years, that's a lot of distance between you and Sam. Are there more of you?"

"Yeah, five more. I'm the oldest and he's the youngest. The only way I can get away to the beach is if I take Sam. So here we are. Jillie's my best friend."

Throughout the introductions Jillie hadn't said a word, just nodded in agreement with everything Sharon said. But it was Jillie I was attracted to. She had more angular, sleek features. Though pretty, Sharon's face was rounder. Beyond her complete silence, there was some mystery to Jillie. Compared to Sharon's bubbly chatter, there seemed more depth to Jillie. I had hoped to sit next to her, but when we settled down, Sharon sat between us. She was definitely running the show.

"You didn't go to school here, or I would have seen you around. Where are you from?"

"New York, New York City."

"Wow, New York City. That must be so exciting. We've never met anyone from New York. What's it like?"

"Well, crowded, noisy, lot's of things going on all the time, lots of places to go. Big buildings, you know, you've seen movies, pictures. It's really exactly like that. There's a lot more than Times Square, that's for sure. Anyway, it's nice to get away from it."

"How come you're here?"

"If you mean the beach, I'm here to get some sun and go swimming, and of course to meet pretty girls and rescue their baby brothers. By the way, do you have any sun lotion?" They laughed. "If here means Jacksonville, I'm in the merchant marine and I work on a ship that pulled in early this morning." There! I finally had a chance to say it to someone. I had been waiting to say it since I had stepped off the gangway this morning.

"Oh that's so cool, the merchant marine." She looked breathless as she shuffled through her beach bag and came up with a bottle of Coppertone.

And then for the first time, Jillie spoke, "Do you get to go to all kinds of places?" Well, she got right to the point, didn't she? What was I going to say— no, I just go between New York and Jacksonville, and maybe exotic Mobile, Alabama?

"Yeah, we go pretty much anywhere. Wherever they need to move cargo. Right now we're doing the East coast, but then who knows, Europe, the Far East. Ship goes everywhere." I wished. But no way I was going to ruin this.

Jillie now emboldened, "What do you do on the ship, do you steer it?"

"No, I work in the engine room, you know with the boilers and all the machines that make the ship go."

"No kidding. How'd you learn to do that."

"Well, you just learn. You have no choice," I said gravely. The reality was painful: there had been no part of my job that these girls couldn't have done as well as I. We sat and talked for a long time. I slathered myself with the lotion and Sharon happily rubbed it onto my back. Eventually Jillie opened up as Sharon quieted down. She must have sensed that I was talking to Jillie, though it was awkward as we had to lean forward and around Sharon. I was getting hungry and asked if there was a place to get something to eat. Jillie said there was a stand near where they had parked their car, and we went there with Sam in tow.

We had hot dogs and cokes and walked back to the lifeguard stand. I asked if they wanted to go for a swim, but they didn't have bathing suits. So they climbed back up to the bench and I stood below within the stand's frame, and with my towel around my waist managed to change into my bathing suit. Talking to them was not my objective, and my objective wasn't feasible, so I ran down into the water until it got deep enough to dive in. I swam around in the warm, placid water, so unlike the ocean in New York. This was fun.

When I got out, there were two guys throwing a football not far away. I could throw and catch a football pretty well, so I walked over and asked if I could join in. There is an established convention around this form of activity. You make the third point of an equilateral triangle and wait to be thrown the ball. If the guy with the ball is aggressive, he fires the first ball at you as hard as he can to see if you can catch it. It's a sizing-up move. He was aggressive. It was a hard throw and I caught it easily with just my hands, not letting the ball touch my body. I threw it to the second guy straight and with a tight spiral, letting him know I could throw it a lot harder. Test over. As far as this game was concerned, I was a player. We could relax. We ran pass routes long and short, made spectacular one hand catches, diving in the sand for some, in the water for others. I was show-ing off. Not for my playmates but for the girls, though from what I could see, they weren't watching. I couldn't remember when I'd had so much fun. After almost an hour I said thanks and we shook hands. After late intro-ductions, Dave, Bill, Peter, I headed back to the girls, dried off and changed back into my clothes.

We sat and talked some more. How was I going to get Jillie alone? I hoped that maybe it was her car and that she might want to have dinner after dropping off Sharon and Sam. But it was Sharon's car, and they had to get home. I said I would probably be coming back some time soon and Sharon wrote down her phone number. I asked Jillie for hers. Sharon answered for her.

"Jillie's going steady."

"That's nice. Why don't you give me your number anyway? A lot can happen while I'm away. And by the time I come back you could be going steady Sharon. Who knows? Jillie blushed and wrote her number on the same slip of paper. They kissed me on the cheek as I patted Sam on the head. They walked to their car and I to the bus stop.

Well, so much for that. Still, it had been a great day. Not bad for my first port of call. Rather than go back to the ship I ate at a diner near the bus station in Jacksonville. I had a chopped steak with mashed pota-toes. Exactly what I would have eaten on the ship for free. But I was on my own.

CHAPTER 10

The Grapefruit and the Kid

The next day was like my first. The ship was unloaded and then loaded. The need to avoid Sunday over- time costs meant that none of that had happened on Sunday. Raul and Michael were rewarded for their minimal chipping efforts by spending all of Monday in the same pursuit. I was back to wiping. Two days of oil buildup on just about everything meant that again I earned my title all around the engine room. Once again I was coated with oil from head to foot. How it got on me I'm not sure, but I was almost as covered in it as the first day.

And it was hot. But I had discovered three things I could do to improve the situation slightly. I now took frequent drinks of water. I sweated it all out, but I didn't feel quite so dehydrated. Someone might have mentioned the other two, but of course…. There were salt tablet dispensers situated around the engine room. As I didn't know what they were, I hadn't used them. It was just curiosity that impelled me to ask one of the oilers. He was surprised I hadn't been taking salt regu- larly. He said he had a tablet every two or three hours.

No wonder I was always so exhausted at the end of the day. Finally, there were air blowers. These were vertical pipes about eighteen inches wide that opened downward about a foot over my head. They blew air from the deck down into the engine room. You could get a moment of relief by standing directly under one of those blowers. It demonstrated the power of relativity. Although the temperature on deck was between 85 and 90, hardly cool, and it must have been warmed on the way down, compared to the 115 at the bottom of the engine room, it seemed like air-conditioning.

Still, it was quite a relief to get to the mess hall for lunch. I sat with Michael, Jack and Max. Jack asked about the beach and I told them about the first two names in my seaman's black book. I bemoaned the fact that they were girls and not women. Girls lived with their parents; women had their own apartments.

"Well, good luck with that," Jack said. And the conversation went on in the same vein.

"Do you guys know women in the places the ship goes?"

"Not really," said Max "We're not around long enough, and it takes too much effort. And besides, we're not gone that long. I've got a woman at home."

Michael joined in. "There's the occasional hooker, but the trick is to get it for love."

As I looked at him quizzically, he went on, "You know, get them to give it to you for free."

"Yeah, right," Jack retorted with a smirk.

"So, have you guys gotten it for free, for love?"

"Peter, you're going to hear all kinds of stories," said Jack. "Maybe some of them are true. But think about it.

That's what you want? Spend your time with whores? Those girls you met today, they sound a lot better."

"Oh, I don't know," said Michael, "I've had some fun with a few. They know what they're doing, and you don't have to battle for it."

"So did you get it for love?" I pressed on.

"Well, truth is I got one to give me a discount because she loved me," he said solemnly.

We all laughed. His heavy brogue made the whole exchange funny and unreal in an Alice-in-Wonderland-way.

But Max felt a tutorial was required.

"If you young guys are going to talk about this shit, you better get the rules straight. First, "it" means getting laid, nothing else. "For love" means you can't pay for it—no discounts. She—and she's got to be a pro, no amateurs—has to give it you out of love. You can buy her drinks and dinner, but no money or gifts. That's it."

Max went on about details and exceptions. Jack described it with a grand wave of his hand as "a noble quest and the Holy Grail of seamen the world over for as long as men have sailed the seven seas—a challenge not always taken up but always in the back of every seaman's mind."

At this point my buddy the steward arrived with some of the food, once again accompanied by a fierce glare clearly directed at me. I looked at him and then at the guys at the table. When the steward left I asked again what was bothering the guy. Max said something about the kid having a chip on his shoulder. It turned out there was a lot more useful information they could have provided.

When the steward returned with the rest of the food he glared at me again. Finally I had enough.

"Hey, what the hell is your problem? Every time I come in here you look at me like I killed your brother. Since the first hour I've been on this ship you've been giving me a hard time. Are you gonna tell me what's bothering you or just glare at me forever?"

Well, I got my answer. "You son of a bitch, look at the floor where your fucking feet are. Look at the mess you make, and you do it man, you slide your feet around so the whole floor is messed up. Nobody else does that shit. You fuck up the floor and I gotta clean it up every time."

Well, how about that. I looked down at my feet and the floor, and indeed there were oil marks. But what the hell was I supposed to do about that?

"Yeah, well I work in the engine room. I'm a wiper. I'm in oil the whole goddamn day. While you're up here being nice and cool—I don't see you sweating— I'm down below doing the worst job on this ship, and you want me to feel sorry for you because you've got to mop a spot on the floor. You expect me not to move my feet? You've got to be kidding. And besides all that, why couldn't you just say something, you know, be normal?"

"I don't gotta say nothing to you. I don't give a shit what you do. I tell you what you do. You fuck with me, you mess up my floor, you got a problem with me. You ask these guys."

Jack tried to smooth things over. "Look kid, he's not doing it deliberately to fuck with you. He didn't know."

"I don't give a shit what this prick knows. He's a wise ass."

I suspected Raul might have somehow contributed to this situation. But I wasn't really thinking at this point. He had gotten to me and my blood was up. I wasn't going to back down from this guy. I was bigger and I was mad. Leaning back and putting my feet further out I looked at him. "Pal, I've got just the solution to your problem. Go fuck yourself!" He glared at me and left. As cool as that might have sounded, I was trembling. I had a strong feeling that this wasn't going to be the end of it.

No one looked at me. There was silence in the mess hall. Had everyone heard this exchange? Then as conversation restarted, now in a muttered undertone, Jack said, "That wasn't exactly the best way to handle the kid. You do have a problem now."

"Why, what's the big deal? I'll try to wipe my shoes before I get into the mess hall. I still don't have to put up with his bullshit. And why do you keep calling him *the kid?*"

"People don't call him kid like they might call you kid. It's Kid with a capital "K," like Kid Gavilan or Billy the Kid. He goes by the name Kid Fonseca and he happens to be the Golden Gloves middleweight champion of Puerto Rico. And he's a nut case."

I felt like I had just been punched in the face. "Why couldn't one of you have warned me?"

"Wait a second. Who the hell expected the two of you to explode like that?

"OK, so what happens now?"

No one answered. As we finished eating, Jack spoke, as if answering my question.

"At some point he's going to come for you. No one's going to intervene. It's tough luck, but it's between you and him. You'll be alright today. He won't try anything while we're in port. But tonight, tomorrow, you're going to have to watch out."

Michael asked comfortingly, "You have a knife?"

"No. I didn't come armed. Sorry, I didn't expect to have to fight for my life."

"I don't know what world you live in, but here you have a knife.

Max escalated the arms race.

"Listen, you've got to protect yourself. Come with me."

With that we all got up from the table. Shaking his head gravely, Michael went out in the direction of the fo'c'sle. I followed Max and Jack. We went into Max's fo'c'sle and closed the door. He opened the lower of two lockers. They were in each fo'c'sle and looked like lockers in a locker-room. He told me to bend down and look up at the top of the locker. There, taped to the ceiling of the locker was what looked to me—and I was no expert—like a .38 caliber pistol of the type detectives used, at least in movies. I looked at him incredulously.

"You've got to be kidding. Come on, there's no way. We cursed at each other. You're not going to tell me that people around here kill each other over that?"

"Maybe you won't need it. I hope not. But if he comes after you with anything more than his hands, this is where you go. It's loaded.'"

I couldn't believe it. Max was nuts. They were all nuts. What had I gotten myself into? Now visibly scared, I looked at them both.

"Can I go to one of the officers?"

"In the ideal world that might work, but here it won't. No one can get into this and protect you. Not one of the officers, not Max or me. On a ship you pick your fights carefully, and when you mouth off you've got to back it up." After a long pause he added, "Or you don't, and you don't want to live with that."

With that we went to Jack's fo'c'sle. He reached under his bed and pulled out a pistol, this one smaller, a silver automatic. As he put it back he showed me that it was attached to the mattress spring with a half-inch wide rubber band. This was just great. I wondered how they imagined I would get to these guns if I really needed one.

"Look, the Kid is a fighter. You look like you can take care of yourself. You'll probably have a fight. We've all had them. The guns, well, just in case it ends up going further."

This wasn't a fight on a basketball court or the school yard. No one was going to break it up. How in hell could I just get out of this. I thought of just swallowing my pride, going up to the guy and apologizing. But I thought life on this ship was not going to take a turn for the better if I backed down and everybody thought I was a coward. The pack always turns on the one they perceive as the weakest. Then again, what would they think if I was dead, or if I shot the Kid?

And what about just having a fight? He was a champion boxer. Why not come at me with his hands. Sure, even though I had weight, height and reach on him, I assumed he could beat the shit of me in a boxing ring. But this wouldn't be a boxing match. I could grapple with him, kick him in the balls, do whatever it took. I would have a chance. And if I got beat up, it would be over, and I would recover. None of this knife and gun stuff made any sense.

There was one big problem with this scenario. I wasn't a fighter. It wasn't that I couldn't fight; I had been in fights. It was that I wasn't naturally aggressive. I had to get mad in order to fight. When I did, I held my own. It started with the fact that as a small kid I was always afraid. Not all that surprising given what I had experienced earlier.

When I was eleven and twelve kids picked on me. I was tall, skinny, my height always way ahead of my coordination. My mother was concerned enough about it—my coming home crying had upset her, more by my description of my fear than by the fact that I had some bumps and bruises—that she enrolled me in a self-defense program, Sigward Health Studio on 51st Street, near the old Madison Square Garden. It was owned and operated by a barrel-chested Swede with a shaved head who had been the fighting instructor for the Stockholm police force before he had immigrated to the United States.

He taught kids, more or less around my age, boxing and judo. This was a very big deal for me: I was scared, and I had more than an hour subway ride each way. I went each Saturday and practiced at home during the week.

Over the course of a year, I developed in two important ways: I learned how to fall without getting hurt, and I lost my fear. We spent the first month doing push-ups and sit-ups and other calisthenics, and falling. We fell forwards and backwards. Starting from my knees, I worked up to being able to fall forward without bending my knees, breaking my fall by slapping my forearms on the mat, just at impact. I could never understand why it worked, but it did. The first time, of course, was terrifying, but eventually I could do it not only on the mat, but on the wooden floor and then even on the concrete sidewalk. I would win bets at school performing this trick. It worked backwards as well though it was a bit more complicated. I would fall with a completely stiff body, hands and arms straight out in front of me, and just at impact slap my arms down and roll backwards, usually doing a backward summersault. Somehow it never hurt. Believing I could do it was the most difficult part, but that accomplished, it became easy.

I did not become a good boxer or judo fighter. I learned how to do everything he taught, but at that age I was too slow to be effective. No part of me was quick. The shorter, stockier kids were more coordinated but more importantly, much quicker. It took a long time for my long skinny arms to move the heavy sixteen ounce gloves. By the time I did, I had been hit, unless I stood in a defensive stance the whole time, and that wasn't the point. So I tried to box. Occasionally I would land a punch and a kid would be staggered, but far more often it was me getting hit. The real issue that never changed was that I really didn't want to fight. Boxing as a sport was OK, but I wasn't mad and didn't really want to hurt anyone. Judo was not much better. I learned the moves, but my long legs and big feet were too slow, and I would trip over them as often as I was tripped by my opponent.

All this would change dramatically as I got older and eventually grew into my body. But I still wasn't naturally aggressive. Even in basketball, soccer and tennis, the sports in which I was rather good, I only got my game into high gear when someone or something got me mad.

***

As I thought about Kid Fonseca coming for me, I didn't feel mad or aggressive; I felt afraid, very afraid. As I spent the afternoon joining Michael and Raul chipping on the second level, there was nothing to distract me from my thoughts. But as Jack had predicted, dinner passed without incident. Then, after a scary discussion on deck with Jack and another AB named Wilson White—everyone called him Whitey—about shark fishing off the ship's stern, I went back to the mess hall for pie watch, television and, hopefully, safety in numbers. Eventually though, I had to return to the fo'c'sle. We were now at sea and it was dark. I walked sideways, my back pressed against the containers. In the open spaces I ran. I didn't know what to expect in the fo'c'sle. What I did know was that Michael, for all his Irish charm and general friendliness, was going to do nothing to help me. He would stay out of it. In fact, if I thought about it rationally—not easy for me to do at that moment—it *was* my problem, not his, and he owed me nothing, certainly not to put himself in harm's way. I was convinced that Raul, on the other hand, was part of the problem.

In the fo'c'sle Michael and Raul were lying in their bunks looking at magazines. If they were talking before I opened the door, they were certainly silent when I came in. I nodded to them and said nothing. As I looked at my bunk I realized I had to make an adjustment in my sleeping arrangement. I had made the bed with the pillow end where I had initially found it, against the bulkhead nearest the door. If the Kid were to sneak in during the night, I would be immediately accessible for anything he might do, unnecessarily so. I remade the bed so that my head was against the far bulkhead and facing the door. If I was lucky enough to wake up—assuming I ever got to sleep—I might have a chance to ward him off with my feet and legs. At least it was better than the previous set-up.

I brushed my teeth and as I looked at myself in the mirror, I wondered whether this was the last time I would see my face. Then, for a moment, I got mad. Bullshit, I thought. I am not going to be terrified of this guy. He's probably going to do nothing, and if he does, he's *not* going to kill me. In fact, if he jumps me in the fo'c'sle, I'll smash his head into the corner of the steel bulkhead and knee him in the balls or in the Adam's apple. With newfound, albeit fragile bravado I marched back to my bunk, lay down, turned off my light, and for the next two hours imagined Raul in various evil roles and Michael with his head turned to the wall, as I rode a rollercoaster up and down between frenzied aggression and abject fear. Eventually, exhausted from the ride, I fell asleep.

I awoke after a night filled with frightening but now ephemeral dreams to a rainy and dark day. The seas were not especially turbulent; it was just a steady rain with a slight breeze. The day went by much like the previous one, except the chipping was succeeded by the inevitable painting. I found the chipping more satisfying. I remembered a line from one of the arias in Handel's "Messiah," "He made the rough places smooth...." The connection was so absurd it made me smile, and that was something I hadn't done in a while.

As I worked in silence next to the other two, the tension palpable, I suddenly realized that the Kid's glare was directly related to what I did just before going up to the mess hall. If I chipped or painted, there was no oil; if I wiped oil there was. I thought it would be no big deal, after one of my more intense wiping days, to get a rag and wipe the bottom of my shoes before going up. The more I thought about it the more likely it seemed that the whole issue would just disappear as more time passed without a new inflammatory incident. After all, the guy couldn't be completely crazy. Why create a huge deal when there was no longer any deal? And after a peaceful lunch and dinner, I was fairly convinced that that's how the situation would play out. After another couple of days, in fact, at a point when it wouldn't look like I was backing down, I would seize the initiative and go up to him and offer to shake hands.

As the rain continued that evening, I was pretty sure there would be no television, but I planned to watch the poker games and maybe even play in the lower stakes game. I must have been early because there was no one in the mess hall when I arrived. There were some issues of *Sport* magazine on one of the tables, so I sat and looked at the magazine while I waited for the players to arrive.

After about ten minutes, I began to have an uneasy feeling. The game should have started by now and there was no one there but me. And it was too quiet. The level on which the mess hall was located also housed the galley and several fo'c'sles. There was always the background noise of men talking or walking or of a portable radio—ambient sound. Now there was nothing. Complete silence. Something was not right. I put down the magazine.

I heard someone approaching the open mess hall door. I waited. OK, the Kid was going to make his move. Everyone was going to stay out of the way, leaving the two of us to settle it. I gulped a couple of times. I was as ready as I would ever be, and started to stand up to meet him as he came through the door. But the vision of what I saw coming through the door shocked me back into the chair.

It was not the Kid. It was Cook. And he was carrying a heavy sixteen inch butcher's knife.

I sat frozen, unable to breath. Jesus Christ! What the hell do I do now? I was totally, ridiculously defenseless against this creature. He was taller and much wider than I. He had to outweigh me by at least a hundred pounds. This guy could kill me with his bare hands. Why in hell did he need a weapon?

In fact you could die of fright just looking at him. He was as grotesque as he was huge. Of course I had heard about him and his legend, but probably out of fear, no one had described him beyond his size. His body wasn't muscular, just enormous. But his head...his head, at least in proportion to his body, looked about the size of a large grapefruit. It would have been the right size for a person half his size. It had a very low forehead topped with a shock of thick, straw-colored hair that seemed to go in all directions, and bisected by a scar that traveled from above the inner edge of his left eyebrow down across his nose to the middle of his right cheek. This was a creature worthy of *The Odyssey*.

As he entered the room, I had no thought of standing up. I wanted to do nothing that would ignite him. He turned and with his left hand, the one that wasn't holding the butcher's knife, closed the door. He stood about ten feet from me and stared, first at me, then in the direction of a porthole, then back at me. His expression was mobile, changing from what looked like hatred to passive to questioning. He seemed to be trying to decide what to do. He looked like an imbecile, a kind of menacing Lenny from *Of Mice and Men*. But he couldn't be. He was obviously an accomplished chef, or at least cook. He had a responsible job. He was responsible for three people and for feeding thirty-three. He had to order food, plan menus. But you could never have guessed it from looking at him, certainly not now. As he stared, I had a fleeting thought of the television program, *What's My Line?* No one would guess.

"You the wiper?" His voice fit neither his body nor his head.

"Yes."

"You're giving the Kid a hard time."

I started to say something, and he took a step toward me.

"Don't say nothing. You mess with him, you mess with me. And now I'm gonna mess with you."

He deftly changed his grip on the knife to a thrusting position and took a small step forward. Standing up would only encourage him; he would take it as a threatening move. No, I had no chance to fight him. Even if I somehow succeeded in kicking him in the balls, unless it damn near knocked him down, I would never get past him and out the door. Surprisingly his movements weren't clumsy. No, my only chance not to get hurt—I still couldn't believe that he, or the Kid for that matter, wanted to kill me—was talking my way out of this.

"Wait a second, just wait a second, goddamn it. If you're going to stab me or whatever you plan to do, first just listen for a second, OK?"

I had no idea where I was going next. But there was no alternative course. I had to buy time and hope that some words would come out of my mouth, words that would make this monster think twice about what he was doing, and that when he thought the second time, he wouldn't be even more determined to hurt me.

"Look, I wasn't messing with the Kid. I don't really know the Kid. Hell, I'm new on the ship. I didn't know my shoes had oil on them. Yeah, there were oil marks on the floor and yeah, I moved my feet around. Who doesn't? But I wasn't deliberately trying to mess up *his* floor. I didn't look down, and I didn't notice."

Cook didn't make another move toward me, but his expression didn't soften. What the hell, I wasn't bleeding yet.

"He could have just said, 'Hey, you're messing up the floor. Wipe your shoes before you come into the mess hall.' What would I have done? I would have

said, 'Oh, OK, sorry, didn't notice.' And that would
have been it. No, instead he just glares at me every
lunch as if I had killed his best friend"—I hoped that
wasn't Cook—"until I finally asked him what the hell
was his problem, just like anyone would. And suddenly
he starts into me, calling me every fucking name in the
book...."

"Yeah, so what of it? You messed with him."

Suddenly—stupidly—I wasn't scared. I was mad.
"No, man, he was messing with me. And I didn't know
what he was talking about. So yeah, I told him to go
fuck himself. OK, I said that, and so would anybody.
Hell, so would you...."

"Nah," he said with a smirk, "I would have punched
him in the head."

"Yeah, well, I didn't do that."

"And that's lucky for you because you'd be dead
now."

"Look, I'm just trying to explain what happened. It
was a misunderstanding. Does it really make sense for
anyone to get hurt over something like this? I've never
seen you before and you've never seen me. And you're
going cut me with that knife, or whatever you came in
here to do? Over what? Because a couple of guys curse
each other out over a goddamn misunderstanding?"

He didn't answer, so I pressed on. "What the hell
did he say happened? Man, go ask Jack or Max; they
were sitting right there. Look, I took this job so I could
ship out, not so I could get into a fight with someone I
never met before."

"You think you're gonna get into a fight with me?"
His tone a combination of mockery and threat.

"No, what the hell? I meant with him, with the Kid. Why would I do that?"

For the first time, he seemed to relax slightly. I changed tack. "I've got to ask you something. I hear the Kid is the Golden Gloves champion of Puerto Rico...."

"Yeah, middleweight, *former* champion."

"Right. What, two years ago? I don't expect he got old and decrepit in the last two years."

"Yeah, so what?"

"So, why does he have to get someone else—you—to come after me?"

His response opened my eyes to a phenomenon I hadn't considered, though I read about it in history courses: a preemptive strike

"He said he thought you were going to go for him with a gun."

"But where the hell did he get that idea? Why would he think that? Jesus Christ!"

"Because you messed up his floor and you made like you didn't give a shit. You told him to go fuck himself— you said so yourself. Nobody messes with the Kid except me. But he figures you're not afraid of him, so you have a gun and you're gonna shoot him, or something like that. You got a gun?"

I couldn't believe it. This was more incredible than Cook showing up in the first place. Because I didn't appear afraid of the Kid and everyone else apparently was, because I had challenged him, in front of others at that, I must somehow be way ahead in the arms race. I had to have a bigger weapon than he did. It didn't occur to the Kid or this monster that I might not know enough to be afraid, or that I might just be brazenly stupid. Or if it did, they weren't willing to take the chance. So he escalated and brought in the big gun. He went nuclear. How about that.

"No, I don't have a gun. I don't have a knife either. Do you guys ever have this wrong."

"You know you talk a lot."

"I have a choice? I'm sitting here reading a magazine, waiting for the poker game. You come in looking like Man Mountain Dean, and you've got a fucking sword. What the hell am I supposed to do, hit you with the magazine? Sure I'm gonna talk. If you're crazy, you're gonna come at me anyway. If you're not crazy, you'll understand that all this makes no sense. Yeah, I'm gonna talk. What else would I do?"

"You could have begged for mercy. Why didn't you?"

"I don't know why I didn't. I guess I didn't think you were crazy." I lied. "But…so that's what this was all about. You come in here to scare the hell out of me and get me to beg for mercy? And then what?"

"You sign off the ship back in Newark."

He now sat straddling a chair three feet from me, leaning forward against and over its back, the knife on the table next to him. He was obviously not crazy. And I was becoming increasingly confident that he wasn't going to do anything to me, and probably never intended to. But there was no way I was going to sign off this ship either. My merchant marine career was not going to end after one week.

He went on. "You've got balls. I'll give you that. Either that or *you're* crazy."

"There's another possibility and it's the truth. You don't remind me of a priest and I'm not Catholic anyway,

but here's a confession for you anyway. I didn't know
anything about the Kid. I didn't know he was a goddamn boxing champion. I wasn't afraid of him because
I didn't know. Simple as that. I didn't know. Balls? I
don't know what kind of balls I would have had if I had
known. Maybe I would have said the same stuff, maybe
not. Who knows? I get mad like anybody else, but I'm
also not crazy."

"Well, fella, you've got a big mouth. It got you into
this and maybe it'll get you out of it."

Way to go, Peter! "And as for you," I got bolder, "if
it makes you feel better about all this, you did scare the
crap out of me. No doubt about that. But like I said,
you don't look crazy." I was working hard to believe
that. "And, not to bring up a sore point—and I don't
want to offend you—but I didn't think a guy who had
killed someone and served seventeen years was going
do something to a guy over nothing." At this I held my
breath.

He looked at me intently and then shook his head
in what looked like dismay. "So you heard all that shit.
It's all bullshit. I don't know where that stuff comes
from, probably Jack, the guy that writes books. I never
killed anybody, and I didn't do any seventeen years. I
was in the army, Fort Sill, Oklahoma. That's where I
learned to cook. I got into some fights, never against
one guy. Near the base there was a fight in a bar. A guy
hit me with a bottle. He gave me this," pointing to his
forehead. "I didn't see who did it. There was a guy and
I hit him, and I kept hitting him. I guess I beat the shit
out of him. But it wasn't the guy with the bottle. Hell,
I didn't know. It was self defense. There were guys all

over the place. I got eight years for aggravated assault anyway. Got out after five for good behavior."

"Why don't you tell people what really happened?"

"Who am I gonna tell? I don't give a shit what these jerks think. They're so scared of me they don't talk to me, and I don't talk to them. And that's just fine with me. Hell, I've just talked to you longer than I've talked to anybody in a year. And what the hell for?"

"Well, wouldn't it be better to have friends or people to talk to than for everybody to be scared to come near you?"

"I got friends."

"Yeah, I know, like the Kid. Maybe someone who asks you to take care of his business with a knife isn't such a great friend. ..."

"That's none of your goddamn business," he said, suddenly angry. But I wondered who he was angry at, me or the Kid.

He abruptly changed direction. "That a baseball magazine?" The magazine was folded on the table showing a full page picture of Hank Aaron.

"Yeah, *Sport* magazine. You know, whatever the sports season, it's about that sport. You like baseball?"

"Yeah, I listen to games all the time. I'm from Baltimore. I listen to them whenever I can get it."

"So do I. I love baseball. You know there was a Baltimore game on TV the other night, against Detroit. You should have come in." I stopped, took a deep breath, looked at the ceiling for a moment, then leaned forward and put out my hand. "My name is Peter, Peter Ernster. I know everybody calls you Cook."

He reached forward and shook my hand—he had the largest, thickest hands I had ever seen. "Joe Wiley."

"Look, Joe, I'm not going to leave this ship. I just got started"

"No, and that's OK. This is finished. I'll talk to the Kid. But at some point you and him, you got to straighten this out."

I told him I appreciated it and that once he talked to the Kid I would straighten it out with him myself. With that he got up, picked up the knife and left.

I sat there, stunned, and exhausted. What had just happened? It felt like a dream. I was sweating and my heart was pounding. But, no, it wasn't a dream. It had been very real. What had just happened was that I had met the rest of the world, and not on my terms but theirs. They didn't go to prep school and college or hang around the Village. They lived a life I didn't know. They lived by different rules. They reacted in different ways, and not only because they had guns. I realized that I couldn't just take the part of this world I liked; the rest came with it. I was the outsider and I'd better watch my ass, and the best way to do that was to watch my mouth.

I picked up the magazine and tried to focus on Hank Aaron. That didn't work. I put the magazine down and stared out the open porthole.

CHAPTER 11

The Quiet After the Storm

I sat alone in the mess hall for another ten minutes before men started to come in for the poker game. The word must have gone out that the coast was clear, that whatever was going to happen either had happened or wouldn't happen. Some nodded in my direction as they came in; others didn't acknowledge my presence. No one spoke to me. That was certainly fine with me. I had no intention of talking about my encounter with Cook, not then or ever.

The higher stakes game offered a pleasant distraction, and gradually I regained my inner composure. Outwardly, I was in poker mode. I was going to reveal nothing of my emotions. Again I thought about playing in the lower stakes game, but it never materialized. Good thing. Concentration would have been impossible. So I watched.

Whitey, the AB who had described the shark fishing off the ship's stern, was a very good player. I watched him intently. No one sat directly behind a player in a position to see his hand. A watcher might turn into a player. Still I could observe his approach to the game and his demeanor. He was quiet but not dour, confident but not flamboyant. If I played, I would model my game on his. But he was cold. This wasn't a friendly game for him. With the money at stake it shouldn't have been for any of them. Still, they seemed to enjoy it. He didn't

After forty minutes of watching, my heart was still beating way too fast. and The poker game was fueling my adrenalin not reducing it. So I went back to the fo'c'sle hoping that I would be alone. Michael was lying in his bunk reading a book. This was new. I had never seen him read anything but comic books or magazines. When I got closer I saw that he was reading my book, *The Agony & the Ecstasy.* How about that. He looked up.

"Hey, how're you doing?"

"Fine," continuing in poker mode. "How do you like the book?"

"Don't give me that shit. What happened?"

"Nothing happened. Why? Besides, you sure weren't interested in talking to me about anything before tonight. Why would I want to talk to you about anything now?"

"Look, you still have a problem?"

"No," I said with an expression suggesting I didn't know what he was talking about, but then added, "I believe everything is just fine. And since you borrowed my book—which I don't mind, as I'm concerned about your cultural edification— why don't you lend me your radio?"

He handed me the portable, shrugged, and returned to the book. I washed up, got ready for bed and lay on the bunk—my pillow still up against the back bulkhead where it would stay from then on—listening to a country music station that I could barely hear. With my arms folded behind my head, I thought about the last two days with disbelief. I was exhausted. Finally, as the last of the adrenaline drained away, I turned off the radio and fell into a deep, dreamless sleep.

When I awoke the next morning I felt like Scrooge in *The Christmas Carol*, waking after being visited by the three ghosts. It was all going to be OK. It was already OK. I was joyous in my relief. I jumped out of bed and gave Michael and Raul each a mock punch in the arm as they were dressing. Yup, this was a hell of a day. And the sun was shining.

I dressed quickly, wanting to get to the mess hall before others arrived. I jogged to the main house. I wondered if Cook had spoken to The Kid by now, but I was sure he had. I went straight to the galley, and we almost crashed into each other. We each took a step back, our eyes uncertain. I came forward. No smile, no words, just my right hand forward. The kid stepped forward and put out his hand. Then, just as he was going to shake it, he pulled it back and launched a fist straight at my stomach. As I flinched, he pulled the punch, his fist stopping at my shirt. He smiled. I smiled and gave him the same mock punch on the shoulder I had given Michael and Raul. Then we shook hands. We looked at each other and nodded. It was over.

***

Although I had the feeling that everyone knew I'd had some kind of interaction with Cook and possibly the

Kid, I had no idea how much of what happened anyone actually knew. I offered nothing. But the feeling in the mess hall seemed very different. No one was solicitous, but there was eye contact. I wasn't invisible any more.

Glen the fireman sitting with Whitey moved a plate out of the way so I could join them.

Max walked in and gave me a mock shoulder punch.

One of my tormentors from the "big shelf" incident asked me if I played chess!

I didn't know if I had somehow proven myself—or had just survived, if I was now an accepted member of the crew. But the hostility was gone even if everyone didn't suddenly become friendly.

***

The return trip went quickly and was without incident, positive or negative. I worked, ate, read, slept and played my harmonica. I expanded my limited repertoire by learning "The Battle Hymn of the Republic." Michael wanted me to learn "Danny Boy," but I couldn't seem to fit the full range of the song on the octaves available on my small harmonica. A work in progress.

As we got closer to Port Elizabeth, despite my somewhat improved status on the ship, I couldn't avoid my feeling of disappointment in everything about the entire experience of shipping out. Even though it had only been a bit over a week, it was clear that I had a lousy job on an outdated ship that went nowhere.

But what the hell did I expect? I hadn't really expected anything. In my usual fashion, I had avoided finding out anything of substance before embarking on the fulfillment of a fantasy. At some level those fantasies must have been influenced by all the seafaring books I had read: *Moby Dick, Horatio Hornblower, Two Years Before the Mast, Mutiny on the Bounty,* and closer in time, *The Caine Mutiny.* Really relevant and helpful. Though to be fair, my fantasy, however vague, would have been a lot closer to reality if I were an ordinary seaman on a ship bound for Europe, or just about anywhere other than Jacksonville, Florida. But if I were ever to fulfill that goal, I needed to stick it out in this job, on this ship, and somehow keep the union aware that I was here and wanted to be elsewhere.

As troubling as this growing concern was, I needed to deal with a more immediate issue: What would I do when we returned to Port Elizabeth? As late as the afternoon before I left New York I assumed I would be with Lorna. But after our last encounter, that wasn't in the cards now, if ever. I thought of calling her. My normal approach to most things was to ignore obstacles and press ahead. But my instinct, however undeveloped, said don't call her yet. The chances of anything positive coming from speaking to her now seemed slim. The risk that it would all end right on the phone seemed great, and I didn't want it to end. I wanted to keep my hope alive.

But the whole situation with Lorna was so confusing. She said she didn't know what to do with me, yet she said she wanted sex too much. What did that mean? What the hell would her shrink tell her? If she asked him, how could he tell her to go to bed with a guy nine years younger than her, have a good time and don't worry about the future? Why was she seeing a shrink

anyway? Was she nuts? How much time did she need? I
had never demonstrated much skill in figuring out how
girls—no less women—thought, or in dealing with any
unanticipated bumps in a relationship. My attitude was
hardly nuanced. Things were black or white. Lynn had
been bright white and then all black. Simple. Lorna
was a rainbow of grays.

I could spend the night on the pull-out couch at my
former roommate Rick's apartment on Prince Street,
the one he now shared with his girlfriend, Carla. But
Carla would make sure to fuck Rick as loud as she could
so that I would be sure to hear it. She had done it
before. Besides, why would I go there anyway?

And my last choice wasn't a choice at all. No way
was I going to stay with my mother. The life of a merchant seaman simply didn't include going home to his
mother. Whatever my level of disappointment, I wasn't
going to add to it with that. And although New York was
still home, I didn't live there now. I lived on the ship.
For a moment, I thought of going into New York and
walking around pretending I wasn't from there. But I
had enough of pretending, enough of living fantasies.

So I would stay on the ship. I would save money.
Besides, it would be hard to get better food than what
Cook put out there every night for free. I certainly
wouldn't be alone. A lot of the guys stayed on board,
both because they had no place to go and to save money.
The ones with family in New York went to see them. I
thought of the Bosun and his perpetual honeymoon
and of my dead predecessor Stanley and his daughter
in Brooklyn. Raul had relatives in Spanish Harlem. I
pictured fifteen people in a one bedroom apartment.

Michael went to an Irish bar on Second Avenue, somewhere in the 70s. He said there weren't any other real
Irishmen there, but he felt at home anyway.

After work on the day we pulled in I took a leisurely
walk up and down the wharf and examined the other
ships. I hadn't paid any attention to other ships the last
time I was here because I was so intent on finding mine.
There were four ships, all larger and newer than the
Rufus Saxton, regular cargo ships with open decks and
cargo-loading booms. They could be going anywhere.

Dinner was different, quiet: fewer men, muffled conversation. It was as if, because we were in port, people
would hear us. Out at sea only the fish. I ate with Jack,
Max and Whitey.

"What are you studying," Max asked.

"European History and International Economics."

"Sounds impressive. What do you do with that?"

"Eventually go to law school, study international
law." This was definitely not what I wanted to talk about.
"Did you guys all ship out during the war?"

"Not me," Whitey replied, "I'm not as old as the two
wise men here."

Getting back to me, Max continued, "So where do
you live, in a dorm?"

"Nah, I live in the village, wherever I can, with guys
that want to share a cheap apartment. So far only
guys..."

Jack interrupted. "So you're in a good school, your
family's got enough money to pay for it, you live in the
village," with that he waived his arms and rolled his
eyes, "you've got a brain—you have a chance at a career
people around here couldn't even imagine, and instead

of that…instead of getting on with it, with this incredible opportunity, you're going to spend *two years* doing this." His expression was a combination of incredulity and exasperation.

What he said, even more his expression and the way he said it, hit me like a two-by-four. Not just because that was exactly what I was set on doing, but because that was exactly how my father would see it…and say it.

I responded as if rehearsing for the eventual encounter with my father, almost starting with "Look, Dad."

"You see it that way, I understand. Me, I see a lot of years ahead, and while it all seems great, it can wait two years? What's wrong with doing something different, and yeah, having an adventure?" I didn't wait for a response.

"You take your years in the war on ships for granted. But you lived it. So this," sweeping my gaze over the mess hall, "isn't much of an adventure, but it's what I've got now." My voice and emotions were rising as if this wasn't just a rehearsal. "And you know, everyone, and I mean everyone, told me I would never get a ship. Well, I got a ship. Now everyone tells me this is the only ship I'll ever get. Well, I'm going to get an around-the-world run. I don't know how, but I will." My bluster was answered by a mocking voice in my head, "Your mother going to help you?!"

"Look kid…Peter, you do what you want to do. It's none of our business. I can tell you, if I had the money I would have gone to college. Jack here did go. Didn't you?"

I looked at Jack.

"Yeah, Hamilton, in upstate New York, but I never finished."

"How about that! I know Hamilton. It's one of the places I was supposed to go instead of NYU. So why didn't you finish?

Jack cut hard into his steak. "That's not part of this conversation."

Max seemed to realize that he had strayed into shark-infested waters.

"Everyone's got his own take on the war. But I'll tell you this, more people—I mean a higher percent—died on these damn ships than in any other branch of the service, if you want to call an unarmed ship a branch of the service.

I thought of the words stamped in red on my seaman's card: "VALID FOR EMERGENCY SERVICE."

"Yeah, you're all war heroes," Whitey cut into the drama. "You want to know about life in the merchant marine, kid? You're looking at it."

There was nothing warm and fuzzy about Whitey. He was sure of himself and didn't seem to care about the others. He was with Jack and Max and me but only to the extent of sitting at the table. It was very much the way he had been while playing poker.

His observations brought the conversation to a halt, and I wasn't comfortable enough to restart it.

Max was. "There's a lot of different people on these ships and they all see this life differently. A lot of guys stay on the ship for months, save money and then blow it. There's a guy we know who works for six months at a clip and doesn't spend a dime. Then he signs off his ship and goes into New York. He checks into the Waldorf Astoria, gets a couple of hookers, orders room service and drinks for however long his money lasts. Then he gets another ship and starts all over again."

They all smiled knowingly.

"We know him alright," Jack added. He's pretty extreme, but most of us do something like that to an extent."

"Except Bosun," Whitey added with the same sarcasm as before.

"Yeah, I saw the picture in his fo'c'sle." They all nodded. Then I asked what had been on my mind since the first evening. "Other than for the married guys, doesn't it get, well, lonely?"

Jack said, "I don't care what these guys say," looking at Max and Whitey, "or anybody else," gesturing around the room, "there's no one in the merchant marine who likes people. If you like people, people in general, you live among them. Your life is about interacting with people. That's what normal people do. They don't cut themselves off from society and live on a floating metal scrap heap with a bunch of anti-social sea hermits. Or," and he looked around the room again, "or they're running away from something or someone."

Max shot back. "Jack, you're full of shit, I've got friends in lots of places, most of the places I've been to often. And I can tell you I'm not running away from anything. I'm on this ship because it's a damn good job. I bid this job because it *is* coastwise and I'm *not* at sea, away from people, for long stretches. It pays better than any other job I could get on land, and it ain't exactly difficult. Jesus Christ. What a load of crap. You may be describing yourself, Jack, but you're not talking about me."

Whitey, who had seemed not to be listening, added, "I'm with Max. The money's good and the food is free." Then he added without either malice or joy, as if just to himself, "I also make a lot more than everyone around here. Hell, I'm here to play poker and take everyone's money." Then just as matter-of-factly, "I can't do that without people. I love people. An awful lot of them want to lose their money."

"Well you're a mean bastard, Whitey, you 've got no friends, sure as hell not the guys you play poker with, and you're not always playing poker but you're always here." Jack was getting angrier. Say what you want; you guys are kidding yourselves. You're on the ship now. You stayed on last week. You didn't get off in Jacksonville. This isn't just your job; this is your goddamn life...and mine too." The last words seem to be the point.

I felt I had to say something. I didn't want to be included in Jack's description either. "I don't know, Jack, like I said, I shipped out for adventure, to see the world...." The others chuckled and rolled their eyes. "Not to get away from people."

"OK, your situation is different *now*, but you keep doing this and you're just like everyone else. But anyway, you don't get it. Adventure or not, it's only certain kinds of people that do this. You really don't agree with me? You think the people you've met on this ship are... regular people?"

I shrugged my shoulders. "Too soon to tell. I didn't really expect to find the guys I was in school with." After I said it, I thought about it. Was it too soon to tell? I thought fleetingly about the dozen or so guys I had met so far, actually talked with. Did they all have something in common? How did I relate to people? Someone turned on the TV, and the conversation—and my musings ended.

CHAPTER 12

Sundays!

Back at sea I had my first overtime day. Doing exactly the same work, on Saturday I made time-and-a-half, almost $25 a day. To put that in perspective, in May I had bought a blue Brooks Brothers, oxford cloth, button down shirt—the very pinnacle of my dress code—for $5. A guy could get used to this kind of money. And as we were at sea, Sunday would be even more lucrative, at double time. Not bad.

Besides waking up at sea on a weekend, or working extended hours on a regular day—which happened only in emergencies—there was another way to make overtime. The union rules enumerated certain tasks as requiring extra pay. On deck, these traditionally involved hazards of one kind or another. But by 1962, these tasks had largely been eliminated through technology or ship configuration.

By contrast, overtime tasks in the engine room were so designated not because of hazard—though they were not entirely without risk—but because they were so unpleasant. There was time-and-a-half work and even double-time work. Legend had it there was triple-time work. Given what I learned of the first two levels, I couldn't imagine what triple-time work might require.

Nearly from the beginning I had heard about overtime work and that if I was lucky I might get some. But in my first eleven days none came up that I was aware of, though I wondered if Michael or Raul were on such a project when I wouldn't see one of them for an extended period during the day.

It all became clear that first Sunday at sea. If you did double-time work during regular hours on a weekday, you made double-time pay for that work. But if you did that same work on Sunday, you only made double-time for the day itself. In other words, you didn't get quadruple pay. Of course, I had imagined making eight dollars an hour doing some damn thing on a Sunday. But the engineers on this ship assigned overtime work only on overtime days. Too bad.

That first Sunday morning at sea I was introduced to my first overtime project: cleaning the ballast filter screen. This was a situation in which First did not assume I knew what he was talking about or would wait to see how much trouble I could get into. No, this needed a full explanation.

Ballast is water let into tanks along the bottom and lower hull of a ship to provide stability. Depending on the weight of its cargo, the ship needs more or less ballast. By opening valves, the water gets in freely. Getting rid of it requires pumps. Because the water used is sea water, it comes along with whatever is in it, living or dead, that can get through the grid on the valve. Over time, whatever was living dies. All of this "sea detritus," First called it, eventually gets caught in filter screens which periodically need to be emptied and cleaned. And that's where I came in.

First showed me the location of the two filters, one along each side bulkhead of the engine room. Each steel cover was about 3' x 18," and was attached by four wing bolts. He gave me two extra large buckets with lids, and saying I might need a wrench to get the bolts started, left me to earn my double time. I had no idea what to expect but couldn't understand why this was such a big deal. You open the cover, take out the filter tray, empty it into the bucket, hose down the tray and put it back. Done. Hell, this was a good job, get to go up to the big shelf and empty the bucket.

I got a small wrench and a screw driver from the board at the front of the engine room and set to work on the first bolt. The covers were positioned low along the bulkhead, so I sat on the deck as I worked. That turned out to be a good thing. Loosening the bolt was a lot harder than I expected. Someone had really tightened it. But eventually I got one loose and then the next two. The edges of steel plate must have been coated with something to keep it tight against the container, since it didn't come away when I loosened the last bolt. I forced the screw driver under the edge and pried the lid open. That was the last thing I did before I passed out.

I couldn't have been out for more than a few seconds. When I came to I saw that I had been dragged about twenty feet from the container and someone was throwing water on my face. The entire watch crew of the engine room, plus my two wiper buddies, was standing over me laughing through the rags they held over their faces. That they were all suddenly there meant that they hadn't been very far away. In fact they had all been waiting behind a boiler to watch the rookie fall for the rookie prank. So what had happened?

All that "sea detritus" was almost entirely made up of dead, decomposing, decaying and putrefying whole or parts of crustaceans of every manner and description. The output of this natural process is a gas so noxious and powerful that inhaling it can knock you out. Without some form of protection, I didn't have a chance. Since I had been working hard to turn the bolts and lastly to pry the cover away, I must have taken a deep breath. The rest followed inexorably, as they all knew it would.

Had I been standing, I would have fallen farther, and the back of my head would have hurt more. But no one seemed terribly concerned about that. I sat up and looked at the men standing over me. Well fuck them! I wasn't going to give them the satisfaction of saying anything. Like a baseball player not rubbing his arm when he's hit there by a pitch, I didn't touch my aching head. First gave me a large clean rag and nodded in the direction of the filter. The fun was over.

***

While the filters took only a couple of hours, some time-and-half work could take all day. One Saturday, I was assigned to chip and paint part of the engine room ceiling. The combination of the intense humidity and higher level of heat collected against the top of the engine room meant that paint peeled there more rapidly than in most other places. It also meant that it was hotter than hell.

A thermometer six feet below where I would paint read 150 degrees. Near the ceiling it was hotter.

I rigged up a scaffold and started working standing upright, reaching above my head. Even alternating hands, it didn't take long before my arms were really tired. There was no way I could keep this up. So I built a higher scaffold and lay on it, my face no more than a foot from the ceiling, the way I imagined Michelangelo painted the ceiling of the Sistine Chapel. That thought amused me for a few seconds until I was overwhelmed by the heat. I simply couldn't stand it for more than a few minutes at a time. I would chip as fast as I could, then get off the scaffold and go out the engine room hatch into the passageway where it was 80 degrees cooler. After a minute I would return and move to another spot. I repeated this process all day. The work wasn't hard; the paint fell easily—usually on my face–but the heat was beyond anything I had imagined.

And then it got worse. The chipping finished, it was time to paint. The heat seemed to have an effect on the paint itself. The fumes of the lead-based paint were not pleasant anywhere, but up in this place the intense heat made the fumes more powerful. I needed wet rags over my nose and mouth in order to breath. I loved those weekends at sea.

***

But the best was yet to come a few Sundays later. There was one double-time job that some people couldn't or wouldn't do. This one couldn't sneak up on you, and when I first heard about it, I couldn't believe it.

Most of the time both boilers were in use. But the ship could actually operate—although not at full speed—with only one. Because some of the oil didn't completely burn and wasn't entirely expelled through the tube blowing process, over time, there would be a deep and heavy accumulation of soot at the bottom of the boilers, as much as two feet of it.. Periodically, the soot needed to be cleaned out.

To accomplish this, one boiler would be shut down and allowed to "cool" for twenty-four hours or so. Then a wiper would "volunteer" to get into the boiler through the steel-covered porthole at its front and clean out the soot. As it happened, Raul claimed to be claustrophobic and Michael had done a boiler the previous month. It was Peter's turn. The fact that I was 6' 4" with shoulders broader than the porthole didn't enter into the equation.

They told me to take off my tee shirt so it wouldn't get caught on the edge of the porthole. The porthole was about four and a half feet off the deck. As instructed, I dropped an empty ten-gallon paint bucket inside, put my head in and grabbed the bottom edge of the porthole with both hands—it would have been impossible for virtually anyone to get in feet first—while Second and the fireman picked up my feet so that I was horizontal.

I couldn't believe what I was about to do. People did this? I squeezed my shoulders together as much as I could and they pushed me forward until I was half-way inside. I lowered my hands and reached in the darkness for the bucket. When I found it, they pushed me further forward until my weight was resting on my hands holding the bucket. The bucket submerged under my weight as they kept pushing. Finally I was completely inside, the top edge of the bucket now several inches under the surface of the viscous soot. I was able to walk my feet down the inside of the boiler until I was standing in the soot, bent over still holding the top edge of the bucket. I stood up. Sticking my head out the port hole, I said, "You people are out of your fucking minds. This is crazy. How the hell am I going to get out?"

"Don't worry about getting out, worry about cleaning it up. Fill the bucket and hand it out the hatch to Michael or Raul. They'll hand you another. You should have it done in an hour. You can't breath, stick your head out. No big deal. These guys have to empty all this crap."

"Right. That certainly seems fair." But he was gone by then.

I got to work. It was hotter than at the top of the engine room, and the fumes were unbearable. I worked in what I thought were one minute units, holding my breath each time. Then I would stick my head out and breath. At first, all I had to do was push the bucket down and it filled with soot. As I progressed I used a dust pan to scoop up the soot. After maybe about an hour—it seemed a lot longer—I was done.

After the inevitable joke of everyone disappearing we started the process of getting me out. "Don't worry." Right. I stood on a bucket, and with my shoulders again scrunched together, I squeezed myself through the port-hole as far as I could. Then while I kept my arms under me, First and the fireman grabbed my shoulders and head and pulled. Jesus Christ! My arms and stomach were getting cut up.   And with me pushing against the boiler once my hands were outside, I was out a lot quicker than I went in.

I looked at myself. I was completely covered in soot. Still, blood found its way through. I looked at First then at the fireman. I shook my head slowly in disbelief. First smiled and told me to get cleaned up—he'd give me some stuff to take care of the cuts—and to take the rest of the day off.

The fireman laughed and said, "Join the merchant marine and find adventure on the high seas."

CHAPTER 13

The Rule of the Second Best Hand
and Other Lessons

As I expected, Jacksonville revisited was a bust. After work on the day we pulled in, I called Jillie from a pay phone near the pier. A man answered. I assumed it was her father. Goddamn girls! Women didn't have fathers answering their phones. Jillie sounded awkward. I told her that since it was a weekday I was only going to be around that night, and asked if she would like to go out that evening. She hesitated and said she was still going steady. I thought about some sort of wisecrack like "Did the last week break the record for going-steady-longevity?" but she didn't deserve that.

"Well, I assumed that you would be. I just thought it might be nice to have dinner…or something, you know, no big deal."

"I would really like to…I just can't."

"I understand." And I did. What the hell did she need me for? She had a boyfriend. Some guy shows up one day and says he'll be around again sometime, maybe, and she's supposed to fall all over him? In the movies. But there *was* something about her, something that made me want to try.

"Why don't you call Sharon? She really wants to go out with you."

"I didn't really just want a date, just someone to go out with in Florida." Definitely not the whole truth and nothing but the truth. "I wanted to see you." True. Sharon with her agreeable round face and enormous family simply wasn't my type.

'Thank you. You're nice."

"So long, Jillie. Who knows, maybe sometime…."

And that was that. I pretended—to myself—as I walked back to the ship, that in forsaking the pursuit of Jillie I had done something noble and manly. But reality intruded: I just wasn't going to get laid in Jacksonville any time soon.

***

Despite the availability of TV in port, it was a two game poker night. The higher stakes game always began first. If there were enough spectators willing to play, there would be a second. It was always understood that the second game was for lower stakes. With betting stakes at $1 and $2 the big winner of the first game might win around $100; in the second at 25 cents and 50 cents, maybe $30. If you could win that much, you could lose the same. $100 was a lot of money–$30 was two regular days' pay for me.

That night there were immediately four ready to play a second game, and Glenn, the fireman—a frequent player—asked me derisively if I wanted to play.

"You play or just watch?

I had watched several of the games. I wasn't going to play in the higher stakes game, and, although I had thought of playing in the lower stakes game, I hadn't found an easy entry. This was it.

"Yeah, I play."

They got one more and we set up the chairs. The rectangular table had four fixed chairs. To these we added a folding chair on each end. It wasn't an ideal configuration for a card game, but everyone was used to it. The game was Dealer's Choice, but by *Rufus Saxton* tradition, that choice was limited to Draw and Five- and Seven-card Stud. Another choice involved the only wild card option, One-Eyed Jacks. That was it. No other wild cards, no other games. Those were the house rules at both tables. And that was fine with me.

But they had added a further refinement. Although the deal rotated as usual, the game chosen by the dealer was played until the deal rotated counter-clock-wise all the way to the player to the left of that dealer, assuring that the same game would be played at least five times in a row. I really liked that. Playing a narrow range of games allowed you to get the measure of the other play-ers. When oddball games like Anaconda, Low-Card-in-the Hole Wild, or even high-low variants were added to the mix, the person choosing that game would always be more familiar with it. That could not only create a temporary advantage, but also completely change the style of the other players. A limited range of games meant that the dynamics of the game were more stable. Some said it took away a lot of the fun of playing. Fun for me was winning.

I knew something about poker. I had been playing regularly since I was fifteen. Maybe not a long time in absolute terms, but it did constitute a quarter of my life. I had played for Saturday night hero sandwiches at prep school, and for somewhat more at various summer jobs and in college. I knew all the games. Though I had never played in the equivalent of the higher stakes game—I simply never had the money, I had played in many games in which I stood to lose enough that I would feel it, particularly since it took so much for me to earn it in the first place.

Cards were in my genes. My father had lost a lot of money playing *Chemin de Fer,* the game played in European casinos, and my mother was a nationally ranked bridge player. Despite the money, it wasn't gambling I was drawn to. I played no other games of chance and didn't even make money bets after I lost one at a young age. (During a World Series between the Dodgers and the Yankees, a boy bet me a whole dollar at 5-1 odds that the Dodgers wouldn't win the next day. Since the odds for any one game were always about even between the two teams, there was no way I could not take that bet. The next day the boy came to collect. There was no game scheduled that day.) But I played poker. I loved the juxtaposition of mathematic probability and chance, the need to control emotions, the opportunity to read people and for acting. I had read that poker was 20% luck and 80% skill, and I thought I was pretty skillful.

As with any other field of knowledge, poker requires that you know what you don't know. I knew I was pretty good compared to the people I usually played with.

But I didn't know these people. That's why I had been watching so many games, that and the fact that for anyone interested in poker, watching Whitey was not only instructional, it was fascinating. He was mostly aloof and silent, but since I wasn't a threat to him—he knew I wasn't going to play in the big game—he gave me a couple of conceptual pointers.

I had learned a few earlier: It is axiomatic that you don't play poker with people you don't know. Another rule is that you don't play with anyone who has significantly more money than you. Someone with more money cannot be bluffed at the stakes for which you are comfortable playing. Without bluffing, not only is it impossible to win more than the occasional hand, you really can't avoid losing in the long term. Of course, by violating the first rule, you can unwittingly violate the second.

Like most of my life lessons so far, I had learned these the hard way. During my summer stint as a bellboy at an Adirondack resort, I was invited to play in a poker game with the kitchen staff. They were in their thirties; I was seventeen. The game was a well-rehearsed whirlwind. Nothing that I tried worked. Whether they were cheating I never knew, but that I had no chance was clear from the beginning. In an hour I lost $55, more than a half a week's pay. I didn't know what hit me.

Now I was again violating both rules. I didn't really know these men at all. From observation, I knew the men at the big game much better, at least how they played poker. By definition, everyone playing even in the second game had more money than I did. On top of that, the sixth player was DeLeo, my antagonist from the "Big Shelf," who was playing in our game only because there was no room in the other. So he not only had more money, he was used to playing for higher stakes. I would have to be very careful.

DeLeo—nobody called him by his first name, and I wasn't curious—was one of those overly chatty players every game seemed to have who narrates while he deals the cards and even when he doesn't. He dealt first and chose Seven Card Stud, nothing wild. Each player put in a quarter—the "ante." Betting would start after each player received two cards face down and one card up. A player could fold, pass, bet, call the bet or raise. This process repeated for each of the next three rounds of face-up cards. The seventh card was dealt face down, leading to the final rounds of bets. Lots of betting, and with six players the pot could grow rapidly.

"So an 8 and a 2, nothing there," DeLeo announced. "A king and a queen, maybe, maybe. Pair of 8s. Too bad you guys didn't meet before the dance. Nothing there." And looking in my direction, two seats to his left, "And our distinguished scholar has got...nothing. And Max, who must have inherited money from who the hell knows, has got a sweetheart jack and 10. Working on a royal flush, are you, Max? And me? Well how about that. A pair of 9s. High hand talks and he's saying half a buck." The betting was limited to a quarter or a half dollar. He was starting heavy. True to form, DeLeo was an intimidator.

And so it went. He never stopped. It was meant both to add humor and lighten the atmosphere, but mostly to disrupt people's thinking. He was a pain in the ass, and I had met several like him before. The trick was not to let him get to me. Easier said than done.

Max, who would be the next dealer, said spontaneously that he would chose the same game, so we would play seven card stud for ten hands in a row. That gave me the opportunity to get the kind of feel that I had hoped for.

One of the most important playing lessons I had learned in college was that unless I had a really powerful hand, one that from the visible cards was highly unlikely to be beaten, it was essential to avoid seriously playing a hand very early in the game. First watch the others and then strike.

So I lost the ante, but not much more, and that was a cheap price for what I learned from watching. Then, having folded several hands early, I bluffed the next bad hand. Nobody had much and I won because everyone folded. I did the same thing a few hands later when I had another really bad hand. My purpose was not to win but to lose, to be caught bluffing. And the earlier the better.

"So we have a bullshit artist. How do you like that guys? Our college kid is a bullshitter. Well, kid, you can't bullshit a bullshitter."

"I don't know, DeLeo, I bullshitted you two hands ago. Or didn't that count?"

This was going to get personal fast. I thought of Cook's observation about my mouth. I did need to watch it. But my point was made. Some would think I was always bluffing and call me on a hand when they realistically had no chance of winning, just not to let me get away with it. Others would stay in a game when

I had a terrific hand, then call—and lose big, when they should have folded long before. All because I was unpredictable.

There were two guys at the table who simply bet according to their cards every time. If they had a weak hand, they folded, and if they had a strong hand, they would bet and play it out. They won; they lost. Because they only played good hands, even when they won they won very little because everyone else, knowing that they had good cards, would fold. Based entirely on luck, one was on his way to being the big loser while the other was just in the black. Over time, people who played that way had to lose. There were simply more bad hands than good ones. But I was glad they were there.

I played mostly defensively, picking my offensive opportunities carefully, whether they were based on a good hand or a bluff. I was preoccupied with the point Whitey had passed on to me a few days earlier. "Avoid the second best hand." Of course, that sounds simplistic. What else would one do? But the fact is, you don't lose big in poker because you have a bad hand, he explained, but because you have a good hand that happens to be second best. That's when the betting gets heavy. The lesson was not to fall in love with your hand, and to think of it only in relation to the others in the game. As soon as he said it I knew how right and important it was. I remembered games when I had played my hand with almost no regard for what someone else was doing. It was such a good hand. No more. This was now my personal motto. Avoid the second best hand. And I was working on doing just that.

We played on. When it was my deal, I chose Five Card Draw, "guts," nothing wild. This was the original game of poker. Each player is dealt five cards face down. He can replace, "draw," up to four cards, four customarily only if he has an ace. Betting occurred after the initial deal and after the draw. "Guts" meant that no minimum hand was required to open the betting, the other alternative being a pair of jacks. Each involved its own bluffing opportunities.

After immediately folding my first two draw hands, I was dealt three queens. This was most likely the winning hand. Now the trick would be to keep others in the game and hope they had semi-decent cards to bet. Fortunately, DeLeo started the betting at fifty cents. No one raised, but everyone called. But when it came to me, I raised. DeLeo looked at me intently. He called. As, amazingly, did all the others. The pot was already worth more than $7. DeLeo drew two cards. Either he had three of a kind like I did or he had three of a suit and was hoping—very stupidly—to pull two more and have a flush. He was definitely not a stupid player, so he had three of a kind. There were only two such hands higher than mine, kings and aces, and ten lower. I liked my chances. Sure enough one of the "luck" players drew four cards. The rest each drew three.

To deceive DeLeo, but also to keep others in the game, I drew only one card. I wanted them to think I had two pair or was drawing to a straight or a flush. By drawing only one card the odds against my achieving my pretended goal were stiffer than those against any of them increasing a pair, their most likely hand.

DeLeo kept up his banter, announcing what he believed everyone had. When I drew my one card, he shook his head and said, "Foolish lad being led to slaughter." The draw completed, DeLeo, the opener, led off. He again bet the maximum. Nothing subtle about him. He went right for it. The ace folded but the rest called. I started worrying about all the hands that could beat three queens, and there were several. Just because DeLeo might not have it didn't mean none of the others did. Stay cool, Peter. I raised again. This time he just looked at me and raised me. Two of the others folded. Max called. There were three of us left. I raised again. Mostly I went with my head. Sometimes with my gut. This time I was going with both. After a call I raised again, and Max folded. DeLeo, visibly frustrated, said, "Bullshit to this. What have you got?" He called. I put down the three queens. He didn't have to, but he showed his three 4s. I won $14. Not bad.

"Well, how do you like that. You kept a kicker. You son of a bitch, you kept a kicker. You know what, guys, we have ourselves a fucking hustler. Son of a bitch."

"I think you better hold on DeLeo," I said, my stomach churning. I told myself to stay cool. Then with a feigned smile directed to the others, "A moment ago I was being led to slaughter. An hour and a half ago I was a college kid. Last week I didn't know shit—you had to "introduce" me to the Big Shelf. And now because you lose a hand, I'm a fucking hustler?"

One of the other guys said, "DeLeo, what's your problem? So he kept a kicker. Smart play. He beat your ass. That's all that happened. I lost money too.

How come I'm not complaining? You want to cry or play cards?"

Well, I had made a new enemy. But I seemed to have gained some friends too, and maybe some respect. The game went on for another half hour without any more fireworks. I came away with $40, more than 10% of my monthly wages! Not exactly small change for me. DeLeo also won, but I was the big winner. Usually I wasn't. Though over the years I mostly won—in part because I didn't play above my head—and never lost big when I didn't, I was usually the second winner. A much lower profile, and a lot less resentment.

I'd have to see how this would play out here. But now what I had to do was try to get to sleep. The one big negative for me in playing poker, and it was a constant, win or lose, was that I got so excited that my heart rate went sky high, and it could take hours for it to drop. Like I said, it was an opportunity for acting. I wasn't actually cool at all, not even a little.

CHAPTER 14

Enter Billy Clayton

B ack in Port Elizabeth I decided to stay on the ship. DeLeo, Glen and an OS named Ray were going into New York to pick up hookers on 42nd Street.

"So, you gonna get it for love?" Max asked, provoking him.

"Yeah, right. Not in New York for sure," DeLeo replied grudgingly.

"Too much time, too much trouble anyway," Ray added.

"So what are you guys really going to do, I mean with the hookers?"

"You want the birds and bees, kid?"

More to persuade himself, it seemed, than to explain to me, Glen volunteered, "We pick them up in the street, in front of the movie theater—there are lots of both to choose from—take them inside, straight up to the back of the balcony. They give us blowjobs. Five, ten bucks, maybe fifteen, depending on what she looks like. They're done; they leave; we watch the movie."

I had walked along 42nd Street many times and seen many movies there, but I didn't recall seeing any hookers hanging around that I would touch with a ten-foot pole. If they got lucky, these guys were going to be in the $5 range, and that would be charity.

"And you guys have done this a lot?" my tone more mocking than I had intended.

DeLeo didn't miss it and responded with "Fuck you," forgetting to add "kid." "You wouldn't know what to do if they were handing it out like candy."

Not getting the supporting glances he had counted on, he turned to leave. The others followed.

***

I didn't play poker that evening. After dinner I sat out on deck as usual, relaxing and looking out over the docks. Michael, with whom I hadn't spoken in a week, came over and sat facing me, cross-legged on the deck. He had never sought me out, really never made conversation, though he was friendly enough whenever I had.

"I need to ask you a question."

"Fire away." I couldn't imagine what he wanted to know that he thought I would know."

"What's Arkansas like?"

If I had to come up with the most unlikely question Michael could ever ask me, this would be right up there with "Who do you think was the more influential historian, Thucydides or Hegel?"

"I don't really know much about it. Never been there."

"Yeah, but come on, you're a smart guy. You don't have to live somewhere to know about it. You must have heard about it."

"Sure, I've heard about it. It's not much. It's probably the poorest state in the United States. It's farms, mostly farms, and I guess poor farms. Why? Max got you doing crossword puzzles?"

He laughed and said, "Nah, I got an offer to work on a farm there. Horses. Guy says it's just like Ireland."

"You want to work on a farm? How come?"

"It's what I did before I left Ireland. I came to New York, I don't really know why, I just did, and this was the best work I could get. I hate this shit, but I don't want to go back either." He returned my questioning look with one that said "I'm not going to tell you why."

"So you worked with horses. I have too. That is I rode them a lot. I did it last summer. In fact there was a groom there from Ireland. Really knew horses."

"Well that's nice," he said sarcastically. "This is a job on a farm with maybe a hundred horses. There's a bunch of grooms. This fella knows one of my cousins. He wouldn't pay me as much as this, but I could get off this stinkin' ship and out of that hellhole down below."

"I don't know if Arkansas is like Ireland. I've never been there either. But what the hell, if that's what you want to do, do it. What's the risk? If it doesn't work out, you can always come back to this."

As we were talking, Jack walked by along the rail smoking a cigarette. Seeing us, he came over.

"You gentlemen solving the problems of the world?"

"Not exactly. Trying to solve the problem of Michael here. He's got a job on a horse farm in Arkansas and wants to know if it's like Ireland."

"Well, I've been to Ireland twice, seen the graves of my ancestors, beautiful country. I've never heard anyone accuse it of looking like Arkansas. But who knows, grass, trees, rolling hills, there might be some similarity. Don't know about the people, though."

"I'm not going there for the people, just the horses."

"I told Michael that if he wants to do it, he should. There's no risk. He could always get another wiper job if it didn't work out or if he didn't like Arkansas. I've also got to believe there are some beautiful parts of Arkansas, probably where the horses are. And as for the people, present company excluded, of course, what's he comparing them to?"

"Well, I am going to do it. I suppose I ought to tell someone, so they can get a replacement. I'd like to sign off in Jacksonville, closer to Arkansas. Can I do that, Jack?"

"You can do whatever you want. They can't make you stay on the ship. They might be happier if you signed off in Newark just because it might be easier for them to get someone there, but I don't know. They might have someone in Jacksonville. But regardless, you still can do what you want."

"OK, I'm going to tell Second in the morning that I'm signing off in Jacksonville. Just have to hope they're happy. Though I don't plan on coming back. Do you know how to get to Arkansas?

"Sure," I said. "You take a bus, probably to Little Rock—only city I know of there. You can get a bus from anywhere to anywhere. Greyhound or Trailways. Best way to get there, maybe the only way. By the way, how did you like the book?"

"Aw, never got very far. The title looked good, you know, agony and ecstasy. I was looking for the ecstasy part, but I never found it. "

With that and a nod to each of us, Michael walked off. He didn't seem very happy or have much conviction. I still wondered why he couldn't go back to Ireland. I came up with a few possibilities.

Jack and I traded a few superficial comments about him, "Seems like a good guy. Didn't really get to know him." And so on. I was more concerned with what his replacement, my new fo'c'slemate, was going to be like.

***

Michael left the ship the morning we arrived in Jacksonville. Raul and I soldiered on without him. It says something about the nature of our work that it would probably take about a week for anyone to notice that one of us was gone.

In the evening before dinner, as I was getting dressed after a shower, a very large guy exploded through the open door. He was my height but easily weighed 230 pounds, very muscular, good looking with curly blond hair. Leading with an olive drab duffle bag *with handles* in one hand and a guitar case in the other, he threw the bag on the floor ahead of him. He didn't seem to notice me as he sang a vaguely familiar country song in full fortissimo.

Bent over tying my shoes, I ducked out of the way of the flying duffle bag. Oblivious as he seemed to be, in the spaciousness of the 9' by 8' fo'c'sle he must have caught the movement out of the corner of his eye.

"Hey," thrusting out his hand, and with a southern drawl so pronounced and slow that I wasn't sure he was going to get it all out, "Billy Clayton, fullback, Southern Mississippi."

This was the kind of introduction I imagined players making on joining a pro football team. Trying to take this all in, I thought of responding with my athletic credentials, but as they would definitely come up short, I just said, "Peter Ernster." As I did, Raul came in carrying his laundry. I made the introductions, leaving out the full back reference so Raul wouldn't counter with, "What's that?"

After shaking hands, Billy picked up his bag and threw it on the lower bunk recently vacated by Michael. Raul made a move toward the bunk, saying he was going to take that one, his assumption being that he was the senior of the two. The cramped upper bunk really wasn't in Billy's plans, though.

"That's OK, fella, you can just stay where you are." And he started making up the bunk. He had such a physical presence that Raul not only couldn't say anything, he couldn't even look at him. He just put his laundry on the top bunk and left.

I would spend the next month with Billy Clayton, and just about every moment would be a unique experience for me. Most important, I had never met anyone who exuded so much physical self-confidence. Not only didn't he fear anyone, he didn't really seem to notice anyone, or if he did, care about his size, attitude or anything else. He just did whatever he wanted and went about his life as if no one else was there. And if he did bump into someone along the way, figuratively or literally, that was likely too bad for the other guy. He wasn't

menacing or threatening.   He just assumed people
would like him or get out of his way. And he was right.

I couldn't wait to take him to the mess hall that evening. His entrance was going to be a lot different than
mine had been, and I was going to enjoy every bit of it.

As he made up the bunk, I started to tell him about
the ship and other things that I thought would be helpful—the kinds of things I wished someone had told me,
but he waved me off with, "I heard the food is good.
Where is it?" So off we went to the mess hall. Unlike my
debut, everyone looked up when Billy walked through
the door. Apart from his physical aura, his body seemed
to move loudly. There were two empty seats at a table with
Max and DeLeo. Billy just sat down. As he did, he stuck
out his hand in the direction of DeLeo and said, "Billy
Clayton, fullback, University of Southern Mississippi.
How y'all doin?" It was like my set-to with the Kid. For a
moment everyone in the room stopped talking.

DeLeo reacted as if Billy were a Martian. But Max,
who was a great sports fan, shook his hand enthusiasti-
cally. A couple of guys from other tables got up and
came over to meet Billy. He was a goddamn celebrity!

"So how come you're not back there practicing?"

"There's a break between spring practice and when
we start up again in August. So I thought I'd just ship
out, see what it's all about. I missed spring practice.
Got hurt early last year, missed most of the season. They
think I lost my spot to some son of a bitch from Ohio.
But I'm in great shape now. You'll be seeing my name
back up in lights this year."

Everybody welcomed him aboard. Even the Kid
was pleasant. What a difference. I wasn't interested

in reflected regard; I had too much of an ego for that myself. But this was going to be fun. Billy ordered three steaks. When I cautioned him about Cook and making sure he finished if he ordered extra, he said with a big grin that we needn't worry about that. Indeed we didn't. I've never seen anyone eat as much as he did that evening. And he did it every evening. I had heard of historical figures and fictional characters described as larger than life. Billy was that in spades.

The questions continued. No, he didn't play poker. He didn't like baseball, never played it, never watched it. He played blues guitar. He liked Jimmy Reeves and, oh yeah, he liked pussy. Everyone nodded in approval. Definitely a good combination. I hadn't heard of the first—which I didn't mention—but heartily endorsed the second. Eventually, he shook hands with everyone in the mess hall, including all the guys that over the past few weeks I hadn't met!

Billy wanted to say hello to the Captain—I had never even seen the Captain. I was all for it, ready to give him helpful tips on where he might find him, but Jack intervened and suggested that the Captain would be pretty busy right about now, what with the ship pulling out and all. To Jack it was clear that the Captain would have no interest in meeting the new wiper. I wasn't so sure. Billy might be the new wiper, but in his eyes, and perhaps therefore, amazingly, in everyone else's, he lived in an existential reality all his own, that didn't readily allow for reduction to convenient and mundane characterization. Besides, the captain might be a big football fan.

Billy and I went back to the fo'c'sle as the tugboat maneuvered the ship away from the pier. He seemed

not to notice. He was intent on getting to his guitar.
He took it out of its case and started tuning. I suggested
sitting out on deck. I grabbed my harmonica and my
rickety chair and we went to my spot. Seeing that the
chair (which I hadn't offered him) might not support
him, he sat on the hatch cover. He finished tuning and
started to play.

As advertised, he played blues, country blues, and he
played well. After a bit I asked him what key he was in.

"C," he said.

"I see you have a capo, so you could play in any key,
right?"

"Yeah, so?"

"Well, I sort of play the harmonica, not as well as
you play the guitar, but I thought I might try to play
along, you know, learn those blues songs. Anyway, my
harmonica is in "G."

"Good harmonica players can play in any key."

He was referring to the technique used by profes-
sional players of actually "bending" notes to create the
sharps and flats of any key signature without an expen-
sive chromatic slide. "Like I said, I'm not a good player,
and I have a "G" harmonica."

Billy nodded and got the capo from the fo'c'sle.
He started playing in "G" and I played along as well as
I could. After some awkward squawks I started to get
the hang of his chord progressions and was able to play
along with the chords. The combination wasn't bad, and
gradually I started to improvise. Occasionally, he nodded in approval. So did I. But sometimes I went astray.

"If you don't know the right note to play, don't just
play any note; don't play."

Right. Good advice, if it were as easy as that. But I didn't know it was the wrong note until I played it. Still, we played for about an hour and I had a ball. I expect that if he hadn't been enjoying himself, he would have told me to shut up. He wasn't exactly concerned with my sensibilities. Occasionally he sang, but mostly he just played. That was a good thing as he had a terrible but very loud voice.

Then he abruptly announced that he was going to sleep. He said he liked to get at least ten hours, and that I should wake him in the morning. He had no questions about the ship, the crew, the work, nothing.

The next morning I woke him at 7:00.

He looked at his watch. "Jesus, it's the middle of the fucking night!"

"Well, we're in the engine room at 8:00, so if you want to eat, this is when you get up. By the way, in case you're interested, it's hot down there, real hot. And so is everything you touch, so I hope you've got work gloves."

I left him to get ready and went off by myself. I didn't think Billy needed any accompaniment. Raul, as usual, was still asleep. I had taken to walking a couple of times around the ship before breakfast, not so much for exercise because it didn't amount to much, but to breath in as much fresh air as I could. I was becoming increasingly convinced that breathing at all in the engine room was killing me.

Billy took my warning about the heat in the engine room seriously. He appeared in the mess hall holding a pair of gloves and wearing a tee shirt...and Bermuda shorts and sandals! I couldn't believe it. I had been way off base at one end of the sartorial spectrum, and Billy had invented the other end. A few eyes rolled but no one said anything. I didn't know what to say. And who was I to say it anyway? With Billy, it was probably going to be just fine. And it was.

Billy reacted as I had on entering the hatch to the top of the engine room, but with more words since he had an audience. At the bottom of the ladder, Second took a long look at Billy's getup but said nothing. Billy's presence had clearly preceded him, but he introduced himself anyway, skipping the fullback part as probably no longer necessary. Then he put an arm around Second's shoulder and in the tone of someone giving grave advice, said,

"Some kinda hot you've got here. Must be shit working down here for a living, I mean all the time."

Second must not have been a football fan, because he gave Billy a withering look and walked away saying, "Take him to the top and let him feel some real heat."

So I introduced him to the engine room ceiling and Michelangelo's scaffold.

Billy complained about everything. He didn't say anything I or others weren't thinking. It was just that only he talked about it. As he did, he was clearly oblivious to how anyone reacted. But he offered fair balance. He really liked the food. And his shorts and sandals, which never drew a comment from anyone, seemed to work out just fine. I thought about getting a pair of shorts myself.

I finally had someone to talk to during work, although besides complaining, he was only interested in talking about football and pussy.

He also wanted to *play* football. That is, he wanted to have a catch. He had brought with him a blown-up, fairly new football, and he wanted to toss it around on deck. On a regular, bulk cargo ship with lots of deck space, this wouldn't have been much of a problem. A refitted container ship with just a few feet between the containers and the rail presented what to me were obvious difficulties. Billy had no concerns. So we stood in that narrow space about forty feet apart, and with his back to the stern he threw the ball. It sailed high. I ran back and jumped, barely able to tip the ball in the air with one hand and then catch it on the deflection. I threw the ball back right at his chest. He caught it easily. His next throw was inches from the wall of containers. Again I had to tip it up before being able to catch it. He was clearly a fullback, not a quarterback. This wasn't going to end well. I didn't want to have anything to do with losing his football in the ocean.

I held the ball. "Look, Billy, I don't think this is such a good idea." Not wanting to offend him, I said, "I'm likely to throw a bad pass, or have one of yours brick off my hands into the ocean. I don't want to lose your football."

"Don't worry about it, I got lots more. I get them for nothing."

"Yeah, well, that's great, but I don't expect you've got any more with you."

After a few more close calls, he called it a day and sat on the deck, with his back against the rail, surveying the ship.

Then, out of nowhere, he said, "It's damn lucky there ain't any niggers on this ship."

Growing up in New York City, and going to prep school in upstate New York, and certainly living in the village, I had rarely heard anyone actually use the word, "nigger." It bothered me. Even here in the isolation of the ship far removed from my experience it stung.

"And why is that so damn lucky?

"I'm not working with any niggers."

"Is that right? That would be a damn shame, to come all this way and have to go right back."

Our body language and tone remained casual, but I could feel the intensity rising.

"You sound like a Yankee nigger lover."

"Well, I guess I am. At my prep school one of my best friends was a Negro, and he was the quarterback of the football team." The term "black" was not yet so commonly used, and the absurd, politically correct, "African American" label was not yet on the horizon. I added for good measure, "And I guess you're a racist bigot." Where was this going to go?

"That's a load of crap. You people up here are no different. You just don't admit it. You don't live in the real world."

"*That* is bullshit. I live in the real world. It's just not your world. Those views are so primitive, they're fucking prehistoric. And that "Old South" stuff is dying out. No, Billy, we are different. I'm sure as hell different."

I needed to de-escalate this. It wasn't out of the question that we would get into a fight over this, and *that* I would surely regret. But I wasn't going to back down on this. He must have felt the same way, though not out of physical fear.

"Aah Peter, I'm just fooling with you. Just wanted to get you going,"

He gave me a slow, mock punch to the jaw and flashed a big grin. I nodded unsurely. And that was that.

***

The evening we arrived back in Port Elizabeth, Billy joined DeLeo and two other guys for the "42nd Street hooker hunt." It was his first visit to New York City. Still, his enthusiasm for the promised $5 blowjob surprised me in light of his girlfriend, Lola, whose picture he had shown me along with a graphic description of her talents. He had a large billfold—the kind you carry in the inside pocket of a suit jacket—that stuck out of the top of the back pocket of his pants. He needed it to hold the rather large picture of Lola. She was Eurasian Hawaiian and the most beautiful girl I had ever seen. More beautiful than any movie actress or model. Absolutely stunning, and more than enough to keep my imagination working overtime. But he didn't leave it to my imagination.

With a huge grin, "And she gives the greatest blowjobs."

Right!

I told him he wasn't going to come across anything like Lola on 42nd Street. He went off undeterred.

***

As promising as the start to Billy's merchant marine career had been, it came dangerously close to ending after a week.   We again arrived in Jacksonville on a Sunday, so Billy and I had the day off. I had told him about Jax Beach when we were tossing the football on deck. The promise of having a catch, maybe even playing some touch on the beach had gone a long way to preserving the football. I also told him he was much more likely to find good looking pussy there than he ever would on 42nd Street, his outing having proved disappointing.

We arrived at the beach by 10:00. Billy had no interest in downtown Jacksonville or the Freedom Tree.   I told him the beach would be deserted that early, but he wanted to get to the ocean. So we walked around, went for a swim, walked around some more to get dry, and then sat up on one of the lifeguard chairs that I now regarded as my personal property. I had borrowed sun lotion from Whitey, whose combination of deck work and pale complexion suggested he might have some, and I applied it liberally wherever I could. I gave it to Billy and he dabbed some on his nose and ears, but said he didn't have much of a problem with the sun. Strange, I thought, given his blond hair and pink skin. But it was his business.

We watched the beach fill up, and Billy chatted up the girls as they passed by our post. After a while we saw some guys down the beach tossing a football, and Billy was off the chair in a flash with his ball. This time he made no introductions, just told me to go long for a pass. I did, and this time he threw it near me and I caught it. I threw it to one of the other guys, and it began.

There were six of us, so a game of touch was clearly on. It was Billy and I and a guy named Chip, against his three friends. What *they* didn't know! Between Billy and me, I was the better passer, but that hardly mattered. It was just a waste to have Billy standing still. So I threw to Billy and Chip. Billy was, to someone accustomed to playing with normally athletic people, incredible, a freak of nature. Despite his size—and in just bathing trunks he looked even bigger—he was unbelievably fast, quick and coordinated. He caught any ball within six feet of him, and any person anywhere. The other team couldn't score no matter what they did because Billy would either bat the ball away from the receiver or touch him before he got very far.

But he really didn't want to play a passing game. There was simply no competition. So, Billy's ball, Billy's game, and no one argued. He had me set up as the center. No more passing. I handed it off to Billy and he would just run. In the rare instances when someone had an angle and could catch up to him, he would fake with his hips and go right by. They didn't have to tackle him, just touch him with two hands. Yet three guys couldn't manage to touch him. Chip and I were supposed to block, but he ran by us too. It was just Billy having fun. Everybody laughed, even the people who had gathered to watch the game. We all had fun just watching.

Girls gathered. Billy had found pussy, or more accurately, pussy had found him. We all swam for a while, then sat around the lifeguard chair, maybe ten of us in all, Billy the center of attention. I had hoped to see Jillie. She was better looking than anyone there, but neither she nor Sharon made an appearance. We all went to the hot dog stand, and as I talked with a small group, Billy walked off with one of the girls in the direction of the parking lot. Eventually I went back to the chair, put on some more lotion, and dozed.

About an hour later Billy climbed up the ladder as the whole structure shuddered. He gave me a grin and a thumbs up.

"OK, not bad. Just played around a bit, but it beat playing football with a bunch of cripples!"

I tossed him the lotion and asked him if she had a sister. Again putting a dab on his nose and ears, and this time on the top of his shoulders, he said, "Go find your own pussy."

We sat there talking and looking at the ocean. Around 2:00 I told him that he was going to get really burned if we stayed much longer. But he didn't want to go back to the ship. Around 3:00, as people were leaving the beach in droves, I noticed that he was getting red. He noticed it too, so we left. By the time we got back to the ship more than an hour later, he was a darker shade of red and not feeling very well. He put a wet towel on his face and lay down on his bunk.

He didn't want dinner and asked me to bring him back a bottle of soda. When I came back with the soda after dinner, he was moaning and shivering. Jesus Christ. He had sunstroke. I had never seen it before, but I remembered the description in my old Boy Scout Manual. I got as many towels as I could find, soaked them in cold water, and covered him with them from head to toe. He was getting steadily darker, and I was getting scared.

I ran back to the mess hall and told a couple of the guys watching TV. One of them went up to get an engineer. I got another drink and ran back to the fo'c'sle. Billy was beginning to turn purple. A few minutes later, First came in. He took off the towels and looked at Billy, who by then was shaking.

"Peter, you've got one stupid friend here. That is the dumbest thing I think I've ever seen. How long was he on the beach?"

I didn't want to add to the problem, so I said, "You know, just a while. We played some ball, swam, walked around a bit. That's all."

"Bullshit. You don't get sunstroke like that after just a while. This stupid son of a bitch has been on the beach all day." He handed Billy a thermometer out of the first aid kit he had brought with him. He had a temperature of over 105! Then he gave Billy some pills and said, "Mister, you stay in that bunk. Take these to get the temperature down. If anyone feels like it, he can keep putting wet towels on you. I hope you're lucky and you don't die. But you're not gonna be fit for work between here and port. So when we get there, you're fired. You just sign right off this ship. You got that?"

Billy didn't answer. He just kept shaking. Billy Clayton's bubble had just burst. Or so I thought.

***

I kept up the wet towels and even Raul helped. Billy was barely coherent. When it got late, I got a bucket of water for the rest of the towels, put a few cups of water along the floor by his bunk, and told him to keep putting on wet towels when the others got warm. And to yell if he needed something. With that, Raul and I turned out the lights and went to sleep.

The next morning, Billy was still purple, but a more maroonish shade. In any event, he wasn't dead. I shook down the thermometer as I had seen my mother do and gave it to him. His temperature was down to 103. He was definitely on the mend.

At each meal, I—and occasionally Raul—brought him something to eat and drink. Occasionally one of the football fans stopped by. He talked, but he was really weak and still trembled from time to time. Raul and I worked as we had the day Michael left, without missing the third wiper. After the first day Billy seemed to recover by the hour, so that by the time we docked in Port Elizabeth, he was a lot better, though he still wouldn't have been able to work.

What happened next demonstrated the nature of the relationship between management and the union, and took just about everyone by surprise. Every time a U.S. ship pulls into its home port—and sometimes in other ports—the steward of the union representing a large contingent of men would board the ship to see that there were no labor issues. He definitely would appear when notified that someone had been fired. Billy had packed his bag and we were walking toward the mess hall, when the union steward appeared.

"Where you think you're going, son."

"Well, they fired me, told me to sign off when we got to port."

"You're not going anywhere, and you're not fired. Can't fire you for a medical disability. I understand you were medically disabled. Is that right?

"Yes sir, I sure was sick. Never felt so bad in my life. But I'm better now, and by tomorrow morning I'll be ready to get to work again."

The union steward could see the sunburn. Billy still looked like a very large beet. Not a problem. The union was there to protect against just such injustices. The steward did advise Billy not to be such a stupid ass again, but otherwise, that was that. Billy Clayton was fully reinstated as a wiper aboard the S.S. *Rufus Saxton*, and the First Assistant Engineer be damned.

On top of that, word that afternoon was that we weren't going to do the Jacksonville run for a while. Billy Clayton, wiper, was going to Puerto Rico. And so was I.

CHAPTER 15

Tommy Arrives and a Couple

of Close Calls

Billy and I stayed on the ship. He wasn't recovered enough to go out on the town and I, again, had nowhere to go. I did call Rick, my former roommate, to see if I had any phone messages. I had told Lorna and my mother that I could eventually be reached through him, as I would call him each time we were in port. Of course, I could call each of them directly, but I liked this plan better since it didn't require regular explanations to my mother, and it avoided putting Lorna on the spot. I also gave them the mailing address of the ship, as I had been told at the union hall that mail would be delivered to the ship at Port Elizabeth. But the only phone message had been from my mother announcing that she was going to Europe to visit friends and would be gone for six weeks. There was no mail. The ball might be in Lorna's court, but she wasn't swinging at it.

While we were eating dinner, a smiling, oddly dressed, leprechaun-like figure made a grand entrance. Maybe 5' 9" and lean, he had a broad, handsome face and floppy, sandy hair, long for the time. Like Billy, he appeared in Bermuda shorts, but to complete *his* look, he wore old, brown, over-the-ankle work boots without socks and an oversized Hawaiian shirt. He received a hearty, almost affectionate, welcome. Everyone seemed to know him and quite obviously liked him. He got hand-shakes, slaps on the back: the prodigal son returned.

"Who is this guy?" I asked, turning to Boson sitting at the table behind me.

"Hey, Tommy," Boson yelled across the room, "I want someone to meet you."

Tommy came over, and Boson, with a grand gesture announced, "Peter, I want you to meet a seafaring leg-end, Mr. Tommy Hill. Ask any of these guys, they'll tell you, Tommy here is the only man alive who truly lives the seaman's dream."

"You're the guy who lives at the Waldorf Astoria?" I asked incredulously as I stood up.

"With its many creature comforts, I should add. Yes sir that is I. As it happens, I just come from one of my most pleasant stays there."

I extended my hand.

"Well, sir," happily adopting the same mock idiom, "I am indeed honored to make your acquaintance. Your fame precedes you."

""What a lot of bullshit," Boson laughed. "Looks like you two will get along just fine." Then, with a wave toward Billy and me, "These two are our new wipers."

Tommy was the happiest, most contented person I had ever met. He seemed to enjoy everything and everyone. He smiled all the time and laughed if given the slightest cue. He was forty and had been in the merchant marine since he was eighteen. Though he had been shipping out for twenty-two years, he was still an OS. (He was the replacement for one of the two passive poker players.) He didn't want the responsibilities of an AB, he said, didn't want to take the tests, too much bother, too much pressure. He was happy as an OS. He'd seen the world several times over, had a great life.

As I said, he was happy. He was also very gregarious and loved to tell stories. It was from him more than anyone else that I learned about the exotic ports around the world, from Pakistan to Belgium, from Norway to Madagascar. In other words, all the places that I had joined the merchant marine to see. Sometimes others would listen in on his stories. No one questioned them.

One evening as several of us were sitting around "my" hatch cover, I asked Tommy to describe his most memorable port experience. I was expecting tales of women in Marseilles and the like. The story he told was quite different and made a powerful and lasting impression on me.

"We were on a Persian Gulf run in 1953. So the ship docks in Karachi, Pakistan. I had a free day and walked around the city by myself. It was just five or so years after Pakistan separated from India, and the Pakistanis were still doing pretty badly. Even though it's big, Karachi's a really poor city, at least the parts that I could see walking from the docks.

"So I walked through this unbelievably poor neighborhood, maybe two miles from the port. There, along a dirt road, there's a row of emaciated, really scrawny, shriveled up, old men. And they're all begging. I don't really know if they were all old, but they looked God-awful. Anyway, next to each of these guys there's a pile of wood around four feet high, stacked in a cart.

"I couldn't figure out what it was all about, so I sat on the ground under a tree about 150 feet away and watched. It was pretty crowded, and a lot of people passed by. Some gave the men coins. After about a half hour a police car came by and stopped near me. I walked up to it and asked the cop on the passenger side why the men were standing with the piles of wood.

"The cops' English wasn't great, but they could speak it. So they look me over, mumble something to each other in what I guess is Urdu, then sort of back and forth between the two of them they tell me, (Tommy now took on a fairly convincing Indian accent.) 'These men, sick, so very, very sick, no food they have, they surely die. No money. No hope for these men. They beg for money to buy wood before they are dying. Very soon they are dying. When die, men get burned on wood. This very good for them, these men.' "

Tommy told this story in a quiet, warm smiling manner, which made it all the more chilling.

***

Billy was back to work the next morning as if nothing had happened. His sunburn was starting to peel and the heat must have made him pretty uncomfortable, but he didn't complain. He lowered his profile several notches, his image having definitely taken a hit. He must have been anticipating his next interaction with First. I certainly was.

As the three of us worked side by side chipping yet another bulkhead, Second came up and motioned to me to follow him. He said with some urgency that he needed me to help him with a problem. I felt honored, really. This would be my first assignment beyond wiping, cleaning, chipping or painting. We walked quickly to a corner of the engine room where a ladder was set up near a long, 12" thick horizontal pipe eight feet off the ground, encased in some sort of hard white material held in place by metal straps. The pipe threaded into an elbow joint which made a vertical right angle.

Steam was shooting out of the horizontal joint through a small crack in the white covering. Second looked at the steam and said it had increased since he left to get me. That didn't sound good. He was clearly concerned. He told me to climb the ladder and wedge my back against the bulkhead well to the right of the joint with my legs hanging over the pipe. When I was in place, he came up and straddled the pipe nearer the elbow, his back braced against the vertical leg of the pipe. The steaming joint was between us. With a pocket knife, he cut away the covering—he said it was asbestos—up to the joint. Then he handed me the knife and told me to do the same on my side of the joint. The knife was sharp, but the asbestos was very hard to cut through. Eventually, using the knife and our fingers we ripped it away from the pipe.

With the joint now fully exposed, the intensity of the jet of steam increased. Wedged against the bulkhead, I couldn't avoid its heat. I didn't need to be an old hand to know that this was dangerous. Second reacted quickly to the increased steam. Ducking out of the way of the steam, he yelled, "Go down and get a number 30 Stilson wrench, fast!"

Right! What the hell was a number 30 Stilson wrench? But this just wasn't the kind of situation where you asked for an explanation. I extricated myself from behind the pipe and jumped down to the deck, not bothering with the ladder. I ran to the wall at the end of the engine room (near the hatch to the engine) where I had seen three very large peg boards each holding an array of very different kinds of wrenches in a range of sizes. But there were no names or numbers.

Someone was always nearby, but not now. I told myself to calm down and think. Two of the wrench types were familiar; the third I had never seen before. While the others were stainless steel, the third type was red. These deserved a name; the others didn't. The red ones also had much larger, heavier, adjustable and serrated mouths. *Yup, the kind you would need to latch onto and turn a smooth pipe.* And if that was what Second was going to try to do, then he would need the largest wrench there. The "number 30" didn't matter.

What felt like a slow-motion reasoning process had actually taken only a couple of seconds. I grabbed the huge wrench off its hook and ran back to the ladder. It must have weighed twenty pounds. I handed it to Second, hoping that I had guessed right. He took it without a word as I climbed back into my position. I felt worthy of some kind of award for solving an inscrutable, ancient riddle.

Second opened the mouth of the wrench as wide as it would go, perhaps not coincidentally, exactly as wide as the diameter of the pipe. He tightened it around the pipe and we each grabbed the handle with two hands and pushed as hard as we could toward the bulkhead to tighten the joint.

I couldn't believe that we would be able to turn the pipe, and at first we couldn't. But as the steam steadily increased so did our effort. I suggested a series of hard sudden movements to free the pipe if it was just stuck. It worked. The pipe turned very slightly. We did it again and again until the steam lessened. With success now a real possibility, we stopped to rest for a few seconds. When we started again, it was still slow, very hard work. After about twenty minutes the steam completely stopped. We had done it. He went for some kind of tar to coat the joint temporarily. When we got to port, he said, pipefitters would fix it permanently.

As I applied the tar to the area closer to my reach, I asked him what would have happened if we hadn't been able to tighten the joint.

"The pipe would've blown."

I had figured that out myself.

"Yeah, and then what?"

"Well, if we were still up there working on it—which is likely since you don't know when it's gonna go, your family would get a lot of money under the Jones Act."

"Right. Good to know."

"Listen, kid...Peter, thanks. You did a good job. I appreciate it."

"Glad to help." And I was. I was on top of the world.

***

A couple of days later, as we were getting ready to wash up, First, who no longer acknowledged Billy's existence, approached Raul and said, "Show Peter how to clean the glass." Raul nodded and walked toward the main ladder. I followed. On a landing near the top of the engine room was a heavy metal structure about four feet high and three feet wide with no visible moving parts. It was painted the same color as the bulkheads and had a small, thick, vertical, glass window near its top, bolted between the front and back of a heavy metal frame. I had noticed this squat thing several times and meant to ask what it was for but never did. Since I didn't know what most things in the engine room were for, this particular lack of information didn't trouble me. It should have.

Raul pointed at what apparently should have been clear glass but which was a charcoal color and completely opaque. I could make out the vague lines of a metal grid with half inch squares behind the window.

"You need a plier to loosen the ...those things behind." He pointed to the wing nuts on the back of the frame. You take the glass out, and clean it and the thing behind it," pointing to the grid.

"Damn, Raul, why the hell didn't you mention the pliers before we came all the way up here?"

He shrugged his shoulders, and we went back down the ladders, and I got the pliers. Returning to the apparatus alone, I studied it carefully. What I should have done instead was think. A little thought, a little sense of self-preservation—and a lot less trust in goddamn Raul—and what happened next could easily have been avoided.

Lids, hatches and thick small glass windows on machines and containers are used to keep what is inside from getting outside. I'd already had some experience with that concept. When the lid, hatch or window is small and held in place by something very strong, there is a great likelihood that whatever is inside is under a fair amount of pressure, and that if given half a chance will get out very suddenly indeed. Unmindful of these inalienable truths, I worked the wing nuts loose and pulled off the top of the frame together with the window.

As I did, I was hit with a blast of scalding smoke and soot. I let out a scream and grabbed my face. I was definitely burned. Damn, it hurt. Because of my height, even though I had bent over to work the wing nuts, the blast had hit the lower half of my face and my neck, not my eyes.

I virtually flew down the ladders cursing in pain. I ran to the sink and grabbed a wet cloth and put it on my face and neck. Someone came over and said that the solvent would be better than water, and it was. After a few minutes the acute pain lessened, but it still hurt like hell. Billy said I had a white grid on my face. As I stood with the solvent-soaked rag on my face, I heard First yelling at Raul.

"What is it with you? Are you fucking stupid? I told you to *show* him how to clean the glass. Now get up there and finish the job yourself. Damn." And then to me, "I'll get you some ointment. Don't worry; it's not that bad."

As First left, I took the rag off my face and balled it up in my right hand in anger. Raul was standing twenty-five feet from me.

I screamed at him, "You're not stupid, are you, you son of a bitch, you're just a fucking bastard. That's why you made sure you weren't up there when I took off the glass." And without really thinking about it, I whipped the balled up, heavily soaked rag at Raul as hard as I could. It was a side-arm delivery that would have made any shortstop proud, and it was right on the mark. With the force sufficient to get a baseball across a baseball diamond fast, it hit Raul just below his left eye at much closer range.

Now Raul screamed. "Jesus Christ, Jesus Christ, you're fucking crazy, man. I didn't do nothing. Man, I didn't know something gonna happen, man. You're crazy, man. Jesus Christ." He put his hands over his eye.

But I wasn't buying any of it. This guy delighted in seeing me get hurt. And now I was going to hurt him. I rushed at him ready to beat the crap out of him, but Billy got in front of me.

"Leave him alone. I'll take care of this shit."

"No, he did the same thing before. He's my problem, and he has been since my first day on the ship." And I tried to push by him. But that wasn't happening.

He walked over to Raul and grabbed his shoulder with one hand and squeezed. Raul danced in pain. Billy spoke very quietly and very deliberately, exaggerating his drawl.

"You know, Raul, you *are* a son of a bitch. But we are a team, and you're part of the team. Only you haven't been playing by the team rules. But from now on you're going to. You're going to show us whatever we need to know, everything. Got that?" Raul nodded. "Then you're going to be happy, Peter is going to be happy and I'm going to be happy. And if you don't, if there's another problem, then, you fucking little spic, I'm going to take your head and shove it in that boiler...while it's on. I really do hope you understand me."

And with that he gave Raul's shoulder an even harder squeeze that sent him to the deck. Then Billy seemed struck by a sudden realization. He gently pulled Raul back to his feet, and spoke to him with a genuine smile.

"And one of the things we need to know and you're going to tell us all about is what to do in Puerto Rico and where to do it. In fact, you're going to show us around. See, when you're a team, you hang around together." Raul just looked at him. Then Billy put out his hand and said, "Let's shake on it." Bewildered, Raul shook Billy's hand. Then we all shook hands.

I could see Raul didn't know what to make of what had just happened. Hell, I didn't either. He went up the ladder to clean and close the window and Billy finished washing up and left, saying he'd see me at dinner. I leaned against the sink and tried to calm down and think clearly.

I wouldn't have called Raul a spic. I cringed at that. My wanting to hit him had nothing to do with my feelings about Puerto Ricans. But was that really true? Hadn't that contributed to the situation from the beginning? No, damn it, I wanted to hit him because of what he had done. But what *had* he actually done? Sure, he was thoughtless, indifferent and maybe even relished the thought that I might get hurt. So maybe he was a shit. But unlike the tube blowing incident when I had no warning, when there was no way I could have known, this time anybody who was awake would have known. I didn't like admitting it, but I got hurt because of my own thoughtlessness and carelessness, whether Raul was happy about it or not. As I went back to the fo'c'sle to shower, I didn't feel very good about anything, and it wasn't just that my face hurt.

That evening as we left for the mess hall, Billy reminded Raul about the "team" and told him that teammates eat as a unit. So the three of us showed up for dinner together. What a sight we made. Billy, the huge blond-topped tomato, Raul with his face lopsided by a large red welt and swelling under his eye, and me with the ridiculous grid decorating my face. The walking wounded. The Three Musketeers of the engine room!

CHAPTER 16

I Meet the Captain

In the morning of the day we passed the southern tip of Florida—we were really in international waters—Second rewarded me for my work on the pipe. At least, I took it as a reward. It was a gorgeous day, the sky a bright blue without a cloud, temperature in the mid 80s, a light breeze. Second found me cleaning near the boilers. He told me to go up to the stackhouse and mend the very long hose inside the house. He said the hose hadn't been checked in some time, and that since it wasn't used frequently, cracks would develop in the rubber.

For me, this was definitely a reward. On a beautiful day, to spend hours on the very top of the ship, in the open air, was as good as it could get as a wiper. I was surprised the deck people didn't get to do this job, but the stack, the stackhouse and everything in it belonged to the engine room. So it was mine.

Armed with a large roll of black electrical tape, I climbed the ladders out of the engine room and then up the flights of stairs to the hatch that opened out onto the small deck surrounding the stackhouse. I had never before been above the mess hall. It was exhilarating just standing at the very top of the ship. I walked to the front and back of the deck and looked out past the bow and the stern. I imagined hanging on to the rigging, standing in the crow's nest atop an eighteenth century man-of-war. This was definitely the place to be.

But I had a job to do. The stackhouse is a structure about ten feet high and wide and about fifteen feet long at the bottom and slightly tapered to the top. Other than the stack itself—the ship's chimney—and the hose, I had no idea what was inside. I opened the large hatch and looked in—this time cautiously.

There was the stack coming up through the middle of the floor, surprisingly only about three feet in diameter, and the enormous coil of hose wound around a seven-foot high, wall-mounted bracket. Nothing else. Whatever the space was supposed to be used for, it wasn't being used for it. It seemed to me that the stackhouse was merely decorative and that the builders had surrounded the stack with a structure more in proportion to the size of the ship than the surprisingly narrow stack itself. Anyway, there was my hose.

I started to unwind the hose loop by loop, bending it aggressively as I did, carefully looking for cracks and taping them over when I found them. After five or six loops, I saw that I had created a chaotic tangle of green hose on the floor of the house, and from what Second had told me, there were still almost 400 feet to go! If I kept this up, I would have no place to stand. Besides, even with the hatch open, it was really too dark to see clearly. I could easily miss a lot of cracks. I was definitely not doing this the right way.

My next approach, which had the added appeal of allowing me to work outside, was to drop the already repaired hose over the side. Soon it was trailing along in the water. As I saw the hose drifting back toward the stern, I worried that it would get caught in the propellers or that one of the sharks the guys were always talking about might come along and bite it. In fact, I couldn't think of any positive outcome of this technique. So, with considerable effort, I reeled more than 150 feet of repaired hose back up onto the deck. The writhing, black spotted, green monster quickly filled the available space. Now what? Damn it, this wasn't the first time anyone had repaired a hose. There had to be a right way to do it.

And then I saw the answer. I slapped my head for not having noticed it right away. There, below and in front of me was another smallish deck with absolutely nothing and no one on it. I could easily lower the hose, all of it, onto that deck, making a pile as high as I wanted and get the job done. While it was unlikely that this was that deck's main purpose, it would certainly serve mine. I gathered up the completed section and dropped it down on to the deck. Then, after unwinding a few coils and examining and mending the hose carefully, I fed it down onto the deck, trying to get it as far forward as possible. I didn't want to fill up the nearer space and then have to try to get the rest of the hose over the large pile.

And so it went. For the next hour I carefully examined and mended the hose and fed it down onto the deck below. Initially, I had tried to make a neat coil on the deck, but that took too much time and effort. I wasn't going to pursue abstract perfection here.

Instead, I succeeded in creating an enormous pile of tangled hose toward the front of the short deck, with several lower tangles near the back.

As I was leaning over the railing, intent on my work, a man whom I had never seen before emerged from the space directly under the stack house. He was still facing the door and saying something to someone inside as he took a step backward. I could see what was going to happen, but I didn't react fast enough to call out. With his next step his foot caught one of the low coils and he went crashing backwards, landing hard on the large pile of hose. As he did, he looked up and saw me. The look on his face—he was little more than fifteen feet away—was a combination of shock, confusion and incredulity.

"What the hell? What the hell are you doing? Who the hell are you?" His bewilderment grew with each question.

I looked at the hose in my hands and then at him. "I'm repairing the hose." And from somewhere out of my usually suppressed survival instinct, I *didn't* add, "What the hell does it look like I'm doing?"

"Do you know what this is?" indicating the deck with both hands.

"Uh, not really."

"Well it's the quarterdeck, and under you is the bridge. It's where we steer this ship. You can't...you can't fill up the quarterdeck with a goddamn hose." He was so exasperated he was struggling for words. "Who the hell are you, and how long have you been aboard this ship?"

"I'm a wiper. About five weeks, sir." The "sir" was more instinct kicking in.

"I'll be damned. I'm the Captain." Then, clearly mad, "And I'm ordering you to get this goddamn hose off my deck. Is that clear, mister?"

"Yes sir." In the moment I forgot the "aye aye." "I'm sorry Captain. I really didn't know. Anyway, I'm just about finished."

"Yes, you are, son. Yes, you are." Awkwardly standing up from the pile of hose, he walked back into the bridge shaking his head.

I had finally met the Captain.

CHAPTER 17

Getting It For Love in Old
San Juan (Part 1)

I didn't see Second again until the next day, which was too bad, since I had a full night to worry about the Captain's parting comment. When I started to describe the hose incident, he stopped me and, laughing, said he had heard all about it at lunch the previous day. Apparently the Captain had a ball describing the pile of hose on the quarterdeck and the wiper holding the hose and looking at him like a bewildered idiot.

"OK. I'm glad he had a good time. Now I have some questions. Am I getting fired?"

"No, Jesus Christ, why would he fire you? For what?"

"Well, he said..."

"I don't care what he said. He's not even pissed off. It was funny, that's all. It really doesn't happen every day. The best part is that because of the height of the bridge windows they couldn't see the hose piling up in front of them."

If I didn't feel so stupid, I would have admired my work too. "So what was I supposed to do with the hose?

I tried unwinding it in the stackhouse. I tried hanging it in the water. Those weren't going to work."

"You wrap it around the stackhouse along the deck. There's enough room to step over it and stand. I should have told you."

"Nah," I said, shaking *my* head, "I should have figured it out."

***

That evening as Billy, Raul and I again ate dinner together, I described my hose caper. They couldn't stop laughing. The day before, I hadn't mentioned it. Even though I certainly saw the humor in it, it wouldn't have been so funny if I had gotten fired.

As strange as it seemed, Billy and Raul were really comfortable with each other. It was as if once Billy imposed his will on him, Raul accepted the situation and his position in it. Whether he truly believed the nonsense about the "team," I was the one who now needed to fit in. Just like that, we were talking like old friends.

"I've got a lot of questions about Puerto Rico and San Juan."

Shaking his head, Billy said, "There are only two questions: where's the best pussy and where's the best food? Everybody clear about that? We're not tourists."

That was fine with me.

Raul grinned. He had brought a small, folded map of Puerto Rico to the mess hall and spread it out on the table.

"This is the ship here." He pointed to the main bay. There were several others. Then he pointed to a bay south of Old San Juan and said, "here, this where I live, Santurce."

"You live on the ocean? I asked approvingly.

"No man, you kidding?"

"So where do you live?"

"Man, you don't want to see that. I show you nice places, nice pussy, nice food. Why you want to see where I live?"

"But we do want to see where you live, because," Billy drawled, "we're a team. If we're in Mississippi, you'd see where I live, ain't that right Peter? And when we get back to New York, we'll go to where you live, right?"

"I think Raul's got a pretty good feel for New York already." I was picturing this crew meeting my mother.

"Yeah, well, Raul, you know, you're the man here. This is your town, and you need to show us. So let's start where you live and go from there."

Raul might be the "man," but Billy was organizing this expedition. I could sense that Raul wasn't happy about going to where he lived, and I was sure Billy could too. Although Raul seemed to revel in the role of local authority and expert, he had no desire to demonstrate his knowledge of what I imagined was squalor.

***

We crossed the Gulf Stream as we approached Puerto Rico, and for the first time I encountered rough seas, with waves more than fifteen feet high. I hadn't expected to get seasick, and I didn't. In fact, I enjoyed it. We lurched around for a bit and I had to hold on from time to time. But overall, it wasn't a big deal.

When I asked Max and Whitey how this weather rated, they said virtually in unison, "You ain't seen nothing." In a couple of hours it was over, and the rest of the way was calm and balmy. And that's the way it was as we rounded into San Juan Bay.

After work we showered and dressed quickly. We approached the gangway at the same time as Max and Bosun.

"Gonna get it for love in old San Juan?" Max taunted.

"That's the long-term plan," I replied. "But we're starting on Raul's home turf, Santurce."

Following Raul, we got a cab and took the twenty-minute ride to the neighborhood where he lived. Santurce is a fairly large and dense part of San Juan, bounded on the north by the ocean. To the west are the fancy hotels of Candado Beach, at that time basically the Caribe Hilton, and next to that, Old San Juan, our ultimate target. The closer to the beach the fancier the houses.

Where he lived, though, could be described as a semi-rural slum. Some of the roads were paved, some weren't. The land and the buildings were shabby and ill-kept. There were no buildings of more than two stories. Businesses were mixed with residential buildings. The houses were white stucco and I guessed were made of cinder blocks. The area was definitely poor. Yet it had none of the squalor and oppressiveness of the urban slums of New York. It didn't seem to me that the people who lived here had a bad life. It was sure as hell of a lot better than Spanish Harlem. And though I knew that Puerto Rico was some kind of territory of the United States, this was definitely a foreign country.

At Raul's house, he got out of the cab quickly.

"You guys, you stay here, OK?" It wasn't a question.

I had no intention of making him feel awkward by insisting that he show us his house and introduce us to whoever else lived there, and I grabbed Billy's arm as he opened the back door of the cab.

"Don't be a prick, Billy. Don't embarrass the guy. I thought he was your friend now."

Billy smiled and sat back. Within a few seconds Raul emerged with a young man whom he introduced as his cousin Jose. Five minutes later the taxi stopped along a ragged road, at a single-story, square, white stucco building with several well-lit windows and multi-colored lights resembling Christmas decorations arranged around its front door. A few old cars were parked randomly in the worn dirt area around the building. This was the bar and restaurant where we would very happily spend the next four hours. On this trip, we would never make it to Old San Juan.

Although it was only around 6:00 when we arrived, the restaurant was crowded and lively. A wonderful aroma of cooking filled the air. Having grown up mostly in New York City, I had some familiarity with Mexican, Cuban and Spanish restaurants. The aroma was very much like those.

Raul and Jose seemed to know everyone in the place, and Raul introduced us to all the men. He spoke in Spanish, and I couldn't pick up a word. Then he turned back to us.

"I tell these guys we work together on the ship. I tell them you never been to Puerto Rico. And I tell them Billy likes to eat a lot. This man, Adolfo, he's my uncle."

I smiled and shook hands with his uncle, the oldest of the group, an intense-looking man in his forties.

"Mucho gusto," I said to each of the four men, largely exhausting my Spanish vocabulary.

Billy tapped Raul on the shoulder and half growled, "Did you tell them I like pussy too?"

At that the men laughed. Their English was just fine!

"No one come here from the ship before," Adolfo said. "This is good you come. Good food, good *cervesa...* beer. You gonna like Puerto Rico."

"I like it already," I said, shaking his hand again.

"Billy shook hands with everyone, but he was pre-occupied with reconnoitering the room. There were several women in the restaurant, young and old, and they received polite nods, but we got no introductions.

All the tables were occupied, but during the intro-ductions some of the men and women rearranged themselves so that by the time we were ready to sit down there was an empty table right by a window.

Raul was beaming. Where the hell had this Raul been? I tried to push that thought away. Where had I been? Had I made any effort to get to know him? Why was it his job to do that? Just because I was new? He was one of only two Puerto Ricans on the ship. No one else took any interest in him. Why should he assume I would? And I hadn't. Billy, for all his bigotry—and I would learn again that it went a great deal further than a passing ethnic epithet—had made an effort to befriend Raul from the beginning. I looked around at this happy place, where Raul fit in so well, and I was the outsider.

One of Raul's friends joined us and they ordered beers all around. I eagerly chose Medalla, the Puerto Rican beer, over the recommended Heineken—I could always have Heineken. It was excellent, with a rich, malty taste. Maybe not my choice forever, but then, definitely.

Billy was unfamiliar with any foreign foods—he had once had Chinese food and wasn't sure he liked it. But he was game. I, on the other hand, couldn't wait. Raul, his friend and Jose argued about the menu. Billy announced that he wanted meat, not fish, but beyond that it was up to them. That settled things quickly. We had wonderful appetizers of puffy cornbread fingers called *surullitos* and *bacalaitos,* crunchy cod fritters— which Billy ate and liked, without knowing it was fish. Then we had a terrific black bean soup. All this took a very long time.

Along the opposite wall, two tables down, were four women— three of them quite attractive. The oldest was in her early forties and had been one of the women to whom Raul had nodded when we arrived. Two were in their late twenties, one attractive and the other quite heavy. The youngest seemed a bit younger than I, but I was not a very good judge of the ages of women. Raul's friend said he knew them all vaguely and that they were not related to each other. In other words, the oldest was not the mother.

During the hour and a half or so that we drank beer and waited for and ate the appetizers and soup, the girl and I exchanged glances at least a hundred times. Everyone at both tables noticed. Even Billy, who was facing the other way, turned around to see what I was constantly looking at. Billy said I should buy her a drink—Raul said the women always had some kind of rum drink. I thought we should buy all of them a drink. I went to the bar, and after some explanations, waving and pointing, the bartender got the idea and the women got their drinks.

They laughed and said, "*gracias.*" The girl blushed. Raul and his friend spoke to each other conspiratorially in Spanish. After some more looking back and forth, while the older woman looked exasperatedly at the ceiling, the two other women kept jokingly prodding the girl. Eventually, she got up and walked past me to the bathroom in the far corner of the restaurant.

After she went in, Raul turned to me and poked me in the ribs. "Go man, go. She likes you."

"Where the hell should I go, she's in the bathroom."

"Yeah, man. Where else you gonna meet her, you know, alone?"

"You're kidding. You want me to go into the bathroom with her?"

"Yeah, go man. You know, you…." He pretended to knock on a door. "If she opens it, that's it, man."

Billy was laughing throughout this exchange, as was everyone else. "What can happen?"

"I can feel like a complete idiot. That's what. This has got to be crazy."

But they kept pushing me, so I got up and walked to the bathroom. I knocked very timidly, half hoping she wouldn't answer. She said nothing, just opened the door and smiled. I went in and closed the door behind me. The bathroom was much larger than I had expected. It had a sink and a toilet that seemed lost in the ten by ten room. She stood with her back to the sink.

"My name is Peter. Hi."

"Dolores," she said, pointing at herself and smiling shyly.

I reached for her hand and I shook it gently. She smiled again. I couldn't believe this was happening. Come to Puerto Rico and meet a pretty girl in the bathroom. And she was pretty, about 5' 3", shapely but slight, with long black hair and light caramel skin and beautiful dark eyes. She wore a thin cotton dress. She kept smiling at me. I asked her if she spoke English. Looking down at the floor and smiling but shaking her head, she said no. Now what?

I put one hand gently on her cheek and the other under her chin. As she looked up I kissed her. She smiled again and I kissed her again. She started to return my kiss as our mouths opened. I held her and she pushed up against me. I pushed her back against the sink. She showed not the slightest inclination to stop me, so I reached under her dress and stroked the inside of her thigh. She pressed harder against me as I found home. We kept kissing and I kept massaging her. Oh boy! Where was this going?

But after a few more minutes of very heavy breathing, she pulled back. She smiled and kissed me lightly on my lips and wriggled free. She straightened her dress and hair and looked at me with a slight awkwardness, but with nothing like the awkwardness I felt. She turned to the door, and as she opened it, she looked back over her shoulder, waved at me lightly with her fingers and walked out. I stood with the door open for about twenty seconds, wondering what had just happened. Still bewildered, I walked back to the table.

Dolores sat where she had before. The other women were in an animated mostly one-way conversation with her. My buddies did much the same thing with me. I couldn't say much.

"Guys, I'm in love." I reached for my beer.

Billy wanted to know what I would do. Raul said there really wasn't much I could do. This was as far as it could go. I had realized that. Maybe the introductions around here were pretty advanced, but there was no way I was going to come here and fuck this girl without marrying her—or getting killed. It had just been a wonderful gift, and that was all. I was happy—horny as hell—but happy.

And we still had the main course to come. Dolores and I kept looking at each other. The women ate some kind of fruit for dessert, then after coffee, they all got up to leave. Again, Dolores waved to me as she walked out the door, not the least awkward now. I waved back. How about that. She had no guile, no ulterior motive. She had just spontaneously—more or less—done what she felt like doing. The very thought of going further in that bathroom with that lovely girl was all wrong. Though this wouldn't qualify as getting *IT* for love, and we weren't in Old San Juan, it had been the nicest unexpected experience I ever had.

Finally our main course arrived, although I was in no hurry. I was having a ball. Jose had recommended the Puerto Rican beef stew, called *carne quisada puertoricana*. I really liked hot food, and though this wasn't hot, it was spicy. It was a lot like a Puerto Rican version of

Hungarian goulash. I loved it. No one could talk Billy into that and he had ordered a steak fried with onions. I suggested that since he had a couple of steaks every night, he might want to try something different. He replied that he had steak every night because he liked it. Right.

We drank more Medalla and talked. We really were in a foreign country. The prices, though in dollars, were ridiculously low. And the feeling of the place was so different, relaxed, easy. I asked Raul why anyone left here, especially to go to New York. I said I know Spanish Harlem and parts of Queens, like Corona. Why would anyone want to be there instead of here? He looked at his friend and at Jose, then quizzically at me.

"You got to be kidding, man. Money. There's no money here. You want to make money, you go to the States. And nobody wants to be alone. We know people in New York, so we go there. Lots of jobs there. Not good jobs, same like here, but the money is way better. Hell, look at me, I make more than any of these guys. And on the ship I don't spend nothing. I bring it home. Next time you meet my wife. I don't want to live in New York. Yeah, it's way better here. Here you can go piss outside because it's open; it's not like New York. But you can't make any money."

I nodded. "Yeah, I understand. I understand. Sorry man, I didn't mean to be so stupid. And, uh, I didn't know you were married"

"No problem, man," waving his hand in dismissal. Everybody married here. OK, not Dolores," he laughed. "You want some coffee? They got really good coffee here, everywhere in Puerto Rico."

225

We all had coffee. I had had more beer than I was accustomed to. Jose asked the owner to call a taxi. As we waited, and then during the ride back to the ship, we talked some more. Looking at Raul and listening to him speak, really interacting with him as a person, I wondered how I could have spent almost six weeks living in an eight-by-nine-foot space with a guy, working with him every day, and not known him at all.

CHAPTER 18

Beauty and the Beast

Leaving San Juan I felt just a bit older. It wasn't the girl. That was a pleasant even exciting moment, a nice memory. It was being in a very different place—really another country—with men, people, quite different from me, and actually interacting with them in their element, not mine. I wasn't just a tourist.

I had spent a summer on a tour of Europe when I was eighteen. Mostly it was looking at great buildings and great art, ancient and newer. We saw people in much the same superficial way, like a photo safari: "See Italian people in their natural habitat!" Except on the two occasions when I left the tour I had no real interaction with the places we visited or the people in them. Although these departures had mixed results—one a pleasant interlude with a Belgian waitress in Paris, the other a motor scooter accident in Florence that landed me in a Rome Hospital for nine days—they were real. I didn't like window shopping through life.

I also finally felt more settled on the ship. I knew almost everyone, and they knew me. Beyond the occasional, sarcastic "Let's ask the college kid—he knows it all," usually followed by some arcane question from a crossword puzzle which I could almost never answer, I felt comfortable enough with the rest of the crew and the few officers I had anything to do with. I thought I had gained a measure of respect, or at least tolerance, and there were no more taunting incidents, even from DeLeo. I imagined hopefully that someone had casually said, "That kid, Peter, he's OK." So they treated me as they treated each other: they left me alone.

This "peaceful co-existence" didn't involve getting to know them, though I tried. Most of these guys simply weren't interested in talking, certainly not about themselves. With some of them my instinct warned me not to try. Even Glen, a mild-mannered, Mr. Peepers-like guy, surprised me. When I asked him at lunch why he had joined the merchant marine, his reaction was to reflexively lean back away from me an ask, "Why, you writing a book or something?" You just didn't ask personal questions. I often thought about the conversation with Jack, Max and Whitey. If these guys wanted to be involved with people, they wouldn't be on this ship, or any ship. I wondered if the crews on around-the-world runs were different, formed closer bonds with each other just because they were together for such a long time. I hoped I would find out.

Between these wonderings Billy and I occasionally played music together. But once we had learned the full extent of each other's limited repertoires, playing the same songs every time got a bit tiresome. He started to teach Raul and me how to play the guitar. I tried to imagine Raul playing the blues and it didn't quite fit. But since that's what Billy knew, he taught us blues chords and we twanged away happily.

Both as a change of pace and because Billy was concerned about getting ready for football practice, we started doing exercises. We did push-ups and sit-ups on the deck and pull-ups on the door frames of the bathroom stalls. Billy was as strong as an ox. He told me he could bench press 350 pounds five times, and I had no doubt. That was almost twice the weight I could manage. Still, when it came to the exercises we were doing, I was king. Actually, I had never met anyone who could beat me—not that it was an activity many competed in. With maximum effort I could do 100 push-ups without stopping—fifty in under a minute, twenty pull-ups, and hundreds of sit-ups. I had won several beers at bars with the push-ups. I didn't know how this particular kind of strength was going to help me, but I had been working on it since I was twelve and was very proud of it.

I teased Billy when I more than doubled his results. Of course, it meant absolutely nothing in a sport like football—or maybe any other. To demonstrate what real power looked like, he had me lie on my back on the deck, cross my legs at the ankles, fold my arms across my chest and hold myself as rigid as I could. With one hand he grabbed my upper leg just above the ankle, and with the other he grabbed my upper wrist. Then in one smooth motion he picked me up like a barbell and lifted me over his head three times. And I weighed over 180 pounds! I guessed the scouts would be more impressed with that than my 100 push-ups! It was no contest. He was strong. I was a curiosity.

Billy would go to sleep earlier than anyone else. I
think more than football, pussy, music and eating, he
really loved to sleep. Sometimes I watched baseball
games at night or read on my bunk. I also talked with
the few who didn't seem to mind talking—Jack, Tommy,
Max, and even DeLeo. I really wanted to hear their
stories about the places they'd been and things they'd
done and seen. Jack was by far the most articulate, but
he was more reserved than the others.

Whenever I could, I played poker. The problem was
that there weren't always enough for a second table,
and there was no way I was going to play in the higher
stakes game. That was one rule I wasn't going to violate.
So, much of the time I watched. The more I saw Whitey
play, the more he impressed me, and the more I wondered why the others played with him at all. Although
they were accustomed to playing for more money, and
seemed to have it to put at risk, I thought I was a better player than several of the men at the table. And I
knew Whitey was much better than me. If you could
somehow equalize the impact of the stakes on each of
us, Whitey would still beat me. Yet these guys were prepared to play with him—and lose to him—regularly. I
wondered what they saw that I didn't, or more likely,
the other way round.

In every game it seems that there is at least one guy
who plays the way the two "luck players" had played in
my first game. I called them "poker dummies," not
because they were dumb, or even because they played
dumb—though they did, but because they were like the
dummy hand in bridge. They might as well have simply
put their cards face up on the table and bet them as they

lay. They just bet big when they had a good hand and folded when they didn't. No exceptions.

Two of the eight that made up the pool of players that played in most of the higher stakes game were poker dummies. Of those one never missed a game. His name was Olinsky and he was an AB who worked the 4:00 to 8:00 watch. Stocky with thick black hair and bushy eye brows, he almost never spoke. When he did it was to Max. After finishing his watch, Olinsky would eat quickly and be the first to sit down at the table. During the game he sat motionless, impassive. The game didn't seem like fun for him, rather like some kind of duty or penance. He lost almost every night.

All things being equal, the poker dummy approach is really not that dangerous a way to play. You win small and more often lose small. But things were not equal. He folded when he had a bad hand, losing just the ante. But when he got a decent hand, he was too anxious to play it. He fell in love with it and bet like hell. He never seemed to consider that while it was a good hand, it might be the second best hand. Too often it was. I had heard of compulsive gamblers, but Olinsky was a compulsive loser.

The night we left Puerto Rico I watched the high stakes game. Seven players rotated into and out of the game. Some ate pie, some just took a few hands off. Whitely and Olinsky played every hand. Whitey wasn't going anywhere while Olinsky was playing.

An hour into the game—seven card stud, nothing wild—Olinsky bet $2 to start. No surprise, he had two queens showing. Whitey called the first two $2 bets. Surprisingly three of the other four stayed in as well.

On the third up card he raised. Two folded and the third called. Olinsky looked surprised. He raised back. It was clear to everyone watching, really everyone, that given how he played, Olinsky had three queens. Whitey raised again. Olinsky clenched his jaw and raised. Whitey smiled at Olinsky and just called. There were going to be no $1 bets in this game.

If Whitey had a "poker face," Olinsky had the opposite. He looked tense, angry and determined. And he certainly wasn't thinking. The fourth up card produced more bets and more raises until the last other player folded. He was no mental giant either.

Whitey knew that Olinsky had three queens. And he knew that Olinsky wouldn't fold a good hand. So bluffing him out of his three queens wouldn't work. So Whitey had to have a better hand. It was so clear I wanted to shout. But Olinsky charged onward like the Light Brigade.

When it was over, Whitey showed his flush and raked in $52. On one hand. Jack, who had been watching said Olinsky shouldn't be allowed out at night without adult supervision.

***

During lunch the next day, Tommy came into the mess hall looking for me.

"Peter, you ever see a dolphin, you know a porpoise?"

"Yeah, in an aquarium."

"Well, I am offering you the opportunity of a lifetime. Step right this way, young man and see one of the wonders of the world...and for the special low price of only…. Just get your ass out here and you can see thirty of them.

So I and a few others followed him out onto the deck all the way to the bow. He pointed to the water. There on each side of the ship, at the very front, swimming effortlessly, at exactly the speed of the ship, were at least fifteen porpoises. They created a kind of wing on each side. At first they just swam quietly. Then, when we started clapping and cheering, they responded by jumping out of the water, one after the other, and then most of them at once, all the time easily keeping up with the ship.

I was amazed by their acrobatics but even more by their awareness of us. They were performing. But the best was yet to come. They must have communicated with each other, because simultaneously on both sides of the ship, they did a wheeling maneuver in which each but the last moved away from the ship, as the last swam under them toward it. They kept up this smooth rotation for about two minutes. We kept cheering, clapping and whistling. Then they went back to jumping and diving.

They were having a ball and so were we. They had obviously put on this show before. Their effortless, graceful movements were truly "poetry in motion." The overall effect was beautiful. As people started to drift away and the cheering died down, the porpoises left too. The show was over, but I smiled thinking about it all afternoon.

"That was unbelievable, wow," I just about gushed to Tommy as we walked away. "I had no idea they could do that. They're so beautiful and serene. I know they're intelligent, but not like that, as a group. Will they come back?"

"Maybe, it's a road show. They'll find another ship. They're beautiful to watch alright, but don't kid yourself; gentle critters can kill too. You should see what they do to a shark. They come at it from opposite sides at thirty knots and smash it."

***

I didn't have long to absorb the observation about killer critters. Late the next morning, while we were still in semi-tropical waters, someone yelled down into the engine room,

"Shark, they got a shark. You gotta see this."

I looked at Second.

"Anyone wants to go, go. That shit's not for me."

Soon, I would understand why. Raul, Billy and I raced up the ladders and out onto the deck. We could see a crowd near the stern house. A couple of guys were walking toward us, shaking their heads as we ran toward the crowd.

There, sure enough, was a shark, or what was left of it. It was about seven feet long and very much dead. It had been savagely butchered. DeLeo and an OS I didn't really know were still hacking away at it, both with red fire axes. Whitey was standing over them breathless, blood spattered all over his face and clothes.

I had never seen—and I hoped that I would never again see—anything so gruesome and horrible. They were viciously hacking the creature apart. Chunks of shark were flying around like large chips from a log. There was blood everywhere and on everyone. The look in the men's eyes was frightening— glazed over in a kind of primal hate. This was cruelty for its own sake, killing for the sake of killing. They did it simply because they could. It was dead now, but not long ago this once imposing creature had been very much alive and doing no harm to anyone on this ship.

When I had heard about the shark trawling line, I assumed the guys wanted to catch a shark to cut steaks for Cook to prepare. I had once seen shark steak on a menu in a seafood restaurant. It didn't sound enticing to me, but who knows? But eating clearly had nothing to do with this slaughter. The moment the bell attached to the line rang, indicating that something had grabbed the meat that was used for bait and was hooked, the men sprang into action. They grabbed the fire axes and poles with large metal hooks and ran to the line. It took several of them to pull in the shark with a small winch.

The thrashing thing must have put up quite a fight as they hauled it over the side with the hooked poles. One of them put had an axe through its eye and then the massacre was on. I learned all this later. At that moment I only knew that I was getting sick and that I couldn't stand to look at what these men had done.

I went back to the engine room in a daze. Billy and Raul just shrugged off the whole incident. But I could never again look at the three killers—there had been others that I hadn't seen—without seeing them in the thrall of this cruelty. What kind of person did something like this. Why? Was being impervious to this kind of savagery required to survive in this kind of world?

CHAPTER 19

Lorna

We docked during the day on a Saturday. That meant I would have two nights available, surrounding a Sunday. I had stayed away from Lorna for more than six weeks. If she hadn't had enough time, she never would. It was going to be now or never. But before calling Lorna, I called Rick, my former roommate, to see if she had called.

"Hey, Rick, Peter. I'm in port for a couple of days."

"So are you returning with your shield or on it?"

"With it so far. It's coming along, but that's all. Say,…"

"Yeah, your mother called just before she left to say she was starting in Paris, then would go to London with her Paris friend, and she would send you a letter with the rest of her itinerary."

"Great, thanks. Ah…"

"OK, Casanova, don't wet your pants. Yes, Lorna, the mystery lady called."

"Well, that's nice. Did she happen to say anything or did you hang up on her?"

"Not much really. She just asked if you were alright since she hadn't heard from you since you shipped out."

"Yeah, well, she said she needed time to think, so I gave her time. When did she call?"

"About ten days ago. She sounds really nice. I…"

"Why don't you just stick with Carla. She likes sex. To put it in your terms, the jury is still out on that with mystery lady. Anyway, how're you doing?"

"Working way harder than I wanted for a summer job. I expected this law firm internship to be a kind of introduction. But the only thing they've introduced me to is a lot of work."

"I bet you get to clean out a lot of boilers at 200 degrees too, huh?"

"Fuck you. No one made you do whatever shit you're doing."

He was right about that. Why in hell was I looking for sympathy? I had made a decision to do something, and I had to take what came with it. Try being a man, Peter, and stop feeling sorry for yourself.

I called Lorna at her office just before she got off work. She seemed thrilled to hear from me. Probably hadn't received a better offer.

"I've thought about you a lot. You never called."

That was something. "I've thought a lot about you too." True…when I wasn't thinking about Jillie or Dolores. "And I'm calling now. Remember you're the one who said you wanted time to think, so I gave you time. You can't have it both ways. Have you and your therapist come to any conclusions?" This wasn't at all the way I had wanted to sound. I was doing everything I could to kill any chance..

"Peter, I said I've thought a lot about you."

But I couldn't get off the roll I was on. "I understand that. So what did you end up thinking?"

"Why are being angry? I want to hear about everything you've done and what it's been like."

"I'm not angry Lorna. It's just that you wanted time to think about, as you put it, 'what to do with me.' Well, you've had time, and now I need to know. If you just want to hear my sea stories, then sometime we can get together for coffee and I'll be happy to recount my thrilling adventures at sea...."

"Peter, is all you have on your mind sex?"

"No, it's not all, but it's an important part. And either it is for you or it's not."

"OK. I want to be with you. Is that clear enough?"

"Yes, that's clear," I said, though I didn't know if it was or not. "I'm here until Monday morning, so I have two nights and all day tomorrow.

"That's great! Stay with me. Let's meet for dinner at the Chinese restaurant again," and after a pause, "and tomorrow morning we can go to the beach."

"Great. See you there in an hour and a half."

"Stay with me," sounded good. But the emphasis was on going to the beach. What the hell? This was a lot more positive than before. And I didn't want to stay on the ship. I had gotten paid a couple of weeks earlier, and with my poker winnings–even after my share of the night in Puerto Rico, I had more than $300—more money than I had ever had at one time—burning a hole in my pocket.

***

Billy and I took the bus into New York. He was staying with friends of his mother's on Park Avenue and 73rd Street. Very fancy, I explained. I told him about the situation with Lorna and what she had said.

He said with absolute conviction, "You're getting laid, buddy, you're getting laid. And that's a fact."

But then he hedged his bet with, "and you better not get back on the ship if you don't." The message was clear: it was up to me.

The trip didn't take an hour and a half, so I was in the restaurant well before Lorna. I had plenty of time to let my imagination run. By the time she arrived, I was breathing hard. Lorna was not. She seemed gentle, even angelic, but not the least bit sexy. Since she had been before—or that's certainly how I had seen her—I couldn't understand the change. It was as if she had a kind of force field around her.

We smiled at each other and I kissed her very gingerly, not sure whether she would break or I would get zapped by the force field. She did seem genuinely happy to see me, and despite my misgivings, I was very happy to see her too. It wasn't just the expectation of sex; I really liked being with her. She wanted to hear about the ship, the crew, Jacksonville, Puerto Rico, everything.

By the time we finished the first beer, Lorna could see the ship. With the egg drop soup and egg rolls, she got the fo'c'sle, meals, poker, Raul and Billy. The second beer brought out Jack, Second, Whitey, the porpoises and the shark. The last was probably not the best introduction to the main course. But with the shrimp in lobster sauce, she got Puerto Rico, though Dolores's part died on the cutting room floor.

They didn't offer dessert, so I was spared telling
any more. Anyway, it had been more than enough for
one sitting. She wanted to pay the check, as a welcome
home present for the conquering hero. As far as I was
concerned, I hadn't conquered a damn thing. In fact,
when push came to shove, I had barely been able to get
out of my own way. Maybe I was being a bit hard on
myself, but goddamn if I wasn't going to conquer the
dinner check!

It was almost 10:00 when we arrived at Lorna's apartment. It was a very small studio apartment. For the
money she traded space for location, right on Riverside
Drive. The point is, she had a convertible couch that
pulled out into a queen-size bed, and other than the
floor, there was nowhere else to sleep. So "stay with me"
meant we were sleeping together.

But sleep was the last thing on my mind. I had
often wondered about people's use of the expression
"sleeping with" someone to mean sex, fucking. A
graduate student I had spent a few days with said she
liked sleeping with me. When I asked her if she like
the sex too, she explained that it was a euphemism.
It made the subject easier to talk about. I liked this
new word, but I worried that it allowed an awful lot of
wiggle room.

Lorna asked if I would like anything to drink. I said,
"No thank you, two beers were plenty." I just looked
at her. I went to kiss her, really kiss her, force field be
damned. She wriggled free and fussed around, pouring
herself some kind of liqueur. I sat on the couch. She
sat at the other end. Stupid me, I should have sat in
the middle. She pulled one leg under her and sat on it

the way girls and women all seem to do when given the chance. She smiled.

For an English class I had read Oscar Wilde's *Lady Windermere's Fan*, and I now felt like we were playing out a Victorian scene. "Would you care to sit next to me, Miss Lorna?" I asked, pointing to the location I had in mind. She moved to the spot, but again sat with her right leg under her, which meant that her body was angled away from me. But her skirt wasn't designed for this position, and it rode well up her left leg. That was well within my reach so I put my hand on her leg and began stroking. She didn't react at all. She didn't push my hand away—which would have been strange since it had been there and a lot higher before—yet she didn't move closer or indicate that she liked it. So I went further, slowly moving my hand under her skirt, all the while smiling at her.

Finally she did *something*. She looked at me intently and returned to a familiar theme. "All you really want, Peter, is sex, isn't it? You're such a kid."

"No, it's not the *only* thing I want, but it is certainly an important part of what I want. I like you a lot, I like being with you, talking to you, being near you. And part of that is having sex with you. Yes, I want that. And when I was younger I was told that sex wasn't for kids; it was for adults. But to you wanting sex is kid-like? Well, that's really too bad...I mean for me."

"Don't be angry, Peter, I'm not trying to hurt your feelings." Then she was managing to without trying. "I mean, there's just so much more. You and I haven't seen each other in more than six weeks. And you expect me to just jump into bed with you and start fucking?"

"No, actually I expected to do a lot of other things before we ever got to fucking, things that, here and there, we've done some of before. And as for the six weeks, yeah, I've been on a ship for six weeks waiting for tonight. And you're right, it wasn't just to talk."

She didn't say anything. She looked at me again, not smiling, with an emotionless expression on her face. Moving her leg from under her, she kicked off her high heels. Continuing to look at me, she started unbuttoning her blouse. She stood up and took it off. Looking at her in her skirt and bra, I was more excited than I could remember being, more than when I had been with any naked woman. I didn't move, waiting for what Lorna would do next,

What she did was walk to her closet which was along the same wall as the couch, open the door which now blocked my view, and stand behind it. Why? She sure broke the mood, however brief it had been. Then she took off her clothes, throwing them on the floor in front of the closet. I waited expectantly for her to emerge naked. She didn't. I couldn't imagine what she was still doing behind the door. Then she emerged...covered from neck to feet in pale blue pajamas. Pajamas! As she closed the closet door and turned toward me, I put my hands over my face and shook my head. Jesus Christ! What the hell kind of roller coaster was this? Seemingly oblivious, Lorna just said, "Help me open the bed."

We opened the bed and took the pillows out of their covers. She turned down the blanket and disappeared into the bathroom. I took off my clothes, folded them on the floor, found my toothbrush in my small blue bag, and waited. As she came out, I stood up, naked, and in a state of visible excitation. Shyness was not one of my problems. She didn't seem to notice as she climbed into bed. When I came out, I was very much in the same state, but she couldn't notice. She had turned out the lights.

I got into the bed next to Lorna and put my arms around her. She didn't pull away or resist. I pulled her toward me and started opening the buttons of her pajama top. Again she didn't resist. As I kissed her, I stroked her everywhere. Soon the pajamas were gone. She didn't resist any of it. She didn't do anything. I knew what would give her pleasure. The graduate student and another woman had each given me very explicit instruction. But when I went in that direction, she did stop me.

"Why?"

"I don't want you to."

"Because you'll get as excited as I am? And you don't want that."

"Because I don't know what I want."

"Well, I do." Certainly that was true for me, for her, clearly not. And I started massaging her seriously. Again she didn't resist. Then we did it. We fucked. More accurately, I fucked her and she let me do it. I wanted to make love—to the extent I knew what that meant, but she wasn't having any part of that. Rather, it was as if she said, "You want to fuck? OK, just do it."

A gentleman, or someone with a bit more maturity than I had, would have stopped, maybe said good night and left, maybe said let's try again another time. But I was bursting at the seams with frustration and had nei-ther the equanimity nor the self-control to do either

It was over very quickly. Clearly, she wanted it to be, and at this point I did too. I held her and kissed the back of her neck as she turned away from me. I said I was sorry, and I was very sorry, though I wasn't exactly sure for what. She put on her pajamas and lay on her side. She hadn't made a sound for over fifteen minutes. I lay on my back with my hands behind my head, thinking. My thoughts alternated between wondering how I had managed to screw this up so badly, to make her so unhappy, and what a shit I was for doing it. But not for long. In minutes, I was asleep.

The next morning I awoke to the smell of eggs and toast. I lay with my eyes closed, afraid to open them. I didn't know in what state I would find Lorna. Part of me wished it was Nebraska. But she was cheery and asked if I had slept well.

She was wearing the pajama top and panties. Damn, was the roller coaster going up again? But she quickly went behind the closet door and came out dressed in a tee shirt and shorts. I forgot; we were going to the beach. As we ate breakfast she said nothing about the night before. I thought about nothing else. I looked at her. She was pretty. She was nice. She was everything she had been the day we met. But we should still be in bed, not having breakfast like an old married couple— or like roommates!

***

Lorna was in such good spirits that I couldn't help joining in her mood. The subway had emerged from the long underground portion of the ride out onto an open stretch in the sunshine, the last leg of the trip before taking the bus to Jones Beach. The car was filled with couples and families on their way to the ocean. I put my arm around her, and Lorna leaned against me as we looked out the window for the first sight of the water. She looked up at me and said, "Let's have a really nice time, Peter."

"Sure! That's what I want too."

We let the ambiguity just hang in the air. The day... and the night would be whatever they would be.

It was 1:00 by the time we got to the beach, and it was crowded. Nothing like Jax Beach, which I described to Lorna. There were people lying on towels everywhere. It was awkward to walk between them. Finally we found a spot, about as private as the subway. We both had our bathing suits on under our clothes, so we were beach-ready in seconds.

We spread out the huge beach towel and sat. Lorna spread sun lotion on my back and legs, caressing and massaging as she did. I did the same for her as she turned her head toward me and we looked at each other intently. (In her case, I assumed it was intently since she was wearing enormous sunglasses.) This was far more sensuous than anything we had done the night before.

There was nothing to do but lie on the blanket or go for a swim. We did both, asking the couple with two small children next to us to watch our things as we went to the water.

We swam around a bit and tried to ride the waves. I held her as we jumped up with the swells. She wrapped her legs tightly around my waist. Maybe we *would* have a really nice time!

Lorna had brought a picnic, and we ate ham sand-wiches and celery sticks.   But she hadn't brought any-thing to drink, so I went off in search of a place to get sodas while she lay on her stomach and read a book. It took me about twenty minutes to find the oasis and return with the drinks. As I walked around, I saw hun-dreds of women and girls lying on their towels, some of them very attractive, and I realized just how happy I was being with Lorna.

We lay on the towel, mostly not saying a word. Our arms touched and my skin tingled. The sun was hot, but heat was something I was used to! But by 4:00 Lorna had had enough of the sun. Of course, we didn't have an umbrella—only people with cars had brought umbrel-las—and there were no shaded areas of any kind. So it was time to leave. Lorna wanted to change out of her bathing suit. Well, that would be a trick. She said all I had to do was fold the towel in half, hold the towel taut, with the fold vertical, and she would stand inside the fold. OK, I thought, I'm game.

I did as she said, and she got inside the towel. Only her head and feet were visible as she took off her bath-ing suit and just stood naked looking at me. I realized she was enjoying this. It was exciting. I could simply drop the towel and there she would be, stark naked in front of a thousand people. And we did have an audi-ence. I told her that, and she just smiled. Then, in no hurry, she put on her clothes. She certainly knew how to get my attention. She could do such sexy things when they had nothing to do with sex.

The ride back was as quiet as the day had been. I felt a real closeness that didn't seem to require words.

I also didn't know what to say. Whatever the mood, it was created by Lorna. If I initiated anything, physical or verbal, it seemed intrusive. When we got back to her place we realized that despite our efforts, we still had sand all over us.

I suggested a shower, together. No, she wanted to take a bath. Well, I could imagine that together too, but so could she and she didn't invite me. She suggested I go ahead and shower, but I insisted that she take her bath first.

Her approach made more sense, of course, as my shower would only take a couple of minutes. But waiting wasn't my concern. If I went first, I would have to dress or sit on the couch naked and force the issue again. No way. This time it was going to be up to her. If, when I came out of the shower she was waiting for me naked, or, as they said in the movies, "in something comfortable," I would know. If she was fully dressed, I would also know. I tried to read one of her fashion magazines while I waited, but my head was elsewhere as my heart pounded in anticipation.

She came out of the bathroom wrapped in a towel. I looked at her longingly as she came toward me, but she walked by and I didn't touch her as we passed each other. The cold water stung but felt good. It also served to keep me somewhat under control. Still, as I dried off, my feeling of anticipation was overwhelming. Not to push the point, so to speak, I wrapped the towel around my waist as I opened the bathroom door. And there was Lorna, standing in front of the open refrigerator, wet hair pulled back, dressed in crisp tan shorts, a long sleeved, blue button-down shirt tied at her waist, and leather sandals, the kind you had to unfasten to take off. How about that.

Every part of me went limp in an instant. I was so disappointed that for a moment I felt like crying. Wow! I couldn't believe it. She was on and then off, like a switch. If she had no desire now, after our time together that day, she sure wasn't going to have it later that night just because it was dark.

"What are you doing Lorna?"

"I'm looking to see what I can make for us to eat."

Made a lot of sense. After all, it was 6:30. We certainly couldn't wait until, say, 8:00 to worry about eating. "Lorna, we need to talk," I said, as I sat on the end of the couch. "Please sit down." She came over and sat on the couch, not quite at the other end. "Lorna, what were you thinking would happen tonight?"

"I would make some dinner, then we could watch TV, maybe go for a walk along the river. It can't be a late night. I have to go to work tomorrow, and you, you have to leave when, by 6:00?"

"Look, I don't know what's going on, what is in your head, but there's something wrong. Yeah, I'm leaving in the morning, and you have no idea when I'll be back. If you don't have any desire for me now, right now, when the hell do you think you're going to have it? You know you are sexy as hell whenever we are in a place where we can't do anything about it, or there's no time to do anything about it. But when we're here, alone, with nothing but time, then you've never heard of sex. It's the furthest thing from your mind. Do you or don't you have any desire for me right now? Can you tell me that?"

"Yes I do, but...."

"There's no but. Either you do or you don't. And if you do, then why are you dressed now? Hell, why were you dressed this morning when I woke up, why were you like a rag doll last night. What the hell is it?"

"You aren't going to understand. You can't understand."

"Oh, but I do understand," and I took off the towel, got clean underwear and socks from my bag and got dressed. "Before I left, I asked you if you were afraid of sex, and you said no, you wanted sex too much. Well, that's bullshit and you know it. You're scared to death of sex. It's not that you don't know what to do with me. You don't know what to do with you!" She looked down at her feet and didn't say anything. But I wasn't done. "You're driving me crazy, and you seem to enjoy it. You're obviously not getting much for your money with your shrink, are you. You see him all the time—how many times have you seen him since I left, fifteen?—and he hasn't even gotten you to be honest with yourself, no less with me." At that she started to cry silently and walked back to the refrigerator.

"I still haven't told him about you."

"Oh that's just great. That's terrific! What the hell are you doing? You have a problem, Lorna, and you know what it is, and you're not doing anything about it. I don't think you want to do anything about it."

"You just don't understand anything."

"Right, you told me that. I'm just a kid and I want sex. Well, you could say, "Peter, I'm afraid," and I could try to help. But you just play this game, and your game is driving me crazy. I don't want to play anymore."

"You're not just a kid. You have no feeling." Now she was really crying. "You're just a bastard, a selfish bastard. Since it's so terrible for you, why don't you just leave?" And then with a sudden burst of fury, "Just get the hell out, now!"

I went toward her, to hold her. But she backed away from me and screamed, "No, get out of here; get out of here!" I stood and looked at her. She picked up one of her clay creations to throw at me. I said, "You don't have to do that. I'm going." I went to the door and turned to look at her as I opened it. I shook my head in bewilderment and said goodbye. As I closed the door behind me, I heard the clay thing smash against the wall.

CHAPTER 20

The Almost Boondoggle

of All Time

Leaving Lorna's apartment I felt dazed, wounded. Yet it was clear that it was I who had hurt *her.* I walked for a few blocks trying to decide what to do. Going back seemed a terrible idea. I clearly didn't know how to talk to her or deal with her at all. I could find a place to eat and stay at my mother's apartment, now empty. But what was the point? No, if I hurried, I could still catch a bus back to the ship.

On the bus, much like the first time, there were very few people. I spread out over two seats and stared out the window, but this time I saw nothing of the passing scene. Instead I saw a vivid replay of every moment of the last twenty- four hours, every moment spent with Lorna. When it came to the last scene, the projector got stuck, and it played over and over again. It had all happened so fast. Her whole being had changed in an instant. I hadn't intended any of it. Why couldn't she just be—I was looking for the word "normal," but what I found myself thinking was—"the way I wanted her to be?" Because she wasn't.   Because she has a problem, and I wasn't interested in her problem.   I didn't want her to have a problem.   I wanted her to be as sexy and full of desire as she was pretty.   I had a fantasy of wild sex with her—and on my schedule—and when it didn't happen I acted like a spoiled kid. And there it was again.

For me, sex was an activity, like exercise, only more fun.   I had the equipment.   I had some idea how to use it, and the rest should somehow just follow.   And sometimes it happened just like that.   But now I had real doubts.   I had once worked for two weeks on a house-framing crew.   One of the men had messed up the joint between a rafter and a ceiling joist.   As he glared at his saw, the foreman said, "When things don't work out, blame the carpenter not the tool."   Well, things hadn't worked out, and perhaps a more experienced carpenter would have known to use very different tools.

***

When I got back to the ship, despite what was surely good reception in port, the TV was off and both poker games were in full swing.   I wasn't really in the mood to play, but I needed to do something that would get my mind off Lorna.   Everyone noticed my "tan"—although it was a lot redder than that—and they asked about Jones Beach, where none of them had ever been.

"So, did you get anything at the beach besides a sunburn?"

I answered inscrutably with what I thought was manly gravity, "I took something with me to the beach and lost it when I got back.   We going to play or just talk?"

I should have just kept talking. Although I was certainly conscious of the money in my pocket, I don't think it affected the way I played. But I lost. I lost big—for me—and quickly. We were playing five card draw—my game—and in the second game I was dealt a jack-high straight, a straight with the initial five cards— a pat hand. Very rare indeed. I bet it big and lost to a flush, a flush that Max had drawn *keeping three cards*. That is something only a fool, or someone with absolutely no regard for the money, would ever do. If it would cost you money to draw cards, you draw to a flush only if you have four suited cards, not three. The odds against drawing a flush with only three suited cards are way too high. Well, he kept three hearts, and goddamn if he didn't draw two more. Since I assumed he had three of a kind, I was willing to take my chances against his drawing a full house. He kept betting and so did I. I lost $24 in one of the largest pots since I started playing.

There was more to come. A few minutes later, still playing the same game, I drew a flush. I had four suited and the betting hadn't been high, so I went for it and got it. Two others bet like they had good hands. But in five card draw, with nothing wild, a flush is a very good hand, so I bet it hard. I drove out one of the oilers, so it was between Bosun, who rarely played, and me. But the poker gods—like the gods of women—weren't smiling on me today. Bosun drew a pair to three of a kind and had a full house! How about that. I lost $22. Just like that, I had lost in two hands more than I had ever won in a night. The curse of the second best hand. OK, Peter, two strikes, thinking back to Lorna. If things happen in threes, what's next?

That night was my worst since getting on the ship—worse than the night waiting for the Kid. Losing all that money really bothered me. I knew it had to happen sometime, but I felt stupid, a failure. It was no consolation that at the next table Olinsky had lost again, this time $190! Nor did it seem to matter that I was still more than $100 ahead overall. It was as if I had thrown *this* money away or left it on a bus.

Even though I couldn't think of anything I should have done differently, I felt, as with Lorna, that it was my fault. I just wasn't ready to deal with what life threw at me like a man. I had handled the situation with Lorna terribly, like a kid. And somehow I had played poker like a kid.

I went to bed knowing that it would be hard to get to sleep. Just when I might have succeeded, Billy came in. He had just returned from New York—someone must have driven him to the ship—and he was drunk. Great. He sang and smashed around the small fo'c'sle for a while, then passed out on his bunk and started snoring. He snored so loud I was sure they could hear it in the next fo'c'sle with the doors closed. Somehow Raul slept through it all, but I couldn't. I tried to wake Billy or to turn him over. I couldn't do either. He just got louder.

There was no way I could sleep, but I couldn't even stand the sound, so I put on my sneakers and went out with my blanket and pillow. I might not be able to sleep, but at least it would be quiet. I lay on the deck looking up at the stars, the absolute peacefulness above and around me in stark contrast to the turmoil I felt inside.

***

Strike three appeared unceremoniously enough in the form of a case of jock itch. Considering the heat and humidity and the fact that I was sweating all day, every day, it was surprising that it hadn't happened earlier. But I had it now, and I couldn't get rid of it. No amount of washing, different soaps, ointments that two of the guys gave me, helped at all. Every day it got worse. From what started literally as an itch, it had evolved into a suppurating, inflamed rash on both sides of my groin. It was ever present, and it had started to really hurt.

I worked through it and didn't say anything about it to the engineers, but I was concerned that someone would notice because I thought it smelled, and I winced involuntarily whenever I moved my legs. The reason I didn't say anything had everything to do with strikes one and two. I didn't really think the engineers would have anything better for the rash than what the guys had given me, but the real reason was what they would think. Who but a goddamn kid would get jock itch on a goddamn ship anyway? And who but a kid would complain about it? But being a man—a very stupid one— wasn't getting the problem fixed either.

I had enjoyed my night under the stars, and a couple of nights before we got to Puerto Rico I decided to do it again, this time with my mattress. It was near midnight as I lay out on the deck, trying to think of anything but the jock itch.

Suddenly I could see movement near the back of one of the containers, though I couldn't hear anything. No one was talking, and as I had learned, with the ambient sound of the sea, rubber soled shoes on a hard steel deck were impossible to hear. But there was definitely someone there.

Early on I had wondered whether any of the crew ever tried to open a container and steal whatever was inside. But when I examined the containers I saw that the door bolt of each container had a thick wire loop through it with a plastic seal. It would be very clear if a container had been opened during its voyage. So what was someone doing skulking around the back of a container, and it was definitely some*one*, not two.

As the moon came out from behind a cloud, I could see that the someone was Tommy. I was in the shadow of the stern house. Tommy was clearly looking for something at the back of a container. He seemed to find it and suddenly smashed his left hand hard against whatever he had found, letting out a curse as he did. What the hell? What had he done? I didn't want to startle him, but I wanted to talk to him. So I started softly playing my harmonica.

He heard it immediately and looked in my direction.

"Is that you, Peter?"

"Yeah. What are you doing?"

"Not too much, except I really hurt my hand, cut it bad. Tripped on something and went to grab the back of the container. Must have cut it on something jagged back there."

"Let me see," I said, as I got up and walked toward him.

"What the hell are you doing out here?"

"Got my mattress, sleeping under the stars. It's nice; you should try it."

"Not for me. Jesus, this hurts."

It was bleeding badly right below the bone between his index finger and thumb. But he had come prepared, as he was already wrapping two handkerchiefs around the wound.

Of course, I could have just let it go, just shut up. But I didn't. Tommy wasn't some crazy tough guy. He was the nicest guy on the ship. "Tommy, don't bullshit me. I saw you smack your hand against the container, and before that I saw you looking around it for something. What's going on?"

"Peter, you're a good kid, but don't push your luck. Don't mess around in something that's none of your business."

"Look Tommy, I'm not messing around in anything. I'm not going to say anything. I don't want to make any trouble for you, hell, for anybody, but particularly not for you. I just want to know what you're doing. It's not as if I was following you around, you know. I was just lying here getting ready to go to sleep."

"OK, you saw what you saw, but if you say a goddamn word about this…"

He didn't finish the sentence. I got the message and nodded.

"OK, here's the deal, you know Eastern Airlines is on strike."

I looked at him as if he might *be* crazy.

"If you have to sign off a ship because you're medically not fit for duty, they've got to get you back to your home port. If there's a bunk on a merchant ship, you go that way. But if there's no room on any merchant ship, just like there's no room on this one, then they've got to fly you back. Only they can't, because the only airline that goes from San Juan back to New York/New Jersey is Eastern and it's been on strike since June 23rd."

Again I just looked at him. I still didn't get it.

"Man, for a smart guy, you're thick as an oak. If they can't get you back, they've got to put you up at a hotel, a hotel that meets the union contract standards, until they can. Well, guess what. The only hotel like that is the fucking Caribe Hilton on the beach in San Juan. This strike could last who knows how long, and I'm gonna live at the Hilton for nothing. That's why I took this job. I had to wait a bit once I was on board, but now, Pina Coladas, women, the beach. You finally get it?"

How about that. I got it. I definitely got it. I just couldn't believe it, and I told him so.

"Come on Tommy, so many things could go wrong. They might not find you unfit for duty. The strike could end tomorrow. Some other airline could fly you to someplace else and then they make you take a bus to New Jersey. They could put you in some dump in Santurce. How could you just hurt yourself like that?"

"Look, with a cut like this, I can't perform my duties. I've got to use two hands and I can't. Period. They fly you back to where you came from. That's what they do. I don't know why. Airline strikes last forever. They just do. And I told you, it's the Hilton. I know a guy, had to stay in PR for some reason, they put him in the Hilton. I'm telling you, I'm golden."

Maybe he was. It still sounded too good to be true. Then, as if it would assuage my doubts, he had another idea.

"Peter, that jock itch I gave you the cream for, if it's not better, a lot better, you should go to the naval station with me tomorrow and have it looked at. Maybe they'll find you not fit for duty too. What do you have to lose? You have to get it taken care of anyway. You go to the naval station, to the medical center. The worst that happens is they take care of it. But who knows, you could be in luck. And let me tell you, that would really be in luck."

Well, how about that. Instead of strike three, I might be about to hit a grand slam! But then I wasn't so sure. Of course, it would be great to have a vacation at the Caribe Hilton, but then what? I pointed out that I would lose my job on this ship and that I couldn't get another one whenever I wanted—as he could. He dismissed that with a wave, saying that when he signed on to the *Rufus Saxton* there had been lots of OS and wiper jobs on the board, way more than a couple of months before.

***

The next day I talked to First about my case of terminal jock itch. He was sympathetic, said he used to get it until he started using some kind of powder every day to prevent it. I told him it was really bad and getting worse every day, and that I wondered if I could go to the medical center at the naval station when we got to Puerto Rico. I had never asked for anything since I was on the ship, never taken an hour off, did whatever they told me to do. He agreed immediately. I didn't mention the airline strike, and no doubt it never occurred to him that anyone could be found unfit for duty because of jock itch.

It had rained in San Juan the night before we arrived, and the humidity must still have been100%. As the cab drove into the naval station the rich scent of bougainvillea—Raul's cousin had identified it for me—wafted in on the breeze. It was a lovely place, clean white buildings, neat and well-maintained grounds, all green and lined with aromatic flowers. What a place to go for jock itch!

Tommy showed me his hand and it looked awful. I don't care how wonderful a boondoggle he might get, I couldn't imagine doing such a thing, really hurting myself deliberately. I had a pretty high pain tolerance, but that just couldn't be normal.

And then there was the complete dishonesty of the whole thing. This was a very different guy than I had thought. But what did I know about him? What did I know about any of them? As we sat in the waiting room, I wondered about the continuing roller coaster. Nothing seemed predictable. But that's what I had said I wanted.

Tommy went first. He was in the examining room for about twenty-five minutes. In that time, I went through every possible scenario, like I imagined a father awaiting the birth of a child. Tommy came out with the doctor, a grave expression on his face, as the doctor told him the injury to the tendon above the thumb was going take awhile to heal. But as soon as the door closed behind the doctor, Tommy's expression changed to a Cheshire cat grin. He thrust his right thumb upward and shook my hand.

Now it was my turn. After explaining my problem to someone I assumed was another doctor, I took off my clothes, and he took a close look. He thought it was a very bad case, one of the worst he had seen. He said he didn't see how anyone could work in the heat of an engine room with something like that. Then he said he would have to get the doctor to look at it. Damn, I thought he was the doctor, but no, *he* was a nurse.

The doctor who had examined Tommy was less concerned.

"Yeah, this is about as bad as I've seen. Surprised it got this bad in just four days."

"I'm a wiper. I work in the engine room and it's over 120 degrees all the time, even 150 degrees and higher in some places."

He was very sympathetic and encouraging.

"It's definitely not going to be a fun-filled few days, but with the antibiotic cream and the other cream I'm giving you it should be gone by the time you got back up north."

"Doctor, do you really think it's a good idea, I mean safe, to work with a condition like this?

He smiled and looked at me with an expression of new-found understanding.

"Son, if you think I'm going to write you up as not fit for duty...for jock itch, well, you've been sold a whale of a sea story."

So Tommy and I went back to the ship, batting one for two. But at least I had stuff for the jock itch and the doctor did say it would be gone soon. I knew I was fit for duty, so I was neither surprised nor disappointed. I really didn't want to lose the job. If Tommy was wrong and there wasn't another job that I could get, I would be out of luck and back in the print shop.

But Tommy was on top of the world. I congratulated him on what might be the greatest boondoggle of all time and assured him that I wouldn't spoil it for him in any way.

Back on the ship, Chief Mate told Tommy to go to the union hall in Santurce and wait for a ship to take him back, and just as Tommy had said, in the meantime he could stay at a hotel, some place like the Hilton. He said he didn't know what ship would have space, and that Tommy should check with the union each day to see how long before SeaLand would just fly him back. He obviously wasn't focusing on the airline strike. Tommy said thank you and went around saying goodbye to the crew. I wished him good luck, and he said thanks but he already had all the luck he needed.

As I slathered the creams on the raw rash, my skin burned like hell, but I could feel the stuff begin to work immediately. I wasn't going to be able to go out that night, but I was going to sleep a lot better. Tommy would certainly be sleeping well. I never saw him again, so I never found out how long he got to stay on the beach. But the airline strike lasted almost another two months.

CHAPTER 21

Missing at Sea

Happily, through the wonders of modern medicine, the jock itch was cured quickly. Also happily, I returned to my moderate winning ways in poker. However, before I could play again, I had to come to terms with two important facts of poker, facts which shouldn't have been so elusive to me: no matter how hard you try to avoid it, from time to time you will have the second best hand and not know it. And because of that, if you play poker enough, from time to time you will lose more than you're ready to lose.

Very much thinking about my father and his gambling, I didn't want to play poker every night. Instead, I continued the occasional long talks with Jack—slowly piecing together the story of his life, played music with Billy, read, and listened to baseball.

On the night before arriving in Port Elizabeth there was another Baltimore Orioles game on TV. I thought it would be a nice idea to see if Cook wanted to watch. When I had told him on "the night of the long knife" that I would tell him when there was a game he didn't seem at all enthusiastic. Still, I had never tried. So around 8:00 I went to his fo'c'sle. The door was closed and I knocked. There was a vague response which I interpreted positively and opened the door. Cook was sitting on his bunk listening to the game.

"Hey, great dinner. The breaded veal cutlet was as good as my mother's, and she's from Hungary where they really know how to make it."

It really was excellent. He nodded but didn't say anything, his look saying, "You didn't come here to talk about the food, so what do you want?"

Responding to the look, I said, "Baltimore game's on TV. You want to watch?"

"Nah, just gonna stay here. Comforts of home."

I stood leaning against the door frame. "You mind if I ask you a question?"

Again he didn't speak, just shrugged his shoulders.

"You know the food is really good. You're a terrific cook, a real chef." He didn't acknowledge the statement. "You could be a chef in a really good restaurant. How come you don't do that?"

He looked at the floor, and the expression on his face suggested that this line of questioning wasn't to his liking. Suddenly he looked up, as if he had changed his mind.

"Other guys have said that. At the army cooking school they said I was good, said I should go to a real cooking school when I got out." Then he shook his head. "Wouldn't have worked out. Could you see me with all those fags?"

"I don't know much about it, but I don't think all chefs are fags."

"Don't have to be all. I don't like fags. But that doesn't matter anyway. I wouldn't fit in anyway. Those jobs, you have to like to work with people. Nah, this is good, right here."

I didn't know what else to say. I certainly didn't want to make it more awkward for him than it already seemed to be. I thought it might be good to listen to the game with him, right there. But he sure wasn't suggesting it, and I was afraid he would think *I* was a fag if I suggested it. So I just repeated that the food was really good, saluted and left.

He would have been an interesting guy to get to know. But I realized that in one way, he was like most of the guys on the ship: if they wanted people to get to know them, they wouldn't be on the ship.

When I got back to the mess hall, I joined the guys watching the ball game. On the other side of the room, oblivious to the loud sounds of the broadcast, Whitey's gang was playing poker. Around the seventh inning, while intently watching the game, we were all distracted by a sudden movement at the poker table. Olinsky stood up, threw his cards on the table, and for ten seconds glared silently at Whitey. Then he turned and walked out.

An important feature of the compensation arrangement on the ship, one used by many of the crew, was the ability to draw advances—as much as 90%—against your base salary. I had resisted the temptation. But particularly on a coastwise run when you were in port often and might need money, it could be very convenient, if not an absolute necessity. Paying poker debts was another common reason for an advance.

Soon after Olinsky left, the poker game ended and some of the players came over to watch the baseball game and talk to Max, Olinsky's friend.

"Jesus Christ, Max, He drew his full 90% for July, and he lost all of it and more, over $900, mostly to Whitey. Kept saying he was going to win it back, but, you know, he just lost more."

"You know, he has a wife and he's going to go home with no money, only a debt?"

They continued on about compulsive gamblers. What would Olinsky do? Would Whitey let him pay it off over time? The one thing they all agreed on was that Olinsky shouldn't be allowed to play anymore.

"I think that's what pissed off Olinsky, Glen said, Whitey kept telling him to stop playing, knowing that would only make him mad and make him play more."

Somebody said, "What the hell, he's not a kid."

***

We arrived at Port Elizabeth at around 7:00 the next morning. As Billy, Raul and I went to breakfast, there was clearly something wrong. There were several guys standing in the passageway outside the mess hall talking quietly. I took a step into the room and saw two men in suits sitting at a table talking with Max. One of them looked up as I entered and gave me a look that said "Get out, now." There was no one else in the room and no food. Stepping back out, I looked at Billy and Raul and shrugged.

Tony responded to my unasked question.

"Those two in the suits are FBI. Olinsky's missing, disappeared last night sometime during the 12:00 to 4:00 watch.

"Jesus Christ, you mean he's dead?" my mouth frozen open, my eyes wide.

"Unless he's hiding or he's a real good swimmer, yeah. That's why the FBI's here. They came on board the minute we docked. Been here for about an hour talking to the crew, one by one. They'll talk to you too. You play poker with him last night?"

"Hell, no, I didn't play poker with him. I never played with him. He only played in the big game. I was in the mess hall watching the baseball game, me and a few guys, and Whitey and Olynsky and those guys were playing on the other side of the room, but I wasn't playing."

"I hear he lost big and got really mad at Whitey. Is that right?"

"Well, he *looked* mad, but he didn't say anything. Just left." I didn't mention what the others had said.

Max came out and asked if anybody had seen Jack or Whitey. The FBI guys wanted them next. Nobody had, so he went off in the direction of their fo'c'sles. I wondered if we were supposed to go to work. Tony didn't know.

Despite my shock I also wondered about breakfast. He knew about that. It was laid out on deck on a table in front of the main house, so we all went out to eat. It seemed the FBI was going to be using the mess hall for quite a while.

I couldn't find a reaction that was the right fit for the situation. I had no emotion. Somebody, somebody I knew, had died, but it didn't seem real. Nine hours ago Olinsky was standing no more than ten feet from me. Now he was dead? How the hell did he die? Did he just jump off the ship? Did he kill himself because he had lost all that money? Whitey would have let him off the hook, given him time to pay. Why wouldn't he? Then I thought about the shark. Still, even though it was a lot of money, you don't kill yourself over $900. I said all that to the guys outside. What I didn't say was that when he left the game and glared at Whitey, he didn't look at all crazy, depressed or confused. He just looked mad as hell.

Bosun offered his perspective. "If someone kills himself, he's gotta be crazy, or sick, or something really bad, so if Olinsky killed himself, no one's ever going to figure it out. But maybe he didn't kill himself. Maybe someone killed him. That sure must be what the FBI's trying to find out."

One thing I knew from my discussion with Max, way back on the morning of the yellow box demonstration: he didn't fall off the ship accidentally. Either he was so upset about losing the money and how he would deal with his family that he jumped—which I just didn't believe—or someone killed him. And though I wasn't going to say it to anyone, I was sure Olinsky was murdered. And I was pretty sure I knew exactly how and when it happened. I just didn't know who had done it.

It had to be during bow watch. Tommy had explained that bow watch goes back to sailing ship days and is a belts-and-suspenders safety measure still used on most freighters at night, despite sophisticated radar. During the nighttime watches, there is always an AB or OS standing at the bow scanning the horizon for the lights of another ship, or anything else that might be out there. In days of yore, if the man on bow watch saw something, he would yell some classic call back to the helmsman. In 1962, he picked up the telephone at the bow.

I had already experienced the effect of the ocean's surprisingly loud, constant ambient sound. Even at the side of the ship I hadn't been able to hear Max coming as close as two feet behind me. The bow cutting through the water made it even louder. And there was virtually no light on the deck between the forward group of containers and the bow. It was clear to me that if someone wanted to sneak up on the person standing bow watch, it would be a piece of cake to do it.

If someone had it in for Olinsky—for whatever reason—all he had to do was sneak up on him while he was on bow watch, hit him on the head with something hard—either killing him or knocking him out—and dump him overboard right there. It seemed to me that the stack of containers would prevent any chance observation by someone on the bridge.

But if it was clear to me, a rookie, it would a lot more clear to the other members of the crew—and for sure the FBI.

Of course, I didn't *know* that's what happened, but it sure seemed more likely than Olinsky killing himself because he had to tell his wife he lost $900! But who would kill him and why? The problem with figuring that out was that I didn't really know Olinsky at all and therefore didn't know anything about his relationship with the rest of the crew except the obvious, Whitey, and I didn't even know the extent of that. Max and Olyinsky seemed to be friends, but Max never talked about him. The FBI guys spent a long time with Max.

My ignorance didn't prevent me from developing a theory, and it was pretty far-fetched even for my sense of drama: Whitey killed Olinsky because Whitey was afraid that Olinsky would kill *him* to eliminate the poker debt? A preemptive strike. I certainly knew where that notion came from. Pretty crazy maybe, but it was the only idea I had. And I certainly wasn't going to open my mouth about it.

That determination was soon put to the test. Just before lunch, First told me to go to the mess hall and talk to the FBI. OK, here goes, I thought. There wouldn't be much for me to say since they would have gotten everything from the others. Wrong. I would quickly learn about stonewalling. The FBI agents introduced themselves and I gave them my seaman's document. They took down the information and consulted a notebook.

"How long have you been working on this ship?"

""About two months."

"And what do you do, your position?"

"Wiper. I work in the engine room."

"What did you do before that?"

"I was in college, NYU. I finished my second year in May."

After an exchange about who I worked with, which was difficult because I knew only the first names of some of the men and only the last names of others, they got down to it.

"How well did you know Frank Olinsky?"

"So well that I didn't even know that was his first name."

When they gave me a blank look, I realized that being a wise guy really wasn't going to play well with these guys.

"He was an AB on the 4:00 to 8:00 watch and I work days in the engine room, so I never had any contact with him. The only times I saw him was during the poker games."

At that they looked at each other and then back at me.

"Poker games?"

Oh shit. Why did I have to add that? But I couldn't believe that I was the first—and only?—person to mention anything about the poker games. Hell, that had to be what this was all about. The rest of the guys must have been afraid of implicating anyone, so they had said nothing about the poker games—nothing at all. And now I had. How about that. Great, Peter. Way to go. Thinking on your feet again.

"Ah...there were poker games at night, sometimes."

"What were the stakes?"

"Well, there were two games, one for a quarter and a half, the other for a buck and two."

"Did you play?"

"Yes, in the lower stakes game."

"How about Mr. Olinsky, which game did he play in?"

"Uh...he played in the higher stakes game."

"Always?"

"Yeah, well, when there was a game. Like I said, they played sometimes."

"How often?"

"It's hard to say. Sometimes we had reception and the guys watched TV. Sometimes there just weren't enough guys, and," I added eagerly, "a lot of times I wasn't there because I was doing something else or just didn't feel like playing."

"But there was a regular game?"

"Yeah, more or less, pretty much." I knew where this was going and I didn't like it at all.

"So who did Mr. Olinsky play with in those high stakes poker games?" There it was. Oh shit. Now what?

"Well, it varied, you know, different guys. It's hard to remember."

"Cut the crap, kid. No one around here even mentions the fucking poker games until you, and now you don't know who played. The games were in this room presumably, and you're sitting what six, seven feet from the game, and they play regularly, and there's only thirty-three men on the ship, and eleven of them are officers, so out of the other twenty-two men you can't recall who played in those games. That's what you're telling us?"

This was going to get bad, which is why no one had mentioned the poker game—that is, until I did. Right. Peter the informer. So I told them who played. Despite their assumption, I did have a hard time remembering everyone, but I made sure to put Whitey casually in the middle of the list, trying not to draw attention to him by mentioning him first or last. I found some comfort in the thought that no one would know who mentioned the poker games. It certainly shouldn't surprise anyone that the subject had come up. But this wasn't going to be the end of this line of questioning. It was just getting started.

"So how did he do, Mr. Olinsky?"

"Look, as I said, I never played with him, so I don't know for sure."

They just looked at me.

"What I heard, but I really don't know, is that he often lost. But…"

"Did he lose a lot?"

"I really don't know." And that, technically, was true. I had heard, but I didn't know.

"Were there any incidents, disagreements, that sort of thing?"

"Not that I know of. They played poker and that was that." The long glare from the previous night was *not* coming out in this interview.

Then one straight out of the movies: "Were you aware of Mr. Olinsky having any enemies among the crew?"

"I told you, I didn't know the guy. I must have spoken to him maybe twice in more than two months. I don't know who his friends were, and I don't know who his enemies were, if he had either. We didn't eat together or work together."

"Thank you very much," then looking at my seaman's document, "Mr. Ernster. You've been very helpful."

And that was that. It was time for lunch when we finished, so I went back outside and had a sandwich from the table with the other guys. No one spoke about Olinsky or their interviews with the FBI. I knew that thanks to me some of them would soon have another. I returned to the engine room.

I had expected the FBI to investigate for days, grilling the crew over and over. They did call one of the firemen back—I saw him leave after First spoke to him, and I assumed they called back all the men I had mentioned. But no one said a word about it, and by the time I finished work they were gone.

No one had been arrested. I couldn't believe that there wouldn't be more. How could they just give up? Hell, how could they leave *me* alone? Once I started them on the poker theme, couldn't they tell that I knew more, that *everyone* knew more? This wasn't the way it happened in the movies. They had to come back. But as unsettling as the situation was, I knew I couldn't bring it up with anyone. This was one time I was definitely going to shut up and keep my thoughts to myself.

By dinner life on the ship had gradually slipped back into its normal rhythm, although no one suggested poker. I stayed on the ship that night, and we watched the Yankees kill The White Sox. I thought again of the posters at the Coast Guard office with the list of men missing at sea. They would be adding another name. As I thought about the list and how strange and unfathomable it had seemed three months earlier, Whitey, the shark killer, sat next to me, unperturbed.

CHAPTER 22

Billy Leaves and My Conversation
with Jack

We were well into August and it had only gotten hotter. At the same time, I had learned to pace myself better. Though I still worked hard, I didn't go around like a whirling dervish trying to prove that I was the best wiper that ever lived. It became clear to me that getting work done before it was expected wasn't particularly useful for anyone. Clearly the ship could have operated with two wipers without any noticeable deterioration in maintenance.

Billy's merchant marine stint came to an end in early August, when he had to get back to Southern Mississippi for football practice. He had intended his experience to last a little over a month and it had. We had a farewell party with Raul at the restaurant in Santurce. Billy's larger than life persona—which was very gregarious and generous in settings like that—had made him a recognizable if not familiar figure at the restaurant, so several people joined the party. Unfortunately, Dolores never made a return appearance while we were there.

It seemed quite remarkable to me how friendly Billy and Raul had become. It wasn't remarkable just because they were so different, or that they knew each other for such a short time, or even that Raul's English was limited. It was remarkable because, as I had learned early on, Billy was an outright racist, and the general sweep of his bigotry included pretty much everyone who wasn't white—with a singular exception for fantastically beautiful Hawaiian girls who gave masterful blowjobs.

Like so many things, I couldn't leave it alone.

"How can you be such good friends with Raul when it's pretty clear he's part negro?.

"Because he's a good guy when you get to know him."

"Don't you think that that might be true of Negros in general, if you got to know them? Some are going to be good guys and some aren't, just like whites."

"Nah, too much history. I'll tell you some more history that will really set you off, good buddy. I don't know how many years ago, my fraternity lynched a nigger."

"You say that like you're proud of it. What the hell's wrong with you? You know what? I think they, your fraternity, should all be hanged, for murder. Then they could just stand there and be real proud of themselves as they got hanged. What do you think of that? Yeah, you're right, that sets me off."

I didn't hide my anger, but all I could do was walk away. It was very frustrating knowing that I couldn't change his views either by argument or by force. Of course, I knew people like him existed. The South was filled with them. But I had never met anyone, let alone worked and lived with anyone, so openly bigoted.

Another part of my frustration had to come from my own self-consciousness about my general feelings about Puerto Ricans. Though my feelings had been benign compared to Billy's, that I had them at all somehow diminished my moral authority in condemning him, and that was too bad.

Though neither of us ever returned to the subject, Billy's bigotry meant that once he got off the ship, I would never see him again. That I wouldn't do. But life on the ship and in port would go on. That was the way it had to be with a small group in a small space—a "team." So we still played blues on the guitar and harmonica, and the farewell party was a good time, though I had a hard time getting my conjured image of the lynching out of my mind.

***

During the afternoon of the day Billy got off the ship, I received a pleasant surprise. While Raul and I were painting the long second level bulkhead, I heard a familiar voice cursing away just below. "Where the fick did tha' spic put the blawdy paint brooshes?" Michael's Irish brogue, which he had laid on extra thick for our benefit, was unmistakable. Well, how about that. Michael. *The Return of the Native*—I spared them the reference.

"So, Michael, they had no use for an incompetent Irishman in Arkansas after all, huh?"

"Aw, you don't want to hear about it."

"But I do. You're now the resident expert on the subject of the great state of Arkansas. What happened?"

"But you know, it was just one misunderstanding after another. It turned out the job was only temporary, and that by the fall the regular groom was coming back. And then, you know, they said I was to be working with the horses when all they really wanted me for was to muck stalls. I didn't get to handle a single horse."

"So they were just bad people who lied to you?"

"Nah, the people were nice enough. It was the guy I spoke to who had made it all sound so different. And, I had to live in a dormitory. This place is bad enough, but a dormitory, with ten people!"

"So what did you do?"

"I called the union in New York and Williams said the guy who had taken my job when I left would leave after a month or so. So, it kinda worked out, and here I am."

"What about Arkansas, what's it like?"

"I don't know. Slept on the bus ride and didn't see a thing. When I got there I never left the farm. So if Arkansas is like Ireland, I still don't know.

***

The collective experience of the crew was enormous. Most had been through World War II—many in the merchant marine. Among them, they had been just about everywhere in the world. I would have liked to talk to some of the mates and engineers who had been at sea for decades and had seen so much of life—and death. But I never had the chance, as I never spent a moment with the engineers after work, or any moment at all with any of the Mates. Most of the other guys had seen a lot but rarely talked about any of it. From their expressions while others described a place or a situation, I could see that they had their own vivid memories, but mostly they didn't share them.

These were competent and reasonably intelligent men, but when they spoke, it was only about what was happening at that moment, not about the past or about anything abstract. Perhaps not surprising from the general level of education, they read magazines and newspapers, but not books. They did puzzles, watched and discussed sports, but seemed never to just sit and think. Of course, I had expected it to be different than my intellectual and academic prep school and college experience. What I hadn't expected was a total lack of intellectual curiosity.

While Max and Tommy did talk about their experiences, Jack was the only one I met who not only had vivid memories and was articulate enough to recount them, but had also thought about and learned something from his experiences and could express that learning as well. Jack was smart and he was educated. In the course of a dozen evening conversations, I had pieced together his story. He was born in Schenectady, New York in 1915. His father was a doctor. Jack was a good student and played football and baseball in high school. He wanted to be a writer and enrolled at Hamilton College, a good school with a top notch writing program. It was not too far from home, where his girlfriend was studying to be a nurse. They were planning to marry when he graduated.

Everything was going well when, during his junior year, while home for the spring holidays, he and his girlfriend were in an automobile accident. She was killed. He didn't share the details, but Jack had been driving and felt entirely responsible for her death. He immediately dropped out of school, not even finishing the semester, and joined the merchant marine. He said he wanted to get as far away as he could

He worked on freighters and tankers as an OS, eventually getting his AB rating. He only bid jobs on ships that would go to the Far East or Africa—ships that would stay away a long time. He said he was trying to get away from his memories.

Eventually, he started writing. At first he wrote about the ships and the people and places that he saw. In 1939, when he was at sea for four years, he invented a character, a detective in Schenectady, and wrote his first mystery novel. Over the years, he wrote nine mystery novels, some with the same character, all published in paperback. He said he didn't have a large following and that the books weren't very good. (He didn't have a single copy on the ship and I was unable to buy one until some time later.) He wrote only on the ship, mostly on an old portable typewriter. He wrote wherever people weren't at that moment—in his fo'c'sle, in the mess hall, on deck, but always on the ship. He never wrote a word on land.

In 1939, once the war started, shipping was concentrated on Europe. The danger for merchant ships and merchant seamen was enormous. Even before the U.S. was at war, U.S. merchant ships were attacked and sunk. By 1942, at the start of the "Lend Lease" program initiated by President Roosevelt to aid the British war effort, thousands of ships were trying to cross the Atlantic.

The merchant ships were virtually unarmed and totally helpless. The huge convoys had a couple of destroyer escorts, but on the whole, they were no match for the German submarines. Jack pointed out the place on our ship where the single .30 caliber machine gun used to be mounted. The fittings were still there on the deck, near where I usually placed my old lawn chair. No wonder merchant seaman had a higher mortality rate than any other branch of service. They were sitting ducks.

Jack described the feeling of being part of a shooting gallery: no one knew which ship would be hit. It was the luck of the draw. The sub would fire its torpedoes pretty much all at once and leave, since its position would be revealed as soon as it fired. I asked why he didn't write about those times. He said he might one day.

Jack made a great impression on me. Apart from his intellect, thoughtfulness, and learning—he hadn't needed college to keep reading and learning—he was wise. Given all that, it is surprising that I should have had the temerity to give him advice. Yet that's just what I did, regularly. I kept telling him that he was wasting his life and that he needed to write full-time and write about the war and…. I was damn near breathless in my admonitions about his career. He said he had thought about all that many times and was still thinking about it. We had this conversation often. Just about every time he told me a story about some experience, I would tell him that was what he needed to write about. There were too many mystery writers, and though there were many who experienced what he did, I couldn't imagine there were too many who had the ability to write about it. This went on for weeks until finally he said that I was becoming a real pain in the ass and should drop it. So I did.

In the middle of August, on our way down to Puerto Rico, he came up to me as I was sitting in my chair on deck playing my harmonica. Billy was long gone.

"You know, you got me thinking. About the writing. Don't get a swelled head. I've been thinking about it since before you were born. But I had stopped thinking about it. And you know what? Now that I've thought about it seriously, I'm going to stay right where I am. For a while I was thinking of burning my seaman's papers and my "A" book, having a ceremony here on deck with all the guys. You would have been invited. But that's *not* what I'm going to do."

"Look, Jack, I wasn't trying to…."

"Shut up and listen. You got me going on this, so now listen to what I've decided and why. Most people can't make it as a full-time writer. I make damn little on the mystery novels. I certainly couldn't live on it. And writers are always looking for the perfect place to write, and many can't find it. Sure, the problem is in their heads, but they keep looking anyway. Well, I've solved both problems. I make a good living shipping out, and I write on the ship—this ship, any ship. Maybe it's the solitude, maybe the peace of a quiet sea at night, maybe the feeling of motion, of moving forward, that gives me momentum. Hell, I don't know. What I know is that when I'm on shore, I wander around and have no peace, and I sure can't write—even my mysteries. But out here I can. So that's it."

"Jack, I think that's great. I…."

"That's it except for one thing. I *am* going to write about the last twenty-five years, the war, the men I've worked with, my life, maybe some of the women…, anyway, the places I've been, and all the rest. It might end up being a crock of shit, but you're right, there is a lot to write about. And one of the first things I learned in my first writing class in college was to write about what you know. So I will."

How about that. What he said made great sense to me. I was too taken by it all to feel very pleased with myself, but I had had a part in getting him to do what he needed to do. Who knows, maybe it would really make a difference. I just nodded my head and didn't say anything. There really wasn't anything else for me to say. But he continued.

"While I was thinking about my life, I also thought about you and what you're doing. And the opposite is true for you. You *are* wasting your life doing this. And that's true in every way. Treat this like a summer job and get back to school. You're bullshitting yourself if you think you'll go back after a few years. You won't. You get caught up in your life, whatever it is, and you stay with it. You'll be making some money, and you won't want to live like a student again. You'll be too old. You won't fit in the life. What you enjoyed before, you won't enjoy then. And then what?" He wasn't looking for an answer.

"The merchant marine is nothing like it was when I shipped out for the first time. It really was a time of adventure. It isn't now, or haven't you noticed? And it's not just because this is a coastwise run. It's all tame and regulated now—a hell of a lot more comfortable, but different. And you think you're going to get a good run. Bullshit. You won't. I don't care what they tell you. Look at the age of this crew. It's like this everywhere. If there's a good run, a good ship, some guy with twenty years seniority will get it, and if you do get it because no one wants it right then, you'll get bumped out of the job as soon as someone does. Everybody's got seniority, and compared to them, you'll never get it. That's because the merchant marine is dying. There's so many fewer jobs now and no new guys. Everybody knows it. It's a dead end."

I just looked down at the deck.

"Peter, you're a smart guy. Everybody can see that. You have a chance to make a really good life for yourself. Not just money, but an interesting life. You think about things. You read, you learn, hell you even remember what you learn. It would be a waste to throw that away. You'll get real tired of this, and then it will be too late. Look, I'm trying to help you. You helped me, you really did, and now, believe it or not, I'm telling you this because I'm trying to help you."

I didn't know what to say. Just as he had thought about the things that I told him, I had thought about all this before as well.

"Jack, I appreciate what you're telling me, and I believe you. I mean I believe *what* you're saying and that you're saying it to help me. Maybe I'm crazy, but I'm afraid of just living my life, with each step just following the other. Going from college, to law school, a job, a wife, a family. I know I told you that a couple of months ago, and I know that's what most people, almost all people, would love to have. But for some reason

I'm afraid of that— afraid that once it all played out, I would be filled with regrets. I have this need for what I call adventure, but it's really just a chance to prove myself, and I don't think I can do that in an office. So I want a chance to get that out of the way—to do it and *then* move back onto the traditional path."

"I understand that. I do. But you're not going to have that chance in the merchant marine. I really don't know what the problem is with the ROTC flying thing, but here's the point. Even if you can't work that out, there is another answer. No matter what the hell you do in your life, whether you become a lawyer or anything else, you can still avoid straight lines *within* your life. It's true for everyone. Just don't plan that far ahead. Be awake to opportunities, ideas that come up, sometimes out of nowhere, and have the guts to grab them when they do. That way, no matter what you do, your future is always wide open. The only way your life ends up being a straight line is if you're asleep or don't have balls. I know this sounds like some kind of sermon, but you really don't need to run away from your life to prove yourself. There'll be plenty of opportunities to take chances, you know, where you can win or lose, right inside whatever life you chose."

Avoid straight lines. How about that.

CHAPTER 23

Getting It For Love in Old San Juan (Part 2)

We were on our last run to Puerto Rico for a while. The word was that we would make a few runs to Mobile, Alabama and maybe to Galveston, Texas. I wasn't looking forward to either. It was a long way to go, each further than Puerto Rico, but when you got there, you were nowhere. Puerto Rico was like a foreign country. Everything about it except the dollar was different. It was OK to feel out of place there; you expected that. In southern Alabama and southeastern Texas I would feel different and out of place in my own country. I expected those places to be filled with Billy Claytons and a lot worse.

While Jacksonville had Jax Beach, no one spoke glowingly of absolutely anything in Mobile or Galveston. The only thing I heard about was a big bar fight in Mobile three years earlier. There is a naval station there, and the watering holes draw the navy as well as the merchant marine, though tradition apparently requires the navy to outnumber the merchant marine. So in all, I was looking forward to my last night in Puerto Rico to stock me with enough memories to last through the upcoming Deep South doldrums. And the only memory worth having was "getting it for love," And where better than Old San Juan?

Since my first night in Santurce, I had returned to Puerto Rico several times but had not picked up the gauntlet. There had been quiet nights in Santurce— with not even a cameo appearance by Dolores, Billy's farewell party, and, of course, the night of the jock itch. But this time, my last opportunity for who knew how long, I, Peter, would take up the merchant seaman's challenge. I enlisted the support of a small group to function primarily as Sherpa guides to take me to some of the suspected lairs of the quarry. And like the Sherpas who get to climb to the top of the mountain, they could join in the quest. While Tommy, who was probably still in San Juan, might have seemed like a logical participant, I felt that his presence would change the nature of the evening, so I didn't suggest it.

Michael and I and two guys from the 12:00 to 4:00 watch, Bart, in his late twenties and Phil, about forty, the replacements for Tommy and Olinsky, took a cab to the center of Old San Juan. Once there, we walked around Plaza de Armas, the governor's mansion, and a few of the other highlights that were nice to see during daylight. Then we walked through countless small side streets until we got to a small Puerto Rican-Cuban restaurant that the guys knew. Again, the food was great, and there were plenty of women, but they were all in groups or with men. As usual, dinner took a long time, which was fine, except that with no apparent opportunities here, I couldn't afford to linger.

It was late in August now, so it was dark by the time we came out of the restaurant. We headed further into the tangle of streets and came to a bar with music. It was loud and crowded. I went to the bar to get four beers, and in the process, reconnoitered the place. This was exactly the kind of place that paralyzed me. There was no way to talk—or more accurately, to hear or be heard. Since I was usually a head taller than most women, having a conversation in a crowded setting was always difficult, but with music blaring and the women speaking and trying to understand in their second language, it was virtually impossible. We all tried nevertheless. But after a half-hour, it was clear that this was not the place for us.

We hit two more bars without success. In one, I did manage to buy a girl a drink, have one dance, and start a Dolores-like conversation—meaning I spoke and she smiled—but she was reclaimed by her group, and they left. Just before 11:00, after walking for awhile, we found a quiet place in a rather seedy area. It was a relief from the noise of the other places. There was a bar at the back and sparsely occupied tables throughout. People were drinking, not eating. If the place served food, it had stopped some time ago. I noticed that the tables were occupied by couples. There were two couples at the bar, one of which moved to a table as we approached. There were also two young, attractive women sitting together at the bar.

There was a man standing next to the one on the left. The one on the right was thinner and prettier, and the chair next to her was empty. OK, I said, this is it. With no hesitation, I sat down next to her and said, "Hi." She smiled and said, "Hi." A beginning.

"My name is Peter, what's yours?"

"Felicia." That answered a more important question as well: she spoke English.

"That's a beautiful name, and you're very beautiful, so the name matches you." Malarkey yes, but true on both counts. She had long black wavy hair, a beautiful face with dark eyes, not unusual for these parts, but still stunning. She had a nice figure in a low cut black blouse and a very tight, very short red skirt. Although I did take all this in at a glance, where my eyes lingered was on her legs. They were long and slender, but what was most striking was that I could see just about *all* of their length. The short, tight red skirt had ridden up so high that she was barely sitting on it. In short she was decked out and presented herself as a beautiful hooker. OK, fair game.

"Can I buy you a drink, Felicia?"

'Yes, but why don't you wait until I finish this one," she said, raising a full glass of what I supposed was rum and coke. I had been looking at her legs, not her glass.

"You speak perfect English," I said with a note of surprise. "It's lovely when Puerto Rican girls speak English with an accent, but you don't have any accent."

"Do you know many Puerto Rican girls, Peter?" As she spoke, she turned slightly toward me so that our legs touched. She didn't move away.

"Not really, just a couple. Why?" Phil was in deep conversation with the other woman, and Michael and Bart got their beers and took them to an empty table.

"I just wondered why you are here instead of with one of them," she said coyly.

"Well, they're both in Santurce. They're sisters, and their father and brothers said they would kill me if they saw me near either of them again."

She laughed. "You're just making that up. That's funny."

"OK, the truth is I just wanted to meet you." She laughed again and pressed her leg harder against mine. "Tell me, Felicia with no accent, did you live in the States?"

"Yes, for eleven years. In New York."

"New York. Hey, that's where I'm from. Where did you live?"

"112th Street between Third and Lexington." She said it with a tone of gloom exactly befitting the address—Spanish Harlem.

"Oh. Right. Well, you made the right move coming back here. I mean it's a lot nicer here than there."

She gave me a look that was a combination of "you'll never know" and "you noticed, huh." Then after a moment she asked, "Where do you live?"

"Well, I live on a ship. I work on a cargo ship that goes mostly between here and New York. But when I'm not on the ship, I live mostly in the Village.

"What village?"

"Greenwich Village, you know way downtown, Prince Street, Bleecker Street, around there."

"I never was there, never even heard of it."

It's probably the oldest part of the city, or one of the oldest. It's nice, but old."

"I guess not a lot of Puerto Ricans live there."

This wasn't going in a good direction and the pressure from her leg lessened. Time to get away from New

York. "So where do you live in San Juan? Near here?" I asked with more hope than curiosity.

"Not too near." Strike one. "I live with a family, my cousins." Strike two. "But you're right, it's a lot nicer than up there."

So where was this going to go, literally? She was obviously here to pick up men. It was almost midnight. What was supposed to happen? As I thought about the logistics, I looked at her—this time at her pretty face. She was in her mid-twenties, though again, I really couldn't tell. She could have been younger or older. In any case, this was a lovely woman. I had a powerful urge to ask, "What's a nice girl like you doing in a place like this?" Of course, I knew the answer. She was here to make money. And I was here to get her to give it to me for love. Just then, Phil, who had left the woman at the bar and joined the other two at the table, walked over to me and said they needed to get back to the ship. Although the port watches weren't that tight, they were already late. He asked if I was staying, and feeling increased pressure on my leg, I said yes. Michael gave me a wave and they left.

Right. I was staying, but for what? This was bullshit. I was wasting her time, and it wasn't fair. I hadn't thought about that aspect of the game before. But the pressure of those long naked legs wasn't bullshit at all. And there were no other customers in sight, so it wasn't as if I was keeping her from someone else. I decided to up the ante. I put my left hand on her leg as she crossed it over the other. She smiled. I began stroking her leg from her knee upward. As I did, she asked me about the ship. I told her whatever came to mind, making up half of it. As she uncrossed her legs and my hand slipped between them, my heart skipped a beat, and I probably told her I was the Captain.

This went on for what seemed like forever, my hand getting closer and closer to the edge of the skirt and then under it. All the while we kept talking. I was now set on reaching all the way up between her legs. What the bartender—or anyone else watching for that matter—must have thought I can't imagine, because in order to make this attempt I had to lean way forward against the bar, twist sideways and reach backward with my hand. It is hard to describe, but was even harder to do. Whether any of this excited her I don't know, but the bulge in my jeans certainly caught her attention, because she finally got down to business.

"I'd like to be with you, Peter. There's a little hotel not far from here. It's only $20."

"You mean the hotel's $20. What about...?"

"Well, that depends. You know, that depends."

Yeah, that much I did know. It was a sliding rate, X for this, Y for that, and for that, Z. I'd heard all about it from several of the guys. They said it was well worth it. A really pretty hooker who knew what she was doing and liked it—you couldn't beat it. None of the bullshit with girlfriends or worse, wives. Get it, get out. I thought I could be OK with that, sometimes, maybe. But what I wasn't OK with was going to this little hotel. That is where I would get rolled and maybe killed.

"Listen, Felicia, you're beautiful, you're nice, and there's nothing I'd like more than to go to bed with you, believe me." Looking at my jeans, she believed me.

"But I don't want to go to your hotel. That's where I get killed, and you know, even you're not worth that."

"No one's gonna get killed. The place is OK." She said that with just enough lack of conviction that I figured that while I might not get killed, beaten up and rolled was very likely on the agenda. Just as she said "OK," my fingers touched home and she shuddered. "Tell you what, let's go in there a minute," nodding in the direction of the bathroom, "and I'll give you a sample. You won't get killed in there, I promise."

She wriggled free of my hand, almost breaking my arm in the process. As she stood up, she looked quickly at the other woman and said something in Spanish to the bartender. I followed her to the bathroom. She locked the door and turned to me. She was relatively tall, maybe 5'6", and with her spike heels, it was easy to kiss her. She pushed her tongue into my throat, and I pushed my fingers hard against her under the very yielding skirt. We held that position for a while—I wasn't going to quit voluntarily—until she suddenly pulled me over to the toilet and sat down. Then she unzipped my jeans and what followed, though not my first such experience, was without question the most enthralling minute of the first twenty years of my life. Then, as suddenly as she had begun, she stopped. It was, as she reminded me with another coy smile, a sample.

Jesus Christ! What do I do now? I wanted her. I really wanted her. There was no doubt she met Max's criteria: she knew what she was doing, and maybe it was just an act, but she certainly seemed to like it. But I wasn't going to that hotel. I wasn't drunk and I wasn't stupid, at least not that stupid.

We went back to the bar, and as we sat, Felicia sat facing me her legs on either side of one of mine, squeezing. She looked at me intently.

"So, what are we going to do?"

"Felicia, the sample was wonderful, and if I could get you somewhere safe, you would already be there. But the guys on the ship told me about the little hotels and I'm not going there with you. I'm sorry."

"OK, that's OK. But I can't go anywhere else, not tonight. And I can't sit here all night just fooling around like this either. I gotta get up and go to work tomorrow morning."

"Go to work, what do you mean?"

"Look, you're a nice guy. I do this some nights because I need the money, but I only go with guys I like. That's it. I've got a real job in the daytime. I work as an accounting clerk in an import-export office."

"Wow, OK, I really didn't know what...you...I mean...."

"I know, you thought you might get it for free, right? Well, you know what? You might, but not tonight. How long is your ship here?"

"We leave in the morning...but we'll be back, soon. I don't know exactly, but soon." I was lying more to myself than to her, I wanted her so much."

"Look, I want to give you something. She opened her pocketbook and took out a small translucent envelope and handed it to me. I looked inside and there was a wallet size picture of Felicia and a tuft of black hair tied with a thin pink ribbon. She took the photograph out and wrote a telephone number on the back, and under it "Felicia Molina." She said it was the number at her office. I put the picture and her hair back into the little envelope and put it in my pocket. I didn't know what to say or do. It obviously wasn't the first time she had given such an envelope to a man—nor would it be the last. Maybe she had a dozen in her pocket book. I didn't care. It was a lovely gesture. I said I would call her as soon as the ship arrived, and that I would take her to the best restaurant in San Juan. She smiled at me shaking her head slowly with a look that said, "Too bad you don't trust me."

What I said next certainly wasn't my head talking.

"Look, Felicia. Are you really telling me that nothing's going to happen, that going with you to this hotel is really OK?"

"Yeah, it's OK. It's not a problem. Ask the bartender."

Right. That was a real help. Not exactly reassuring. But she was. I felt like a kid again. I told myself that If I wanted to get laid, if I wanted to have this beautiful women, if I wanted to be a man, I would have to have the balls to trust her and go with her. So I said, "Let's go." And with that and a hopeful glance at the bartender, I put my arm around her and we walked out the door.

Outside the night was as dark as on the ship's deck at sea. It was well after midnight and the street lights I had passed coming to the bar were no longer on. There wasn't any light coming from any of the low buildings on the street. Still, the ambient light from other parts of Old San Juan was just enough to see where we were going. And Felicia knew the way.

Walking with my arm around her, I tried not to let the pressure of my hand on her waist give away the fear I felt. There wasn't a sound other than the clicking of Felicia's high heels on the sidewalk. After three blocks I asked her how much further we had to go. "Not much further," she said. It bothered me that she didn't say anything. She seemed preoccupied with something, and the only thing I could imagine her being preoccupied with was the hotel and what was waiting there.

When we had walked another block I saw some movement ahead of us on the other side of the street. I stopped. What was I doing? People walk on streets at all hours of the night. Hell, we were doing just that. We walked on.

The movement materialized into three men walking toward us. In an instant my heart was racing. I felt Felicia tensing. I took my hand from her waist and reflexively both hands became fists. Three men walking around on a dark street in Old San Juan: not good. My first thought was anger with Felicia; she had set me up after all. It wasn't going to be the hotel but the street. Why hadn't I thought of that? My anger quickly—too quickly—turned to fear.

And my fear was not misplaced. The men were crossing the street and moving diagonally toward us when one of them shouted, "*Chica, Felicia...* " followed by a torrent of Spanish delivered in a taunting and menacing tone. I couldn't understand the words, but I understood the tone.

Felicia shouted back as the men approached. My two years of junior high school Spanish and my recent contact with Raul didn't help much, but I understood enough to know she was telling them to fuck off. She turned to me and said, "I know what you think, but I didn't do this. These guys aren't with me."

"But they know you."

"Yeah, and I know them. They're trouble."

The men were right in front of us, close together in a triangular formation, with the leader standing directly in front of me, his face twisted in a threatening sneer. They were all of medium height and build. They didn't look physically tough, and their tough demeanor came from the power of their numbers. They looked like the Puerto Ricans I had encountered unhappily more than once in New York. And like them they wore their shirts untucked so there was no way to tell if there was a gun or a knife stuck into a waistband.

"So you Felicia boyfriend tonight?"

I didn't answer. I was scared, but thinking back to the situation with the Kid, I was surprised I wasn't more scared. Though I knew where this was going, I didn't panic. This was a mugging, a New York City mugging.

"I think you buy us some drinks boyfriend." Only the leader spoke. The other two imitated his expression: a combination of a grin and a sneer. An expression that said we've got you and we can play with you. And then, "Maybe you just give us your money and we buy drinks. OK, Felicia, he give us his money?

Since this was in English, and pretty well-practiced English at that, she answered in English. "No Antonio, it's not OK. You leave him alone. You leave us both alone."

Whether her protest was just for show I didn't know. What I did know was that no guns or knives had appeared, and if they had them, then showing them would have certainly made their demand more compelling. Antonio—he was clearly part of Felicia's circle even if an unwanted part—had moved within an arm's length of me. His sneering grin reminded me of my first encounter with Raul in the fo'c'sle. Only there was no ambiguity with this guy.

The situation was only going to get worse and my options were limited. Give them my money. I had almost $300 in my pocket, and I wasn't going to give it to them; and buying my way out for less wasn't realistic. Fight them. I could throw a few punches and hurt someone, but against the three of them, even though I was larger and stronger, I would get the worst of it in the end and lose the money as well.

I took the third option which came to me as Antonio moved close. It was a move I had first learned as a twelve-year-old in my judo class and over the years had practiced with friends. I wasn't going to score any points with Felicia for bravery, but I might just be able to get away from these guys.

As I hadn't said a word or otherwise reacted, they had no idea that I would do anything. Without warning, I stomped as hard as I could on Antonio's left instep and held my foot there. At the same instant I pushed him hard at the shoulders. It is impossible for anyone to keep his balance against such an attack, and he didn't. As he went sprawling backwards and to the left, he crashed into one of his buddies, taking him down as well.

I had no intention of following up this move. I turned and ran. One was still standing but in the confusion didn't move. I ran as fast as I had ever run, right down the middle of the street, hoping that a car would come. They ran after me, but I had a half block head start, and I was betting that I was in better shape than they were. I wished I wasn't wearing loafers, but in the moment they were as good as track shoes.

Felicia called out as I ran. "I'm sorry Peter. I didn't do this."

Felicia was not my problem. My problem was that I didn't really know where I was going, but I couldn't stop or slow down until I got there. I tried to retrace the route I had walked that evening with the guys from the ship, but I hadn't been paying much attention. I had to get back to the Plaza where I hoped there would still be taxis or maybe a police car, hell, just some people. But the route hadn't been straight. I remembered that we had turned corners as we went from bar to bar. It couldn't be that far, I hoped more than believed.

After about a minute of running I could no longer hear them behind me, but I had to assume they were still there, and they could certainly hear me. So I ran. I ran toward the brighter lit sky near what had to be the center, the Plaza. I zigged and zagged through narrow streets that never went exactly in the right direction. It was like tacking into the wind on a sail boat.

After another minute of running very indirectly toward what I hoped would be the Plaza, I took a chance and stopped long enough to turn and look for my pursuers. If they were still following, I couldn't see them. But it was so dark I couldn't be sure, so I kept going, now at a jogging pace. My heart was still racing, though now more from running than fear.

Suddenly, as I turned another corner, I was at the Plaza. I had no idea how far I'd run. If it had been in a straight line it would have been less than a half mile. But it had been anything but straight. It was a typically hot summer night and I was panting and sweating. I walked along the edge of the Plaza and stopped in a dark doorway and waited. I could see in all directions but I couldn't be seen. Nothing. Still, they had to know I would go to the Plaza. They could have followed slowly and be waiting for me to move.

As I got my breath back and my heart slowed I thought, come on Peter, cut the drama. These guys tried to mug you, you got away, game over. They're not into chasing people around San Juan–followed by my usual bravado after the event, "Fuck 'em, let 'em come." And with that I ran diagonally through the plaza to the corner where taxis were lined up with their lights on.

CHAPTER 24

The Storm and What Followed

The next morning was dark and wet and I felt like hell. I was not used to having just four hours of sleep, and the prospect of the moving inferno awaiting me below didn't make me feel any better. We left port sometime after breakfast, and by the time we got out into open water the sea was churning.

The combination of too much to drink—although I hadn't really noticed at the time—not enough sleep and the heat was enough to give me a pounding headache. As I very rarely got headaches, I didn't handle it well. Taken together, it was the worst day I'd had on the ship. Each noise of the engine room—usually impossible to distinguish—hit my head separately like so many individual hammers. I could *feel* the noise. The heat, the noise, and the pain in my head were all part of one driving force. Then, not to be left out, my stomach joined in. I was supposed to be painting, but the powerful smell of the lead-based paint would have taken me over the edge, so I opted for what I thought was the lesser evil—chipping. Of course, that involved more noise, with hammer striking chisel striking steel bulkhead, but that couldn't be helped. At least it didn't bring another of my senses into the mix.

I made it to the lunch break, but eating lunch wasn't in the cards. I poked my head into the galley and asked the Kid for a piece of toast. With a coke—I had heard it worked to settle your stomach as well as remove paint—and with the toast I went to the fo'c'sle and collapsed on my bunk. I wanted to sleep but was afraid I wouldn't wake up to get back to work. I must have dozed anyway, because I awoke with a start. There had been a loud crash. I looked at my watch and I was twenty minutes late. But when I tried to stand up, the ship rolled so hard that I fell back onto the bunk. I looked out the porthole, which I had closed because of the rain, and it looked as if we were underwater. Then the shipped rolled again and we weren't. I knew I needed to get back to the engine room, but how the hell was I going to do it if I couldn't even stand up?

OK, Peter, this is a storm and we're in rough seas. You stand up and balance yourself and anticipate the movement of the ship. Fine. Then there was a sudden crash as an enormous wave hit the bulkhead, and down I went again. Goddamn it, I had been knocked down three times in the space of one minute. Was that a TKO? Keep your cool, Peter. This was what the guys were talking about during the last storm when they said I hadn't seen anything. This is what I hadn't seen. You want to go to sea, well meet the sea! Get outside and look at it—and get back to the engine room.

I managed to get up again and lunge for the door. Then I lurched along the passageway to the outer hatch. As I opened it, a wave crashed over the side. First I had to get to the containers and find some purchase there, then make a rush for the main house. Easier said than done. As I looked to the port side, the ship rolled that way and a wave loomed above me like a mountain. It must have been more than thirty feet over my head. It came crashing down and the ship rolled to starboard. I still hadn't moved.

I told myself that seamen did this all the time, so get on with it. I staggered toward the first row of containers and lunged for a handle along the back. Now I was shielded from the waves by the containers—as long as the waves kept coming from the same direction. I inched along the back of the containers from one hand-hold to the next. Then it was open deck between me and the main house. I watched the waves rise and crash against and over the side of the ship.

I tried to get the rhythm of the waves. Where I was standing at that moment, the danger was that a mass of water would hit me and send me crashing against the opposite side. As I got amidships the solid steel side became rails, and one could be swept over or through them into the sea. Neither scenario was appealing, so, using my best judgment, I just said the hell with it and staggered as fast as I could until I crashed into the back of the main house.

Once inside, I sat on the floor of the passageway catching my breath. I was soaking wet, my clothes and shoes soaked completely through. I had often thought that the only thing the engine room was really good for was drying clothes—I had even asked Second (with the expected result) if I could hang some of my wash on one of the railings. Now I would see how fast it worked.

I noticed that while I didn't feel good, I felt a little better than before this game had begun. All in all, I wasn't the worse for wear, so I climbed back down into the engine room.

There, things deteriorated quickly. My somewhat improved state turned out to be transient—the result of adrenaline produced by fear. Now seemingly out of harm's way, the adrenaline left, and in its wake, the pain in my head and the discomfort in my stomach returned with a vengeance. At least it couldn't get worse, I thought. But it did. By mid-afternoon a new phenomenon overwhelmed me. I got seasick. It started gradually as the movement of the ship became more rhythmic. It became impossible to work. Just staying upright was difficult.

As I had never been seasick before, at first I didn't distinguish it from my general physical distress. Suddenly it became very clear. I was going to puke all over the engine room. I staggered to the ladder and climbed it as fast as I could. Then I ran out to the rail and let it go. I wasn't given to nausea. Even on the student ship I'd had no experience with this violent spasmodic feeling. I had no control over it. It was a reflexive expulsion of everything inside me. I thought my guts were coming out. Through it all, the ship rolled heavily and the waves crashed as I held onto the rail for my life. Then, exhausted, I retraced my earlier course back to the fo'c'sle. As I was letting go of the railing, I recalled my concern of the first morning, about how I would be able to walk on the deck during a violent storm, balancing my 60-pound sea bag on my shoulder. I now knew the answer!

Though my clothes had dried quickly in the engine room, they were now soaked through again. I took them off and put on my pajamas and a sweatshirt. I was freezing. Even under the blanket I was shivering. And the nausea, though not as intense—only because I couldn't possibly have anything left inside me— was ever-present. I slept intermittently and stayed in bed for the rest of the day. At dinner time, Michael and Raul came in. No one seemed to have missed me all afternoon, so I had to explain that I had been in bed for the last two hours, that I was seasick, felt sicker than I had ever felt in my life, and that I wasn't going anywhere. When they asked if I wanted anything to eat, I said I wasn't eating again, ever.

Later, when the storm died down a bit and the trip between the stern house and the main house no longer meant putting one's life in jeopardy, Jack came in with some tea in a thermos. He said we'd had at least thirty-five-foot seas. Not the highest he'd ever experienced, but right up there. He said it was not uncommon to hit a storm as we crossed the Gulf Stream. Still, the severity of the storm was unusual. I said it was pretty obvious that I wasn't handling it very well. He suggested graciously that I might be sick, not just seasick. I said, no, it just hit me like a ton of bricks when the going got really rough. I didn't make any connection between the seasickness and how I had felt before getting seasick.

We passed through the storm during the night, yet my seasickness never let up. The slightest roll of the ship—and it rolled constantly—made me nauseous. The night passed slowly. I slept from exhaustion but awoke often from the nausea. From time to time, I staggered to the toilet and threw up—though I thought there was nothing left inside me— or just gagged with dry heaves. In the morning I asked the guys to tell Second that I couldn't work. I had hoped until the last moment that I could will myself out of the bunk, into my clothes, and down into the engine room, but I couldn't do it. I had dreaded the decision. It was an acknowledgement of failure, the most fundamental failure I could have experienced on a ship as a seaman. There was a storm, the first really big storm, and the kid got seasick.

Later in the morning, Second came to check on me. I told him I was really sorry, that I had never gotten the slightest bit seasick before, and that I couldn't understand it. I assured him I would recover quickly and get back to work. But I didn't. I spent the entire trip back to Port Elizabeth in my bunk. The seasickness never left me. My diet consisted entirely of clear liquids and just enough of those to keep me from becoming completely dehydrated. I was so weak that getting to the bathroom and back took an extreme effort. I just wasn't getting better. No one could understand it, but there it was.

The evening before we arrived in port, Second came in again and asked if I felt like I was improving. He added that he wanted an honest answer. I was close to crying when I shook my head and said no. He said I needed to get to a doctor as soon as we got in, and that since there was no way of knowing when I would be fit to work, I would have to sign off the ship. He said he was sorry, but there was no alternative. Maybe they'd get someone to fill in for a couple of runs. I said I understood and that I hoped that I could get this job back. He said that he hoped so too and that he was sure I'd be OK in no time.

And that was that. There was so much more I wanted to say, and at the same time I didn't want to say anything. I just wanted this to go away and get back to work, anything not to have to give up. But in the morning I packed my bag and Raul carried it down the gangway. The union steward was there and confirmed that my signing off the ship was appropriate from the union's perspective. He said he would drive me into the city. Then I walked around to say good-bye to everyone I could find. I said I'd see them all soon. Everyone went along with the pretense. They joked that I had to come back soon because it would be too tough to replace an old hand like me. I said that with me gone, at least for a while, they would have to find someone else to give their money to in poker.

It had ended so suddenly, and I felt a deep sense of failure. Still, I was determined that I would give it another go and fully expected to be back on a ship soon, though the likelihood that it would be this ship was slim. If someone bid the job, he wasn't going to leave it in two weeks, and I certainly couldn't bump him. More important, this would be my chance to get another ship, one that was going somewhere—maybe around the world or to the Persian Gulf.

So shouldn't there have been more of a farewell? My experience on this ship, with these men, had been so important to me. Yes, to me. But to them? Guys come and go. And as Jack said, if people mattered to these guys, they wouldn't spend their lives shipping out.

***

The doctor at the Coast Guard medical center in Brooklyn was encouraging. He said that what I had was *not* really seasickness but some kind of stomach flu. It had simply eliminated my system's natural defense against seasickness. He was quite certain about that when I told him that I had never been even slightly seasick before, even during a previous storm. That buoyed my spirits considerably. Whether or not it made sense, it was definitely what I wanted to hear. Jack had been right after all. I wasn't a failed seaman—just a sick one—and not too sick at that. He said that this kind of illness was usually viral, that he couldn't give me anything for it, but that rest should take care of it in a week to ten days.

As bad as I felt physically, I was exuberant. I would be back at sea in no time. The doctor said he would have to certify me unfit for duty. He added rather unnecessarily under the circumstances that I couldn't get another ship until he examined me in ten days or so and certified me fit again. I assured him that I wasn't going anywhere but home to bed. And that's what I did. I managed to stock up on Melba toast and a few other bits of food that I thought I might manage to keep down, and went to bed. My mother wouldn't return from Europe for a week, and I would have the apartment to myself until then.

By the time she did come home, I was almost fully recovered. I had lost quite a bit of weight and was still weak, but I was eating regularly again and started to gain it all back. The evening of her return, as a welcome home celebration, I took her to a local Italian restaurant. I plied her with questions about her trip and mostly succeeded in avoiding any real discussion about the ship, except to say that I would be returning to it soon. Since it was the end of August and classes didn't begin until September 16th, that didn't raise any immediate red flags.

By the eighth day I was back to normal. I went for a run in the park, went to a Chinese restaurant with Rick, and even called the graduate student who liked "sleeping with me." There was no answer, so I went to a movie.

Knowing I would pass my physical with flying colors, I made an appointment with the doctor for what would be my eleventh day off the ship. On the tenth day, I got a call from one of my best friends from prep school and college, who had just returned from a stint as a counselor at a large summer camp in the Adirondack Mountains. He said that two very attractive female counselors were staying in New York for two nights before going home to Tennessee and asked if I wanted to have a double date that night. I said sure, and he added that these girls were definitely "action." Well, I thought I was definitely ready for action.

When I arrived at the lobby of the girls' hotel, it was immediately clear which was my date. My friend was 5'9" and one of the girls, Madge, was around 5'2". My date, Suzanne, was every bit of 5'10" and, though she had a terrific figure, was a substantial person and looked like an athlete. She had short, straight blond hair, blue eyes and a beautiful smile. The girls were very pretty and tan from a summer in the sun.

Suzanne and I hit it off immediately. She was gregarious, confident and warm. This was going to be fun. And it was. The girls were very taken by the fact that we were both named Peter. We joked—not for the first time—about this being a Peter party. We ate at a nearby fancy Chinese restaurant. Peter and I both had money—though the $1000 I had pocketed dwarfed his counselor's salary and tips—so I felt we could go anywhere. It was an intoxicating feeling that I wasn't used to at all. We ate a great meal, drank crazy tropical drinks and talked. We stayed for three hours. After dinner, rather than going somewhere to drink or listen to music, we went to Peter's parents' apartment, which was both available and close by.

Pretty soon, Suzanne and I found a bedroom and began what would turn into a four-hour marathon of passionate kissing and fondling. Even though she shed much of her clothes, and she clearly wanted to, Suzanne said she was "not one of those girls who 'do it' on the first date." Right. Here we go again. But this time I wasn't giving up. And giving up was the appropriate term, since some of the time I felt as if we were in a wrestling match. At about 2:00, just when I thought victory was at hand, there was a knock on the door followed by Peter saying that Madge wanted to leave. Suzanne quickly put herself back together and went to confer with her friend. Apparently Peter had upset Madge in some way—not hard to imagine. Suzanne wanted to stay but had to go with Madge. So we took the girls to their hotel. Suzanne and I agreed to meet the next afternoon after my doctor appointment for a walk in Central Park and then...maybe Madge and Peter could make up and go...someplace. Suzanne and I would then spend the evening in the hotel, that evening being the critical *second date*. Now *that* was a plan.

I returned home around 3:00 and went to sleep on the pull-out couch in the living room. Since her return, my mother had been busy getting the apartment painted, and my room had been first in line. I was asleep in seconds, the long session with Suzanne having exhausted me.

Some time before 5:00, I awoke in a cold sweat and feeling terrible. I started to sit up and suddenly my head felt like it was spinning. It started slowly, but as I moved to steady myself, the spinning got faster. Then it was no longer just my head. My entire body was spinning, faster and faster. I tried to lean against the wall but it was spinning too. I was scared. I leaned back and grabbed the sides of the bed, but it was spinning with me. I must have moved reflexively, because the spinning changed. Before, I was spinning along the axis of my body; now I was spinning like a gyroscope, on many planes and in many directions at once. I fought to regain my balance, but whatever I did made the spinning worse. I was no longer on the bed. I must have tried to stand up because I crashed into the coffee table. I was on the floor, flailing violently with my arms and legs, trying to regain my balance. I was also screaming.

Sometime during all this my mother came into the living room. I heard her calling my name, but I couldn't speak. I could only scream and spin. There was no up or down, no ceiling or floor. Furniture was flying around and breaking as I crashed uncontrollably from one place to another. I had no sense of time, but while I was terrifying her and myself, my mother had the sense to move whatever furniture she could from the center of the room and call 911.

And then the paramedics were there. It took three large men to subdue me. They thought I was fighting them. What I was trying to do was to hold on to them to stop spinning. Eventually they manhandled me into a straight jacket, put tape around my ankles, and carried me still screaming to the waiting ambulance. From their perspective, I was no longer moving. From mine, I was falling and spinning out of control, much like I had felt as a child when I had been given ether before an appendix operation. The paramedics must have tired of my screaming and moaning because after a while I felt a needle in my butt and I quieted down.

I was taken to Madison Avenue Hospital, where our family doctor was an attending physician. As I lay strapped to a gurney in a quiet hallway, I tried to think, to make some sense of what was happening. But I couldn't focus. My only conscious sense was panic. Any movement at all, even of my eyes, and the spinning went into higher gear. As the sedative began to wear off, I moaned louder and louder. Then I heard a lot of talking near me, and soon I felt another needle. This time I was out for the count.

**

I awoke in a bed with tubes inserted in various veins in my arms, my arms and legs fastened to the side and foot railings of the bed, and rather disturbingly, my head in a padded vise. I couldn't move, which, of course, was the idea. To minimize the movement of my eyes, a nurse gave me a pair of opaque glasses, the type sometimes used by the blind.

While I was wearing these, a neurologist came to see me. I never did see him. He explained that I had been and would continue to be sedated to minimize my urge to move.

"You've got a condition known as Meniere's syndrome. It's an infection of the inner ear. Part of the inner ear is a very small canal that contains a small amount of liquid. The canal and the liquid act like the liquid and bubble in a carpenter's level, and like that instrument, it's what keeps us "level." When the system works, we maintain our equilibrium. But with an infection, the canal gets inflamed and swells, forcing out the liquid, and drying it up in the process. The result is that the carpenter's level no longer works. To lesser degrees, it's not that uncommon. In your case the canal shut down completely, and you've lost 100% equilibrium.

"Usually, the condition lasts for a few minutes to a few hours. Yours is much more severe and will last— is already lasting—a lot longer. So you're going to be like this, sedated and strapped up, until the antibiotic which is dripping into your vein eliminates the infection. Then the inflammation goes down, the canal opens, and your body will regenerate the fluid. All of that is assuming the infection is bacterial and not viral."

So I was really sick. What now? "What if it's viral? That's what the doctor at the Coast Guard said it was."

"You mean you had this before?"

"No, I was just very seasick, and he said it was a stom-ach virus."

"Well, I don't know what it is at this point, but we'll see. I think the antibiotic will take care of it. And you're lucky you don't have the other symptoms that usually go with this." I couldn't wait to hear how lucky I was. "Hearing loss and a constant buzzing in your ears."

Now I had something else to worry about. And with that, the invisible doctor was gone.

Over the next nine days, I improved steadily, as the antibiotic did do its job. First the straps and then the vise were gone. Finally, I got out of bed. The doctors said I would make a full recovery, but with my mother often around, I didn't want to start a dialogue with the medical staff about when I would be fit to return to sea.

When I checked out, I was weak, wobbly and very demoralized. I certainly didn't need to be in a hospi-tal any longer, but even I knew I was in no condition to show up at the union hall looking for a job. Still, I did need to know what the likely time frame was going to be, and for that, the opinion of the doctors at the hospital would be interesting, but the only opinion that would matter was the Coast Guard doctor's.

Push was very much going to come to shove. Whatever recovery time frame the doctor determined, I would finally have to cross the Rubicon. Whether it was soon or more like a month, I would have to tell NYU and the AFROTC—and deal with my mother. In either case, I would have to make an important decision—one that I had made in my mind several months ago, but which until now, despite my declared conviction, had been only hypothetical. Until now, I hadn't burned any bridges. Except for the guys on the ship, I hadn't ever told anyone. Now I was going to quit school for real—for a while. I thought of all the effort I had put into learning. I thought of Jack's words, "Wasting my life," I "would never go back." On the other hand, none of the reasons for shipping out had disappeared or changed.

During the subway ride to the Coast Guard medical center, I sat in the first car looking out the front window at the darkness of the tunnel ahead. It was early afternoon and I was almost alone in the subway car. As the train rattled forward, the tunnel seemed to get steadily darker, intensifying my doubts. I fought it. I was going to do this. I had decided in March! I couldn't back out now.

I regularly did so much thinking, so much fantasizing, only to come in contact with reality from time to time, usually with a hard bump. The examination by the doctor was yet another collision. I sat on a chair at the side of his desk as he went over the discharge documents from the hospital. I described what had happened since he had seen me. As I spoke, he casually got up from his chair and moved around the room, stopping just behind me and to my right. Suddenly, he yelled "Peter!" I turned to look at him and nearly blacked out as my feet flew up in front of me and the chair went careening backward. He was expecting it and stopped the chair from falling over. I regained my equilibrium in a few seconds and we sat looking at each other.

"I'm sorry I had to do that, but I needed to know. You needed to know."

"But doctor, I knew I wasn't fully recovered. What I need to know is when I will be, when I will be fit for duty, so I can get another ship."

"OK, let me be very clear. I wouldn't let you back on a ship for at least two years and even then who knows? You have a severe case of Meniere's syndrome, and you have had a severe infection, which has made the condition more serious. You aren't close to having recovered. On top of that, once you have this condition, it generally returns regularly. It can be brought on by all kinds of things, sinuses, a cold, anything. You'll think you're fine, and then something simple like turning your head suddenly will send you crashing into a wall—or into a bulkhead—or off a ship. Once you have it, you stay susceptible to it for a long time. It can take years before you'll fully be rid of it. I'm sorry, but that's the way it is. You are going to have to find another line of work—and better not too soon for that either, but that's your business. Being on a ship, that's my business."

"Isn't there a chance that you're wrong, and that I will recover completely and much sooner?"

"No. And even if there were a chance, I'm not going to take it. I'm sorry."

And just like that, my dream died. I was no longer a merchant seaman. I would not see the world or have a chance to prove myself in what I saw as the real world. I thought of Felicia, of all of it. It was over. I tried to convince myself that I hadn't failed, that it was just one of those freak things that happen. But it had happened to *me*. I had gotten sick, been too frail. I didn't make it, and the rest was all excuses.

I no longer had any decisions to make; they had been made for me, taken out of my hands. I thanked the doctor—I wondered later what I had thanked him for—and sat in the waiting room for a half hour, not ready to leave. I needed time to think, to come up with a Plan C, before I could leave and face the world. But there was no Plan C. I would re-enroll at NYU and start my junior year in a few days. Fleetingly, I thought of actually asking the doctor for his opinion about my continuing the AFROTC flying program, but the answer was so obvious that I didn't want him to think I was as stupid as l was sick.

***

After lunch on the first day of classes, I arrived early for what I expected to be an interesting European History class. I saw a pretty young married woman with bobbed blonde hair whom I had spent a lot of time looking at in a class the previous semester. She smiled at me in recognition, and we talked as we entered the classroom. She was friendlier than I had remembered her being. As we sat down, she asked me what I had been doing the last few months. When I told her, she looked at me seemingly both impressed and bemused and said, "What a great summer job!" Giving her a look of deeply conflicted gravity, I nodded and said, "Yeah, I guess it was." Then I noticed her hand. The wedding band that had quietly discouraged me months ago had been replaced by a gleaming band of white skin that screamed at me from her tanned finger.

APPENDIX:

The Merchant Marine

To understand the work situation on the *Rufus Saxton* and among American seamen in general, one needs a sense of the state of the United States Merchant Marine at that time. In 1962, the United States Merchant Marine (that is, American-owned and operated vessels flying the American flag, as opposed to so-called flags of convenience, such as Liberia and Panama) and their crews, was in a steady decline that began after World War II and would continue to the present.

At the end of the war the United States was the runaway leader in both international trade and in the size and share of its shipping fleet. Although the very high 1946 figure of 2000 vessels is impressive, it is misleading as a baseline, as it still included the hundreds of Liberty Ships and other similar vessels constructed during the war to deliver war and post war materiel and civilian supplies. 1950 is a more representative year. With 1100 self-propelled Ships of over 1000 tons gross weight, the U. S. fleet represented 43% of the world fleet. By 1960, the fleet was down to 431 ships and represented only 5.8%. (Today the percentage is less than half that.)

During this period there was a parallel reduction in U. S. seafaring billets—merchant marine jobs. Again discounting the huge, immediately post-war number of 160,000, by 1950, the figure was still well above 60,000. But the decline, even after its precipitous post-war phase, continued, so that by 1962, it was around 47,500. (That would continue unabated until more recently the figure was about 19,000!)

Alongside, and to some extent causing, this phenomenon was the rapid expansion of the U.S.-owned foreign flag fleet which would eventually grow to more than double the U.S. flag fleet. Since U.S. trade was increasing (even though its world share was declining) and overall use of ships for trade was also increasing commensurately, why was this happening?

The answer is complex, but like most economic phenomena is mostly about costs. In the case of the U.S. Merchant Marine, the primary factors were legislation and unionization. Both were necessary but costly. Several federal statutes passed in the first half of the twentieth century (the Jones Act and the Merchant Marine Act being the most important) created appropriate shipboard safety rules, workload and living standards for seamen, and granted them legal rights against their employers for injuries suffered in the line of duty. In essence, these statutes brought the rights and conditions of merchant seamen up from the 18th and 19th Century to the level of modern shore-based workers. This legislation also established the requirement that U.S.-flag vessels be manned by American crews.

Organized labor was an important part of the pressure that led to the passage of these laws. The unions representing merchant seamen went beyond this effort to establish wage standards and funded pension programs common to land-based unionized work situations. All of this enhanced the security and quality of life of U.S. merchant seamen, but added significantly to the costs of U.S. ship companies. And while over the years the annual percent increases in unionized seagoing wages were not significantly greater than their non-union counterparts, the baseline costs were much higher.

The union factor added another cost for the U.S. ship company: labor unrest. There were many strikes in the 50s and early 60s. Some were about pay and work conditions while others were the result of jurisdictional disputes between unions. For example, in 1961, the year before I shipped out, at the end of their three-year collective bargaining agreement, the two largest unions (the National Maritime Union and the Seafarers International Union) forced two major work stoppages within three months. A total of 59 operating days were lost, affecting 391 ships.

The labor risks—and attendant costs—were exacerbated by the multiplicity of unions representing the different seagoing functions. In 1962 there were eleven unions that might impact a U.S. flag ship company. The NMU and the SIU (ultimately merged in 2001) represented mostly deck personnel, though they represented some other functions as well, such as wipers. There were other unions for masters, mates and pilots, for licensed engineers, for oilers, firemen and water tenders (the last harking back to an earlier time), and for cooks and stewards. Some unions represented only seamen on the west coast operating in the Pacific trade. The result was that while labor peace and stable costs might be established with one or two unions, other unions would be unaffected and could be counted on to create economic pressure on behalf of their membership. Moreover, several unions would be represented on any given ship—as they were on the Rufus Saxon, complicating work rules and other matters.

Ship companies have many variable costs over which they have little or no control, such as fuel. But at least one variable cost could be controlled: Labor. And Labor represented a very significant portion of total costs. By flying a foreign flag, U.S. ship companies could reduce their labor costs significantly by hiring non-union foreign crews. These men would receive much lower wages and have few, if any, of the benefits accorded to U.S. unionized seamen.

As in other, older industries, the number of men working a position was often more a product of tradition than actual necessity. Therefore, adding further to the reduction of U.S. billets was the downsizing of crews based on technological advances. Also, by 1962, the unions were forced to negotiate productivity improvements to avert an even more precipitous decline in jobs.

Beyond financial concerns, there were also social forces at work. The average age of the U.S. merchant seaman was much higher than his foreign counterpart and continued to rise steadily. Seniority added to labor costs, while at the same time discouraging potential entrants from seagoing careers. As there were ever fewer jobs, and the best of these would always go to much more senior seamen, a new entrant could expect only the least desirable jobs for a very long time. This could even mean that a man qualified as an able body seaman could only get a job as an ordinary seaman. Altogether, these factors created much less of an incentive to join the merchant marine than in years past.

At a more fundamental social level, the allure of life at sea seemed to have diminished. Perhaps men had become less adventurous. More likely, with the rapid growth of the U.S. economy, there were simply more (and more attractive) opportunities on land.

The perverse result of all this was that while there were ever fewer merchant marine billets, there was a shortage of seamen to fill them. Because of the many reasons why seamen might not want, or be able, to work at any given moment, the labor supply needed to be quite a bit larger than the number of actual billets. That margin had, over the years, narrowed dangerously with the result that, again, the least desirable billets had an uncomfortably low number of applicants. So, to put it plainly, although the union made it appear that it was doing college students a great favor by allowing them to ship out, the truth was that those students (including this student!) got those jobs because the union was having an increasingly difficult time finding union members to fill them.

ACKNOWLEDGEMENTS

This book owes much to the insights and suggestions of my editor, Catherine Adams of Inkslinger Editing, to whom I am most grateful. It would no doubt be a better book if I had followed all of them. I also want to thank Dr. Sarah Russell Hankins and Paula Goldstein for their careful and helpful reading of early manuscripts, and James P. Hall for that as well as for his tireless assistance in research. I want especially to thank my wife Catherine Grace for her perspective as a writer, for her several readings, and most for tiring of my many stories and suggesting that I write this book as a way of dispensing with them once and for all. Finally, I must acknowledge a polo pony named Tina, whose untimely buck at speed put me in a condition that assured ample time to get started.

6318129R00194

Made in the USA
San Bernardino, CA
05 December 2013